DATE DUE

DE 5 '05			
AP 17 '06			
SE 30 '06			
SE 9 '06			
JE 11 '09			
FE 15 '13			
OC 28 '15			
NOV 14 2019			
Cedar 12.9.19			

Demco, Inc. 38-293

BERTHA BARTLETT PUBLIC LIBRARY
503 BROAD ST.
STORY CITY, IA 50248

BERTHA BARTLETT PUBLIC LIBRARY
503 BROAD ST.
STORY CITY, IA 50248

Pride In Our Hometowns.

P·O·R·T·R·A·I·T·S
OF
Iowa

Great places to spend the day – or a lifetime!

Copyright ©2004 Nonpareil Publishing
All rights reserved
First Edition
ISBN 0-9745410-3-6

Pride In Our Hometowns.

P·O·R·T·R·A·I·T·S
OF
Iowa

ACKNOWLEDGEMENTS

PUBLISHED BY NONPAREIL PUBLISHING

JOHN BRIDGE

Creative Design Editor

JON LEU

Senior Editor

TOM SCHMITT

Project Director-Editor

PROJECT CONTRIBUTORS

Pride In Our Hometowns: Portraits of Iowa is a cooperative effort of 25 Iowa newspapers serving the communities feature with the pages of this book. Our thanks to the following newspapers:

Adel – *The Dallas County News*
Algona – *The Algona Upper Des Moines*
Ames – *The Tribune*
Boone – *News Republican*
Charles City – *Charles City Press*
Cherokee – *Chronicle Times*
Clarinda – *The Herald-Journal*
Clinton – *Clinton Herald*
Council Bluffs – *The Daily Nonpareil*
Denison – *Denison Bulletin/Review*
Indianola – *The Record Herald/Tribune*
Le Mars – *Daily Sentinel*
Logan – *Logan Herald Observer*
Mason City – *Globe Gazette*
Mt. Pleasant – *Mt. Pleasant News*
Nevada – *Nevada Journal*
Orange City – *Sioux Co. Capital-Democrat*
Oskaloosa – *Oskaloosa Herald*
Ottumwa – *Ottumwa Courier*
Pella – *The Pella Chronicle*
Shenandoah – *Valley News Today*
Sioux City – *Sioux City Journal*
Spencer – *Spencer Daily Reporter*
Storm Lake – *Pilot Tribune*
Woodbine – *The Woodbine Twiner*

Nonpareil Publishing appreciates all the efforts and contributions from everyone involved in this publication. Special effort was made to ensure the accuracy of the information for each story and picture. However, historic reviews were, many times, based upon limited available sources.

Portraits of

IOWA

TABLE OF CONTENTS

ADEL – *Growing With Pride*	5
ALGONA – *On The Right Track*	13
AMES – *Where Life is Replenished and Visions Thrive*	21
BOONE – *Close To The Rails*	33
CHARLES CITY – *America's Hometown*	43
CHEROKEE – *A Strong Agricultural and Industrial Region*	53
CLARINDA – *Where The Work Ethic Still Works*	63
CLINTON – *Iowa's City Of Good Fortune*	71
COUNCIL BLUFFS – *Iowa's Jumping Off Point*	83
DENISON – *It's A Wonderful Life*	95
INDIANOLA – *Come See What's Up!*	105
LE MARS – *City Of Growth and Success Stories*	115
LOGAN – *Bridging The Old and the New*	125
MASON CITY – *America's "River City"*	133
MT. PLEASANT – *Growth, Prosperity and Contentment*	145
NEVADA – *Heartland, Heritage and Horizons*	155
ORANGE CITY – *Discover The Dutch!*	165
OSKALOOSA – *Pride, Progress and Tradition*	175
OTTUMWA – *The City Of Bridges*	185
PELLA – *City of Refuge*	197
SHENANDOAH – *The Garden City*	207
SIOUX CITY – *The Heart of Siouxland*	217
SPENCER – *Gateway To The Iowa Great Lakes*	229
STORM LAKE – *Always "The City Beautiful"*	239
WOODBINE – *The Best In Iowa Small-Town Living*	249

Pride In Our Hometowns.
P·O·R·T·R·A·I·T·S
OF
Iowa

FOREWORD

While the state of Iowa has many outstanding attributes, at the core lies its people and the communities they forged. These cities line the endless roadways that crisscross the state. While each is unique in its own way, all have a common trait - all have played a key role in making Iowa one of America's best places to live and raise a family.

Each community has its own colorful history. Some community histories date back long before Iowa became a state in December of 1846. The history of others are shorter but are rich in success.

Some family names have a long history in their community, histories that date back for generations. Some families date back as far as when the community's roots were first planted in Iowa's rich soil. Other residents are likely relatively new and may now be establishing their roots in their new found home. Yet others, who may have moved on, remember with pride and love the place they once called home. Regardless of the length of time a family has been associated with a community, if they remain there today or not, an endless number of people lovingly call these communities "my hometown!"

As a two-time non-native resident of Iowa, I have chosen to live in this wonderful state because of its moral fortitude and the promise it holds for the future. I brought my family here because I wanted them to live in a community they could proudly call "my hometown!"

<u>Pride in Our Hometowns: Portraits of Iowa</u> focuses on but a small sampling of Iowa's favorite hometowns and the stories behind them. These portraits provide readers with glimpses of the pride each community holds and the promise each projects. As readers turn the pages of this book, they will discover why these hometowns have become some of America's favorite places to call home or just spend time visiting. Each community is: *A great place to spend the day – or a lifetime.*

Whether your roots date back for dozens and dozens of years, or you're relatively new to the Iowa - even if you're simply passing through this outstanding state - <u>Portraits of Iowa</u> will give you a fantastic tour of a state where lives have blossomed in the past and are provided the opportunity necessary to grow in the future. I know you will enjoy this picturesque tour.

Tom Schmitt
Nonpareil Publishing

Pride In Our Hometowns.

P·O·R·T·R·A·I·T·S
OF
Adel

ADEL

GROWING WITH PRIDE

Dallas County's rich history begins with its namesake, George Mifflin Dallas, Vice President under James K. Polk. Gold seekers made their way west through this region during the gold rush of the 1800s. Native American artifacts found in the area provide evidence of earlier residents including the Sac and Fox Indians.

With the westward expansion came the eventual organization of what is present-day Adel.

Pride In Our Hometowns.

P·O·R·T·R·A·I·T·S
OF
Adel

GROWING WITH PRIDE

The Brenton Arboretum provides visitors with a fascinating glimpse of the many facets and species in nature.

A SNAPSHOT

Home to approximately 3,500 people, Adel is located about 13 miles west of the intersection of Interstate 80 and Interstate 35.

The city, with its historic courthouse standing among businesses which line all four sides of its square, has experienced steady growth over the years while maintaining its small-town feel.

Adel was originally surveyed and platted in May, 1847 as the location for the county seat. It was the first town in Dallas County. When first laid out it was originally called "Penoach" or "Panouch," an Indian word meaning "far away." That name was soon changed to "Adel" in honor of "a very pretty child with a prettier mother." The name was also appropriate due to the ground which it lies on is a natural dell, surrounded by high ground of every side. According to Native American beliefs, it is precisely because of this location that the city is protected from cyclones.

Ironically, they were right, as

Adel

Adel is home of the legendary University of Iowa football player Nile Kinnick, who attended Adel High School then went on to eventually win the Heisman Trophy for the Hawks. The U of I football stadium is named after Kinnick and a beautiful park in Adel bears his name as well as another former famous Dallas County resident, Major League Baseball Hall of Famer Bob Feller.

The first house in Adel was constructed by J. C. Corbell in the fall of 1847. The population did not increase rapidly as, just eight years later, the city had just 25 houses and three businesses. That would soon change, however.

As the county seat, Adel's courthouse was, and still is, the centerpiece. The building is a superb example of French chateau architecture, and has majestically presided over Adel's central business district since 1902

The first county courthouse was a log cabin built in 1848. This building was replaced in 1853 by a one-story frame building which was used until 1858, when a third courthouse was constructed.

The third courthouse came about after an election authorized its construction by a vote of 401 to 240. This $20,000 structure was two stories high and

*Left: The Dallas County Courthouse is located in the county seat of Adel.
Right: A huge clock tower is perched atop the Dallas County Courthouse in Adel.*

constructed of brick and located on the town square. The present-day courthouse was dedicated in 1902 and is listed in the National Register of Historic Places.

Interestingly enough, the naming of the county seat did not come without controversy.

Before railroads came into the county, Adel was a natural county seat due to its accessibility in the center of the county. Eventually the railroads, led by the Rock Island Line in 1868, moved into the southern part of the county, followed by the Fort Dodge Line which was built a year later and stretched from the southeast to the northern boundary, passing through Dallas Center.

With neighboring cities, including Waukee and Perry, clamoring for the right to be named county seat, a group of Adel businessmen, assisted by others in Redfield and area farmers, was successful in bringing a railroad which extended from Waukee, through Adel, and eventually to Panora.

The question of building a $65,000 new courthouse was put before the tax payers in 1898 and was soundly defeated, 2,281-1605. Two years later, however,

Right: Fishing is a popular sport in Dallas County. Left: More beauty from The Brenton Arboretum.

public sentiment had changed although the price tag had been increased to $85,000. The vote carried this time by a 3,338-2,049 vote.

The new building was completed on April 1, 1902, and was dedicated later that year in September. The famous clock which is housed at the apex of the courthouse tower was purchased by the citizens of Adel at a cost of $1,000.

Adel was one of the first communities to boast of a brick and tile factory in the state. Established in 1882 by Robert Kerns and A.C. Hubbard and called the Dallas County Brick and Tile Company, it was later renamed Adel Clay Products. As such, the factory churned out over 20,000 bricks per day. The plant was later torn down, rebuilt, and bought by United Tile Company in 1926. The plant has had undergone physical and technological changes over the years, most recently a multi-million dollar investment which turned it into a state-of-the-art brick making facility.

The cities and communities in the county, while woven together by that common thread which makes Iowa a special state in which to reside, still proudly maintain their own identities and traditions.

Located near Des Moines,

History is alive and well in Adel.

The Raccoon River runs through Dallas County.

Each summer brings the rodeo competitions to Adel.

Iowa's capitol, the charming community features numerous turn-of-the-century homes and buildings and brick streets.

The Adel Library and Community House buildings, both built as churches in the 1860s, also have been preserved and help create downtown Adel's unique character. The rebirth of downtown has been a product of hard work, dedication and enthusiasm by residents and the local Main Street program, which was founded in 1993. Downtown Adel is known throughout central Iowa for its unique giftwares, and many other fine retailers and restaurants who provide friendly service and quality goods.

Adel is an example of how a city can maintain its unique character while remaining true to its past.

The city has a variety of civic groups and organizations, a strong school system and an Adel Partners program that helps maintain and promote a strong business environment.

A big drawing point each year is the annual Sweet Corn Festival which brings thousands of people into the community to enjoy free sweet corn and the many events which accompany it.

The city also boasts the Adel Historical Museum. Built in 1857, this was the first two-story school house in Adel. One of Adel's oldest standing buildings, it currently houses the Adel Historical Museum as well as Adel Partners

THE ARRIVAL OF FALL BRINGS A PLETHORA OF COLORS TO THE REGION.

Right: Just south of Adel is the Bob Feller Museum in Van Meter.
Left: Residents gather the day before Adel Sweet Corn Festival to help shuck the corn.

Adel IOWA

A boy and his dog have some fun playing in the water during the Dallas County Fair.

Main Street Chamber Offices. Other city features include the Community House, which was built in 1860 as a church, and eventually renovated by Raccoon Valley State Bank in 1995 for use as a community group meeting place.

The Clarke House served as home to former Iowa Governor George W. Clarke from 1913 to 1917. Clarke first opened a law office in Adel in 1878 and soon formed a partnership with John B. White. The White and Clarke firm continued on for over 50 years, with Clarke's son, Charles, succeeding his father in the business. Governor Clarke served as Lieutenant Governor from 1908-1912.

Clarke nearly didn't have the opportunity to take Iowa's highest seat. In 1895 Clarke narrowly escaped being shot at during a robbery of the Adel State Bank. The story as told by his son: "White and Clarke occupied an office over the bank and my father was the junior member of the firm. He heard shots in the bank below and rushed down to see what was going on. He threw open the bank door and started in and the man with the shotgun whirled and

Right: Summer community parades are a staple in Dallas County.
Left: The library in the Hotel Pattee in Perry, northwest of Adel in Dallas County.

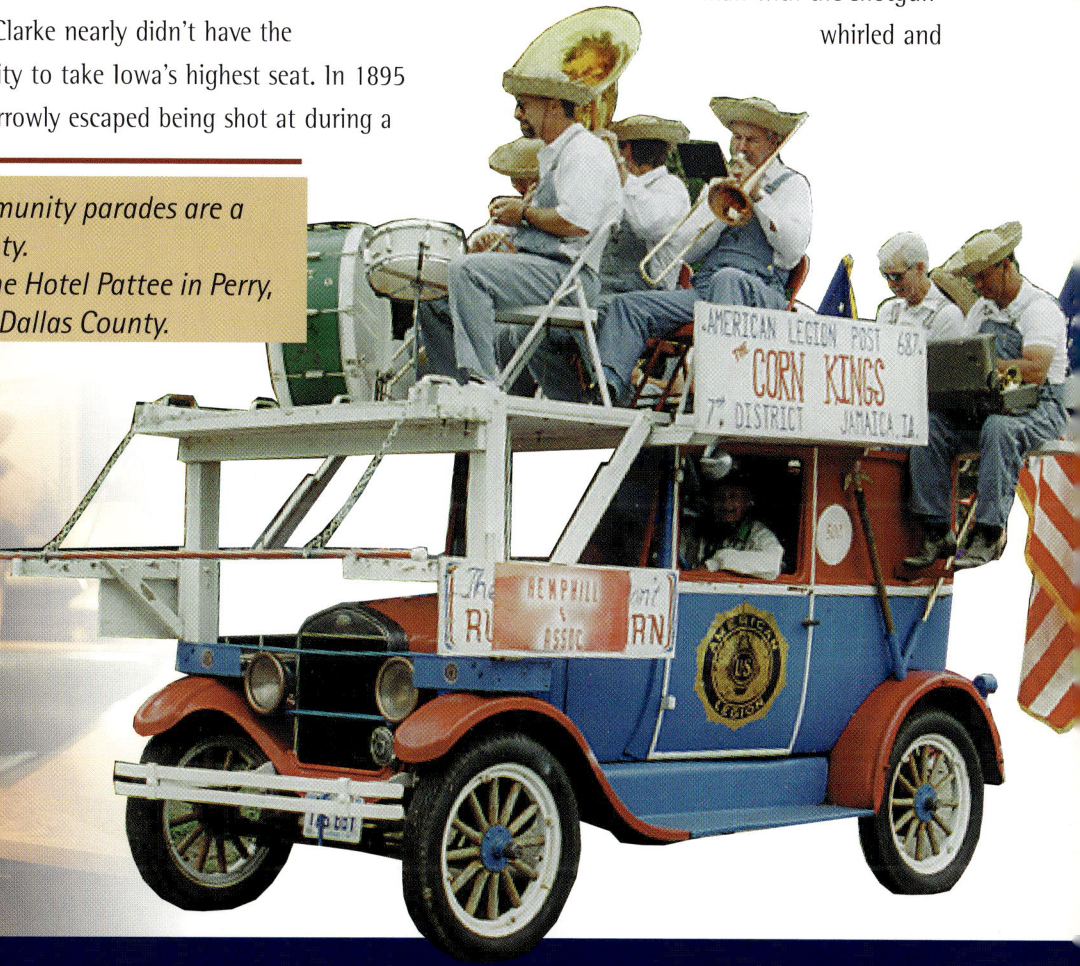

pointed it at him and pulled the trigger. The gun misfired. The shell failed to go off and the bandit worked the lever and threw the shell out on the floor and another from the magazine into the barrel. By the time he was ready to shoot again father had gone out the door and into the street."

Amongst the many things the city offers recreationally is the Raccoon River Valley Trail which weaves its way along a 56-mile route from Clive to Jefferson, serving more than 75,000 cyclists annually.

The small village has grown into one of Dallas County's golden locales. Its growth continues to this day and its inhabitant's view toward the future is reflected in its welcome sign which reads: "Adel, Growing With Pride."

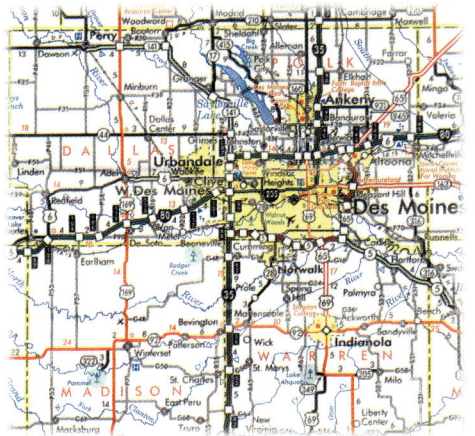

Learn More

Adel is located in Dallas County, Iowa, approximately 13 miles west of the intersection of Interstate 8 and 35.

For more information, call the Ma Street Adel Chamber of Commerce at 515-993-5472,
or visit the Website at:
www.adeliowa.org

Story Contributors

The information provided was gathered from various local history books, literature and city groups and organizations.

Left: Adel is one of the few communities remaining which has brick streets.
Right: Kids enjoy while learning at school.

Pride In Our Hometowns.

P·O·R·T·R·A·I·T·S
OF
Algona

ON THE RIGHT TRACK

Blessed with a topography rich with black soil and located amidst rolling hills bordered on three sides by the East Fork of the Des Moines River, the area that is now Algona was an easy draw for its founding fathers who ventured west in search of cheap land.

The first settlers arrived here in 1854 prescient of the agricultural hub Algona now is. The arrival of the railroad in 1870 keyed growth for the city and Kossuth County, putting the town "on the right track" and that phrase still serves as its de facto slogan.

ALGONA

Pride In Our Hometowns.

P·O·R·T·R·A·I·T·S
OF *Algona*

ON THE RIGHT TRACK

Each year thousands of former Algonans join the town's current residents for Founders' Day, which is held in July, to commemorate the first white settlers' arrival on July 10, 1854.

Today, the Algona's economic base has expanded from its agricultural base to one that includes high-end manufacturing, many small businesses, and a growing healthcare industry. The city's picturesque beauty, affordable living, good schools and numerous recreation opportunities continue to make Algona a desirable place to live.

Following some economic hard times associated with the 1980s farm crisis, Algona has enjoyed revitalization in the 21st century. But bouncing back from adversity is nothing new to this gritty community whose history is marked with instances of rebirth and transformation following the ravages of weather and economic hardship.

A SNAPSHOT

Through it all Algonans have persevered.

In 1854, Ohio brothers Asa and Ambrose Call set out to find a suitable place in which to start a settlement. They traveled much of the Mississippi River Basin and into Minnesota to the present site of Duluth, before finding a place with all the amenities they were looking for. The Calls found that place on July 10, 1854.

"When for the first time the two Call brothers passed over the rolling tract of land on which the city of Algona is now located, and beheld not only the picturesque scenery which burst upon their view, but also the natural advantages which the site afforded for founding a promising city, Asa C. Call remarked to his brother: 'I think, Ambrose, this is the place we are looking for.'" (History of Kossuth County, Vol. 1 © 1913)

Algona's rolling hills were rich with groves of hardwood forest. The river supplied plenty of water, which as an added benefit would turn waterwheels powering various milling operations. And the soil, which sprouted

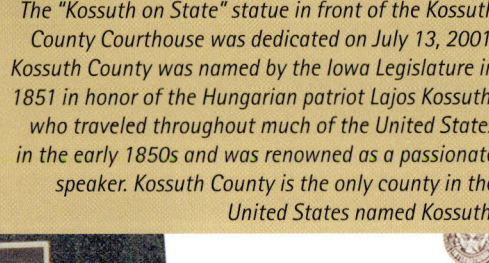

The "Kossuth on State" statue in front of the Kossuth County Courthouse was dedicated on July 13, 2001. Kossuth County was named by the Iowa Legislature in 1851 in honor of the Hungarian patriot Lajos Kossuth, who traveled throughout much of the United States in the early 1850s and was renowned as a passionate speaker. Kossuth County is the only county in the United States named Kossuth.

Ambrose Call

Asa Call

Asa and Ambrose Call were still young men when they first set their sights on the land in a curve of the Des Moines River. The two are credited as the founders of Algona, the first to claim land at this site and leaders throughout the town's development years. Asa, the elder brother, was later elected county judge, and known for the rest of his life as "Judge Call." Ambrose, the younger of the two, built the first cabin in the new settlement, and later built a grand home and an opera house, which were both landmarks in the community for decades. He also operated one of Algona's first newspapers, the Algona Pioneer Press, started in 1867.

numerous native grasses and wildflowers, was obviously fertile.

In 2004, Algona celebrates its Sesquicentennial, but a century and a half have done nothing to dim Algona's sparkling beauty. It still boasts a great many trees — having been selected by the National Arbor Day Foundation as a "TreeCity USA" three years running — and offers 138 acres of parkland. A new skate park, a paved radio-control car racetrack, a new Aquatic Center, and new YMCA are among the many amenities that make Algona an ideal place for raising a family.

Family has always been a community building block in this part of Iowa. In Algona's earliest days, large families provided the manpower necessary to make a living on the farm. Look through the local phonebook and you'll see many family names repeated over and over again throughout Kossuth County. Some of those families date back to Algona's beginning. It is not uncommon to encounter locals who can trace back their ancestry in this area as far as seven generations.

As Algona's early families grew in size, so did their agricultural holdings and the city itself. In 1869 local newspapers reported that nearly 5,000 acres of prairie land had been converted into farm ground over the course of the previous year. (Times Remembered Algona: 1854-2004 © 2003)

The aforementioned arrival of the Milwaukee Railroad in 1870 helped transform the town into a growing city with a variety of businesses, churches and schools. By the 1880 census, Kossuth County had 6,178 residents (nearly a third of its present total) of which 1,295 were foreign born.

Those earliest of settlers struggled through severe weather — the winter of 1856-57 was reported as being particularly bad — and other acts of nature. Grasshopper plagues devastated local crops in the 1860s and 1870s. In 1874, the grasshoppers were so plentiful that pioneers reported that at times they "darkened the skies" and "destroyed everything" (History of Kossuth County). And in 1894, a killer cyclone struck the area, wiping out farms, schools and

The recent equipment at Central Park has been very popular with children. The playground is dedicated in the names of Wes and Mary Bartlett and ALgona's Kiwanis Clubs, who contributed to the project.

Algona IOWA

It appears as if the grasshoppers were resorting to eating the wooden picket fence in this photo from 1874. According to the notation found with the photo, a heavy infestation of grasshoppers that summer "destroyed everything."

homes and killing 15 people. Despite such setbacks the town's leaders forged on and the period from 1881 to 1905 saw dramatic growth in Algona. In 1881, the Chicago Northwestern Railroad arrived, giving the town a north-south rail route.

By the early 1900s, farmers began installing drain tiles to turn what had been swamp into productive farmland, expanding agricultural opportunities by many thousand acres. It was also during this time that some of the cities architectural landmarks, including the Carnegie Library, the Methodist Church and the Call Opera House were built.

It was also during this time that two former rival newspapermen, Harvey Ingham and Gardner Cowles, Sr., became partners and began their path to regional renown as the managing editor and publisher, respectively, of the Des Moines Register.

Cowles came to Algona in 1882 as school principal and later married one of the teachers who worked for him, Florence Call, daughter of town co-founder Ambrose Call. At around the time of his courtship of Miss Call, Cowles bought a half-interest in the Algona Republican. Cowles' ownership share of the Republican drew public scrutiny from Ingham, who was half-owner of the Upper Des Moines. Ingham, an Algona native, objected to a school official delving into the heavily politicized world of turn-of-the-century newspapering.

STRUGGLES

Despite some public jousting, the two later became great friends and, in 1904, joined as partners to buy controlling shares of the Des Moines Register and Leader. The two turned the fortunes of the paper, which had been losing money for 16 months, and had it in the black after just eight months. They remained on the job into the 1930s. (Kossuth County Advance, June 25, 1979)

The Great Depression affected Algona much as it did the rest of the nation. "In the wake of dismal crop prices, poor yields

Each fall bands from throughout Iowa take part in the Band Day parade and field competition.

In April 1937, the Call Theater itself became the sho as crowds gathered in the streets to watch as firefighters battle the blaze that eventually destroye it. The theater was originally built as an opera house

and a land boom at the end of World War I, banks close at rapid rates. Only one newly-organized bank in Algona, with few loans, survives the Depression." (Times Remembered) But like the hardships before it, the Depression was not enough to crush Algona's spirit. The town and the county actually grew. Kossuth County reached a peak of 26,630 residents in the 1940 census.

The 1930s saw the zenith of Republican politician Lester J. Dickinson's career. An Algona lawyer, Dickinson served six terms in the U.S. House of Representatives (1919-1931) and one in the U.S. Senate. He is the only Algonan to have held such a high government post.

During World War II, Algona and Kossuth County chipped in to help with the war effort with farm production. In 1943, more than 4,000 acres of county land was designated for growing hemp, primarily for ropes. The county was also home to the main German prisoner of war camp in the Camp Algona system. The camp, part of a chain of camps spread over four Midwestern states, was home to a total of 10,000 German prisoners between April 1944 and February 1946. The prisoners' labor helped local producers process nearly 2.6 million cases of canned peas that helped out in both the war effort and here at home. (www.pwcamp.algona.org)

THE HISTORY

The German prisoners were made to work, but they were also treated fairly. As a thank you for their treatment, a group of prisoners built a nativity scene out of wire-framed concrete finished in plaster, at half life-sized scale, and dedicated to the city of Algona in December 1945. The scene remains a popular tourist draw to this day.

The post-war period witnessed the rise of Algona's most-famous son, musician Dick Dale, with the Lawrence Welk Orchestra. Dale, who was born in Algona in 1926 started playing saxophone in junior high and was playing with popular area bands in high school. He served in the Navy during WWII, and returned to playing music after the war, landing with Welk's band in 1951. Dale sang, danced and played sax for the band that grew in popularity with the national airing of the Lawrence Welk TV Show, which aired weekly until 1982, and can still be seen in syndication.

In 150 years, Algona has weathered good times and bad, droughts, blizzards, floods, and tornadoes, and more. And its residents have proven time and again that they're up for any challenge that comes their way.

Downtown Algona is undergoing a multi-million dollar renovation of State Street, that includes a new infrastructure of storm and sanitary sewers, a new water

The Algona Aquatic Center, completed in 2001, draws families from throughout the region during the summer months.

Algona IOWA

main, a new concrete road, and new curbs, gutters and sidewalks complete with pavers in a herringbone design. The street will also feature new streetlights, planter boxes, benches, and public restrooms. The Downtown Project is expected to be another piece in the puzzle that will help encourage businesses to stay in downtown as well as to draw new businesses to the area.

The new Pet Kingdom pet store is an example of what downtown Algona can be. The store's extensive remodel was complete in late 2003 and its chic setting for pet supplies of all price ranges has been a draw for curious customers from cities throughout the area. Many Downtown Algona buildings date back into the 19th century giving travelers a glimpse of what the bustling city must have looked like before automobiles ruled the road.

Some of the area's most successful businesses date back to those early days, while others have grown strong in recent times.

Pharmacists Mutual, which insures pharmacists, is the only company of its type in the nation. Founded in 1909, the company now employs over 200 people and has 35,000 policyholders in 45 states. In 2003, Pharmacists Mutual added on a $1.4 million 7,500-square foot expansion.

Among other large employers in the city are:

GROWTH

• Snap-On Tools, which has been a part of Algona for 50 years, is located on the site of the old hemp processing plant from World War II. Snap-On Tools' Algona plant manufactures tool storage units for professional auto technicians and industrial customers. The company has approximately 300 employees.

• Pioneer Hi-Bred International, a seed corn producer, has been in business here 66 years. It employs 38 full-time and 100 seasonal employees and produces approximately 1.7 million units of seed corn that is shipped to customers in eight states.

• Kossuth Regional Health Center, which got its start as St. Ann Hospital in the late 1940s, now has 150 employees including 11 health care providers. KRHC is a 24-bed critical access hospital that includes two physicians' clinics. Its employees also provide home care, hospice. The facility also is home to public health nursing agencies.

• The Algona Hormel plant, which opened in 1970,

Nearly anyone living in Algona at the time can tell you where they were and what they were doing that June day in 1979 when a tornado ripped through the community, causing millions of dollars in damage and killing two people.
It came into Algona from the northwest, seen here bearing down on the Colonial Motel located at the "four corners" intersection of Highways 18 and 169. The motel was owned at the time by Bob Schmidt, who purchased it from the original owners, Lyle "Bud" and Katy Anderson, who built the motel in 1959. The motel was destroyed by the tornado and never rebuilt.

Left: Kossuth Regional Health Center has 150 employees including 11 health care providers. KRHC is a 24-bed critical access hospital that includes two physicians' clinics.
Right: A suspended walking track above the main gym has been a very popular addition to the Algona Family YMCA. The YMCA underwent a $1.6 million expansion in 2001 and is one of the nicer YMCAs in the country for a community this size.

> Roads, permanent buildings, lights and a sound system that reaches throughout the entire 140-acre area have turned a former elk ranch northeast of Algona into A.B.A.T.E. of Iowa's Freedom Park. The park is the home to the annual Freedom Rally, which draws 10,000 or more motorcycle enthusiasts to the area each July 4 weekend.

employs 175 employees. It primarily produces pepperoni products for retail sales, food service suppliers and food manufacturers.

While these larger employers help support the city's economic base, the local economy is bolstered by many smaller businesses. Specialty businesses have added to the city's reputation for producing top quality manufactured goods.

That group of businesses includes:

- KOFAB, an Algona based food processing equipment manufacturer;
- SBEMCO International Matting by Design, a custom mat manufacturer whose clients include Target, Nordstroms, Marshall Fields, Kohl's, Mervyn's, and Disney;
- Universal Manufacturing, which specializes in engine rebuilding, and engine parts manufacturing;
- and Cozzini, formerly AFECO, also a custom food processing equipment manufacturer.

Those types of businesses would not thrive if it were not for Algona's fine educational system. Algona has both a public and parochial school systems and branch campuses for Iowa Lakes Community College and Briar Cliff University. The Algona Community Schools system, which includes Algona High School, has a scholarship endowment fund of $14 million. The fund's total is believed to be among the highest in the nation.

The Catholic school district, which includes Bishop Garrigan High, has a $10 million endowment fund.

Between the two endowment funds nearly $900,000 in scholarships are awarded to Algona high school graduates each year.

While the city provides well for its citizens in terms of education and job opportunities, it does not neglect the other aspects of their lives. Algona has 12 churches and the townspeople attend church in high numbers.

When not at work or worship, there are many recreational opportunities available for locals and tourists alike.

The city offers 138 acres of parkland. Ambrose A. Call State Park – named for the brothers who

> A paved, striped oval with a control tower was built at Algona's Veteran's Park in 2003. The track draws radio-control car enthusiasts from throughout the region during the summer months.

19

Algona IOWA

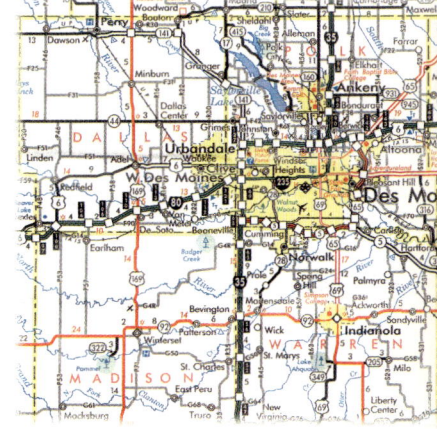

founded the town — features hiking trails, camping, a shelter house, and an authentic pioneer log cabin.

Another popular tourist site is Smith Lake, a 53-acre reservoir just north of town that offers camping, fishing, two swimming beaches and picnic areas.

Twenty-acre Veterans Park, located just off Highway 169 on the south side of the East Fork of the Des Moines River in town, offers a full complement of outdoor activities and is home to a new track for radio-controlled car racing.

The Algona Family YMCA is a state-of-the-art exercise facility with more than 40,000 square feet of exercise space. The YMCA features two gymnasiums, an indoor walking/jogging track and a full complement exercise equipment. The facility was updated with a $1.6 million expansion in 2001.

Algona's new Aquatic Center drew more than 44,000 visitors in the summer of 2003 and many of those are coming from outside Kossuth County.

Algona is also home to two museums. The Kossuth County Museum, housed in an 1867 schoolhouse on the corner of E. Nebraska and S. Dodge streets. The new Camp Algona POW Museum at 114 S. Thorington St. will open in time for the Sesquicentennial, July 8-11, 2004. It is believed to be the only museum of its kind in the nation.

Many other Iowans have learned of Algona's scenic beauty by visiting here for the annual Band Day Festival. The fall festival has been held annually for 55 years and last year it drew 27 high school bands and thousands of spectators for the parade and competition.

Thousands more tourists are becoming familiar with the area via their association with the A.B.A.T.E. Freedom Rally. The event, which has been held over the July 4 weekend in each of the two previous years, has brought in more than 20,000 total visitors. The motorcycle rally is held at A.B.A.T.E.'s Freedom Park located just north of town.

Those seeing Algona for the first time will see the best of small-town Iowa — a city graced by good schools, strong churches, a vibrant business district and intriguing neighborhoods that mix the best of old and new. Those traits are what will keep Algona going strong for years to come.

"Algona has been and continues to be a progressive city where people make things happen. ... There is no better place in the world to raise a family," wrote Algona Mayor Lynn Kueck in the foreword to Times Remembered.

LEARN MORE

Algona is located in north-central Iowa at the intersection of US Highway 18 and US Highway 169. It is 43 miles north of Fort Dodge, 54 miles west of Mason City, and 47 miles south of Blue Earth, Minn., and the intersection of US Highway 169 and Interstate 90. To learn more about Algona, contact the Algona Chamber of Commerce at 515-2957201 or at www.algona.org, or the Algona Upper Des Moines newspaper at www.algona.com.

Many Algona area residents remember watching a lake being built in the 1960s as the first park in the county conservation system. The Kossuth County Conservation Board was created in 1962, with the first land acquisition in April 1965 along Highway 169 north of Algona. In 1965 and 1966, a lake was built on the 120-acre tract, originally named Kossuth County Park and Lake Smith. By 2003, the system had grown to manage 1,500 acres in 24 different areas, ranging from natural prairie to the Smith Wildlife Area with its maple sugar shack. There are now five full-time employees and two seasonal employees. Presently, efforts are under way by an independent Kossuth County Nature Center Foundation to raise funds for a new nature/educational center on the west side of Smith Lake.

STORY CONTRIBUTOR

Jeff Robinson is the editor of the Algona Upper Des Moines newspaper.

Pride In Our Hometowns.

P·O·R·T·R·A·I·T·S
OF
Ames

WHERE LIFE IS REPLENISHED AND VISIONS THRIVE.

Built on the skeletal frame of the westward railroad, fleshed-out by the growth of what is now one of Iowa's leading universities, Ames has established itself as a hub for regional needs, a draw for national acclaim and a fertile land for dreams to take root – whether those dreams involve reclaiming the prairies or creating new technology.

From marshland beginnings to award-winning metropolis, Ames has continued as a wellspring of opportunity where life is replenished and visions thrive.

   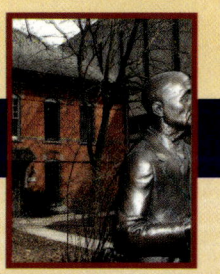

AMES

Pride In Our Hometowns.

P·O·R·T·R·A·I·T·S
OF
Ames

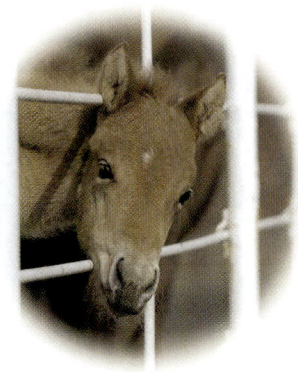

A foal pokes its head through the fence at Iowa State University Horse Farm.
Photo by Andrew Rullestad

WHERE LIFE IS REPLENISHED AND VISIONS THRIVE.

A SNAPSHOT

Ames is a picture of idle beauty; a whisper of all that Midwest cities should be and so seldom are.

It is burgeoning trees overhanging long sidewalks, children playing on the front steps of Victorian homes, old men packing up fishing poles to take a drive to the lake, and summer concerts at Bandshell Park when the municipal band takes on Dixieland jazz.

It is the beauty of swans floating on Lake Laverne at the foot of stately, century-old buildings at Iowa State University, and the pageantry of students running for their classes.

It is Ames, Iowa: A city built on the dream of uniting the country in the fading days of the Civil War, and nurtured by a vision of new ideas and diverse knowledge.

Within one year, 1864, the town was platted in barren marshland along the chosen route for the transcontinental Chicago and Northwestern Railroad, and the Iowa Agricultural College, predecessor to ISU, became the nation's first land-grant college.

That interconnection and mutual growth pattern – more than half of the city's population attends the university – continues today, whether it is as simple as residents attending Cyclone football games and the ISU

(Foreground to background) Christa Heiligenthal, 8, Harry Heiligenthal, Eric Bradly, Miles Bousquet, 7, Andrew Heiligenthal, 13, and Forrest Bousquet, 10, (standing) enjoy sledding at Veenker Memorial Golf Course
Photo by Nirmalendu Majumdar

lecture series, or as weighty as the city helping to carve out the award-winning CyRide transit system that offers free service to ISU students.

By blending together, a love of culture and a reverence for knowledge has been woven into the fabric of the community. The ethereal concepts of "a sense of place" and "quality of life" are written into city documents.

Artist exhibits, theater presentations, concerts and open mic nights are prevalent in Ames. The city sponsors a revolving display of outdoor public art in parks and in front of municipal buildings. The new Ames Main Street Cultural District is creating a welcoming cultural destination of coffee shops, boutiques, street music and art displays in the downtown area.

The Ames Public Library is well-known in the region, and has been ranked eighth in the nation among cities of comparable size, based on circulation numbers and funding sources. The K-12 Ames Community School District has a far-reaching reputation for excellence in the state and the nation.

Ames is a deliberate balance of the past and the future, of history and forward motion, of lush greenery and steel-edged innovation. It is a city with a vision to be a leader in the bio-technology industry, and a people who value small town ideals above all else.

The past is respected. Many locations are listed with

CY-IOWA STATE MASCOT

The east face of the Memorial Union
Tribune File Photo

the National Register of Historic Places, including the eight block residential area of the Ames Old Town Historic District. The old 1913 Municipal Building was renovated to become the headquarters of the statewide Youth and Shelter Services, while the 1938 downtown high school building was restored to hold the new City Hall and the police station, plus a city gym and auditorium.

The city is a growing metropolis. Evidence can be found in the amount of land that is being annexed into the city, the number of apartments and subdivisions that are popping up. Yet in many areas, the city and public are working together to create design standards and regulations for that growth.

A recent success has been Somerset, a "village concept" subdivision that is developing in a variety of uses and architectural designs for single-family homes, townhouses and row houses. A centralized commercial area, complete with clock tower, gives a small-town feel.

Commerce-Industry

However, Ames is more than Midwest charm. It is a center for commerce and industry – such as 3M, Sauer-Danfoss, Ball Plastics Corporation and Barilla – as well as cutting-edge research and development companies that are reaching out to touch the nation and the world. Iowa Thin Film Technology has contracted with the U.S. Army to design lightweight solar panels to create a power source in tents; ETREMA Products is working with the U.S. Navy on sonar equipment; and New Link Genetics is the first human pharmaceutical research company in Iowa.

As Ames reaches for its bio-tech vision, one of the motivators will certainly be the ISU Research Park that links technological discoveries with the business savvy and development assistance needed to get ahead.

Ames also is home to federal laboratories, such as the National Animal Disease

Sculpture by artist David Dahlquist, at the intersection of Kellog Ave. and Main St. in Ames. Photo by Andre Rullestad

Bandshell Park

Dr. William Swanson, Veterinarian from Cincinnati Zoo, demonstrates surgery on a domestic cat during National Veterinary Student Conference at ISU. Photo by Nirmalendu Majumdar

Center and the Department of Energy's Ames Lab, as well as university entities, such as the ISU College of Veterinary Medicine, which is one of the leading vet schools in the nation.

The city of Ames rests near the center of the state and at the crossroads of two major thoroughfares, where it has become the hub of regional shopping, entertainment, education and medical services.

Mary Greeley Medical Center, public hospital, partners with McFarland Clinic to make the community a health care hub. The facility recently opened a state-of-the-art William R. Bliss Cancer Center in its new addition.

Serving as a regional center is not new for this area. The lush, resource-rich lowland that is now Ames – a network of waterways and sloughs between Squaw Creek and the Skunk River – have always been a source of nurturance even before the town settled. Before European settlement, Mesquakie Indians returned to the land each summer to fish, hunt and replenish their stores.

And like that time so long ago, Ames is a "transient" city – a touchstone for students passing through their university years, families seeking its safe streets and good schools, and entrepreneurs staking a claim. Few of the city leaders and community advocates were born within its boundaries.

But for most, no matter how long they stay, Ames is never forgotten.

The city in all its beauty and charm, all its fertile opportunity, becomes their home. In memories, Ames remains a place where life is replenished and dreams can thrive.

SHE WAS A WOMAN TO BE RECKONED WTH...

She was a woman to be reckoned with, by all accounts.

Cynthia Duff was a woman who would drive an open wagon 30 miles to State Center to haul back lumber for an addition on her house in the new village of Ames. She was a

Left: Stan Hyer of Ames tries his hand at ice fishing at Hickory Grove Park. Photo by Michael L. Palmieri
Right: Josh Boetel of Lake Park flips beef kabobs at the County Cattlemen's Grill-Off during the 2003 Iowa Cattlemen's Association Summer Conference and Trade Show held at the Scheman Building in Ames. Photo by Jon Britton

Ames IOWA

woman who would help found the first faith congregation in Ames, open her home to the first services, see that a church building was erected, then help putty the windows herself.

She was "considered by some to be eccentric," wrote Farwell T. Brown in the first of his trilogy on the history of Ames, "(but) those who knew her best knew her true value." One friend mentioned "her usual spirit of bravery and patience" in a letter quoted in Brown's book.

Perhaps it was that bravery that brought Cynthia Duff and her husband, Alexander, to the untamed land of Story County in 1863. But once here, it was thought to be her perseverance in working with area landowners that allowed the couple to purchase 200 acres of marshy land in Story County.

She and her husband sold a portion of the land to railroad magnate John I. Blair for the original town and the right-of-way for a new rail line that would eventually link Chicago and San Francisco. The town was platted in December 1864 and recorded in January of 1965, just months before the Civil War ended.

Cynthia Duff asked that the new town be named after her home county, Onondaga, in New York State, but Blair had other ideas. He named the town after his friend, Oakes Ames, a Congressman from Massachusetts and a Congressional supporter of the railroad.

The history of the city and Iowa Agricultural College sprang up almost

Left: Victor Kraatz, Germany, and Shae-Lynn Bourne, Canada, perform for an audience during Champions On Ice at Hilton Colliseum in Ames. The couple have won nine national titles since 1993 in pairs skating. Below: Journey band members Jonathon Cain (left) and Neal Schon perform their hits at Hilton Colliseum in Ames. Photo by Andrew Rullestad

BIG SHOWS!

Marcus Savage, 12, of Ames catches some air on his skateboard at the Ames Skate Park. Photo by Jon Britton

simultaneously within a handful of years. As the town took root, so did the Iowa Agricultural College across the creek.

The college and Model Farm were chartered under a grant from the new state of Iowa in 1858. Two years later, the Farm House – now a campus museum – was the first college building erected

But it wasn't until 1862 that Congress passed the Morrill Act, which created a new type of university based on the belief that higher education should be accessible to all. The college in Ames became the first land-grant college in the nation. The first Iowa Agricultural College class of 26 students graduated in 1872.

In the first years, the campus and the nearby city of Ames were separated by what was often miles of mud, impassable for even the horse-and-wagon transit system.

In 1891, the Ames and College Railroad trolley began the loop between Main Street and the campus, joining the two entities for the first time. The "Dinkey," as it was dubbed, shuttled students, faculty, mail and even freight.

The People

The fight with muddy roads at the turn of the century was a national problem, and in 1913, Ames became a part of the 12-state Lincoln Highway that ran from Times Square in New York City to Lincoln Park in San Francisco.

Cynthia Duff was not the last of those in Ames to show bravery and the perseverance to follow a dream.

Ames High School

Iowa State University junior Leah Kastner walks home in the rain on West Street from her job at the University Bookstore. Photo by Jon Britton

Ames
IOWA

Billy Sunday, a baseball player who became the first nationally acclaimed evangelist, was born on his grandparent's farm in Ames in 1862.

Carrie Chapman Catt, who came to Iowa Agricultural College in 1877 despite her father's wishes, went on to be one of the leaders in the fight for the 19th amendment and a woman's right to vote.

George Washington Carver became the first black student at Iowa Agricultural College in 1891, receiving his bachelor and master's degree in botany, and went on to become the first black faculty member. Carver received national and international fame in his life, but is most noted for his creation of 325 products from peanuts.

Henry Wallace was the young son of a faculty member at Iowa Agricultural College when he became friends with George Washington Carver, and often followed him into the field. Wallace went on to graduate in 1910 from what was then Iowa State College. He served as U.S. Secretary of Agriculture in 1993, Franklin D. Roosevelt's third-term vice president and lost a bid for the presidency. Wallace founded the company that would become Pioneer Hi-Bred.

Ada Hayden, who was born in rural Ames, studied botany at Iowa State College, graduating in 1910 as the first woman to receive a doctorate. Hayden continued on at the college as an assistant professor where she was known for her work in prairie preservation. She collected over 30,000 plant specimens of plants, which is the basis for the ISU Ada Hayden Herbarium.

Julia Loughlan, the widow of a railroad man, is believed to be the only woman stationmaster in history. She served at the Ames Depot from 1917 until the mid-1920s.

Neta Snook Southern is believed to be the first licensed woman pilot in Iowa, and flew as a civilian pilot in Canada during World War I. She returned to Ames after the

A balloon passes through the Veishea parade on the Iowa State University campus.

Trent Grover, Ames, uses a pair of shutter glasses to watch a virtual reality video at Prairie Logic in Ames. The company offered a product that delivers live-action three-dimensional video. Photo by Andrew Rullestad

war, where she rebuilt a wrecked airplane in her backyard. It was when she was a flight instructor in California in the 1920s that she taught Amelia Earhart to fly.

Herman Banning, whose family moved to Ames in 1919, became the first black aviator to complete a transcontinental flight in 1932. Banning had studied engineering at what was then Iowa State College in Ames, when his interests changed to flying.

R.E. "Dad" Carr was a contractor in Ames when a 1926 bond referendum to fund a new swimming pool failed at the ballots. Within months, Carr began construction of a privately-owned and funded "public" pool for the kids of Ames on his land along the Skunk River. Carr Pool was purchased by the city in 1973.

John Vincent Atanasoff was an Iowa State College alumnus and professor in the late 1930s when he began to work on what became the first digital electronic computer.

Malaysian Iowa State University student Iwin Lee stands in front of his country's flag at the Malaysian cutural booth during the FACES (Families in Ames Celebrating Ethnicities) festival held in downtown Ames. Photo by Jon Britton

The Present

Today, the university has a student population of more than 27,000 from all 50 states and nearly 120 countries. That diverse population adds unique aspects to the Ames community. There are more than 40 different faiths and denominations represented in the area's faith centers. The Ames Human Relations Commission hosts the annual fall FACES festival to celebrate the cultures represented in the city.

And today, the city of Ames is a thriving community of culture, knowledge and commerce, and has a growing list of amenities. The city boasts of an ever growing network of 56 miles of bike and pedestrian trails, and 1,200 acres of parks – from skate parks, to disc golf courses, to woodland nature trails.

Ada Hayden Heritage Park is the newest

Left: The Iowa State University Campanile is pictured. Photo by: Joel Becker
Right: Fans cheer as the Cyclones take the field. Photo by Jon Britton

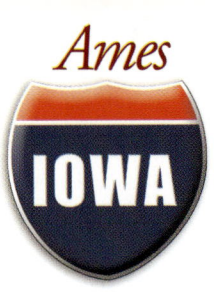

Ames IOWA

showpiece, with five miles of trails, a 1.2 billion gallon lake and naturally-filtering marshland set among native prairie plantings, wildflowers and look-out stations. The 437-acre site was once a strip-mining gravel quarry, but working in partnership with ISU, the Iowa Department of Natural Resources and the Story County Conservation Board, the city of Ames has recaptured and carefully restored the land to a heritage park.

"In 50 years, where will your kids go to find solitude?" asked Nancy Carroll, the director of Ames Parks and Recreation. "In 50 years, they are going to feel when they walk into this park the way the land was 150 years ago."

The multiuse park is open for recreation, bird-watching, boating and fishing, with a launch for non-motorized boats. But it is also used as a conservation education site, an ISU research station, and a back-up water system for the city of Ames.

As with Ada Hayden Heritage Park, the university and the city of Ames continue to move in tandem, with many of the town's amenities found on the campus.

The Iowa State Center is a complex of facilities – Hilton Coliseum, Stephens Auditorium, The Scheman Building and Fisher Theater – that provide an array of programs from concerts, to touring Broadway companies, from basketball games to lectures.

Lower: Steve Carter sits among photos of the Iowa State Business Park, Wednesday, Mar. 5, 2003. Photo by Andrew Rullestad
Left: Ada Hayden Park in early spring is shown here from the South.

Ryan Murray of Ames practices teeing off with a 5 wood at Veenker Memorial Golf Course. Photo by Jon Britton

The PrISUm Spectrum solar-powered car competed in the American Solar Challenge, a race that covered 2,300 miles from Chicago to Los Angeles. Photo by Andrew Rullestad

With its multi-use rooms and kitchen services, The Scheman Building is the first choice for conferences and workshops. It also houses the ISU Brunnier Art Museum.

Nearby Reiman Gardens, Iowa's largest public garden, covers 14 acres with a variety of plantings, paths and benches for viewing. The flowers also find their way indoors to a glassed-roof conservatory and the unique Christina Reiman Butterfly Wing, styled in the shape of a glass butterfly. Behind the scenes, the garden is an ISU horticulture research site.

Art and green spaces continue downtown with curbside plantings, small parks for picnicking and the Octagon Center for the Arts, featuring local and national exhibits, as well as art classes and a museum gift shop.

Shopping in Ames is an eclectic event, from major chains to tiny boutiques. Downtown Ames holds a variety of floral, gift and clothing stores, as well as consignment household goods and clothing. Eateries range from a quick deli sandwich to a gourmet meal.

Meanwhile, the Campustown area in the heart of the university district caters to the younger crowd, with late night bars, ethnic restaurants and even pushcart service. Campustown shops center on books, backpacks and student needs, as well as the more broad-minded, such as bead shops, game stores and tattoo parlors.

Ames is also the

A once popular campus and local "hangout"– Cy's Roost" in Ames. Staff photo by Jack Jorgensen

Ames IOWA

Iowa State University senior Tom Calgaard, walks in the snow to Howe Hall on campus. Photo by Jon Britton

location for many annual events, such as the summer Iowa Games statewide amateur sporting event, and the Iowa Special Olympics Summer Games, which brings special needs athletes from across the state. The city has been chosen to host the first-ever Special Olympics National Games in 2006.

But it is not the events, the festivals or the amenities that give a city character. It is the people.

It is true today, just as it has been true for the past 140 years, that the people of Ames will continue to find pride and comfort in the town they have created, and will continue to reach for the stars.

They are a people who will take a stand for what they believe in.

And what they believe in is Ames.

Iowa State's coach Dan McCarney walks to the field with players before a home game in Ames, Iowa. Photo by Nirmalendu Majumdar

Story Contributor

This article, by Ames Tribune staff writer Beth Anderson, is based on research taken from the books of Farwell T. Brown.

Brown was named the official historian for the city of Ames in 1986. He is the author of many books on the subject, including the trilogy: *Ames: the Early Years in Word and Picture*; *Ames in Word and Picture: Further Tales and Personal Memories*; and *Ames in Word and Picture: Tales From Two Old-Timers*.

Learn More

For more information, call the Ames Convention and Visitors Bureau at (515) 232-4032, or (800) 288-747 or online at www.amescvb.com.
Or visit the city Web site at www.cityofames.org.

Ames is located in central Iowa at the crossroads of Interstate 35 and U.S. Highway 30.

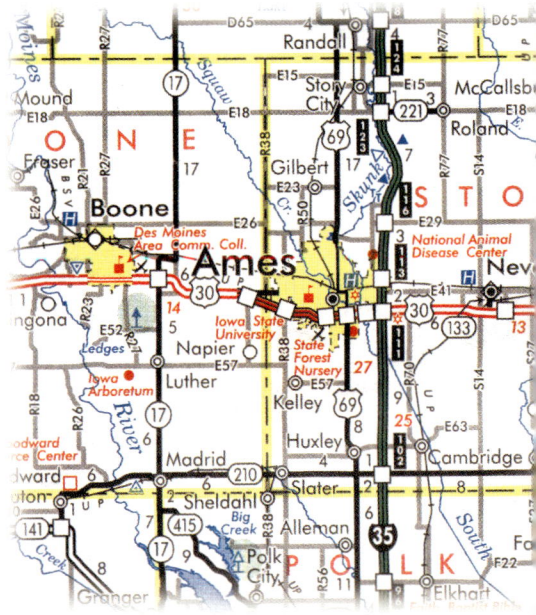

Pride In Our Hometowns.

P·O·R·T·R·A·I·T·S
OF
Boone

CLOSE TO THE RAILS

More than 60 trains pass through the heart of Boone daily – going east or west on the double track that cuts through the heart of the 12,800-populated central Iowa community. Once the flashing lights and crossing gates lift as the Union Pacific train whistles its way through the city, life in Boone moves on.

While the city is nestled in railroad heritage, a busy Boone has numerous other attributes and attractions to promote.
Boone's tourist attractions and annual activities deliver a compromising balance that feature activities and events of today, yet satisfying the thirst of historians who want to dig deeper into the roots of Boone's past.

BOONE

Pride In Our Hometowns.

P·O·R·T·R·A·I·T·S
OF *Boone*

CLOSE TO THE RAILS

It was 140 years ago when the town plat for the town of Boone was filed for record by John I. Blair, who had previously purchased a large portion of the land where the city of Boone is now found. It happened that Blair was the manager of a railroad project built from Marshalltown to the Missouri River. A railroad line was built to Marshalltown in 1862, to State Center in 1863, to Nevada by 1864 and the track was placed in Boone in December 1864.

Boone County itself, organized in 1849, was named as a tribute to Daniel Boone and his son, Col. Nathan Boone, of the U.S. Dragoons. Boone was among the first white men to explore this region. Captain Boone was in the expedition that marched from Old Fort Des Moines where Montrose, in Lee County, now stands to Wabasha's village in

A SNAPSHOT

Minnesota, about where the city of Winona now stands. Wabasha was a great chief among the Sioux Indians, and the intent of Boone's expedition was to establish a treaty of peace with the Indian chief.

The expedition left Old Fort Des Moines on June 7, 1835 and marched along the divide between the Des Moines and Skunk rivers. On the evening of June 23 that year, Boone's army camped in what is now Boone County.

Boonsboro was the original county seat of Boone County.

A Pufferbilly Days highlight is the huge parade of bands and floats.

Boone Station, which later changed its name to Montana and then to Boone, was also incorporated in the 1860s. A petition in circuit court changed the city's name from Montana to Boone effective August 1871.

Top: The annual Johnny Appleseed tree planting progra Boone has introduced 7,800 trees to Boone over a span years. Right: This town clock was put in place in 1915 c corner of Story and Eighth in Boone and it gives perfect to this day.

The two towns merged into Boone, which became the county seat in 1887.

Boone has its list of legends, too. Mamie Doud Eisenhower, wife of U.S. President

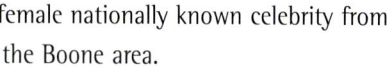

Dwight D. Eisenhower, was born at 718 Carroll St. in Boone Nov. 14, 1896. Her father, John Sheldon Doud, came to Boone in the early 1890s and established a meatpacking company with his father, Royal Doud, of Chicago. Her mother, Elivera Carlson Doud, was born in Boone May 13, 1878. One year after Mamie was born, the family moved to Cedar Rapids.

The house was later owned by several families, and then remodeled into apartments. It also served as a Sunday school location. A Mamie Doud Eisenhower Birthplace committee formed and the home was moved to a donated site at 709 Carroll St. in Boone in 1975, and the Birthplace was dedicated June 22, 1980. The home has been restored to the 1890s period, looking at life from the era of Mamie and her family. Much of the furniture in the five-room Victorian home was provided by Mamie's family and the master bedroom furniture includes the bed in which Mamie was born.

Mamie wasn't the only female nationally known celebrity from the Boone area.

When Kate Shelley of Moingona was 15 in the year 1881, she braved a raging rainstorm to warn passengers of a night express, telling those responsible that a railroad bridge at Honey Creek had been washed out. She crawled over a railroad bridge that spanned the Des Moines River, from Boone to Moingona, where the train was to arrive, and she helped avert a terrible catastrophe. For that effort, she became known nationally through books and films for her heroism.

There's a museum in nearby Moingona dedicated to the heroine that show artifacts and photographs relating to Kate Shelley's life. More information about Boone history is also available at the Boone County Historical Center.

They named a bridge after the heroine – the Kate Shelley High Bridge is the longest, highest double-track railroad bridge in the United States. It stands 185 feet above the Des Moines River at a length of 2,685 feet. Union Pacific trains now cross the bridge

Mamie Doud Eisenhower

The History

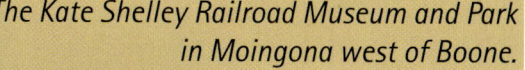

The Kate Shelley Railroad Museum and Park in Moingona west of Boone.

Mamie Doud Eisenhower's birthplace is preserved for tours conducted by curator Larry Adams.

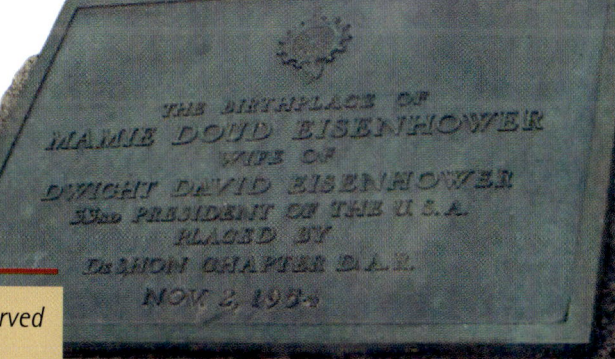

Boone, IOWA

continuously. Within the past few years, the bridge has been reinforced to continue serving the railroad industry while also being a popular tourist attraction.

One of today's national celebrities from Boone involved in the entertainment industry is Jamie Aaron Kelley, who has a national fan base. Kelley is an Elvis performer and a solo artist who has appeared on national and international stages. He has recorded several CDs in Nashville. Yet he often comes to Boone to perform for charitable causes. He's recreating history by bringing the songs of Elvis back to life.

History is being well-preserved in Boone, too, in many more venues.

The Boone County Historical Center is a plethora of historical collections which show many pictures and genuine artifacts reliving the stories of the past of Boone County. In the spring of 2004, the historical center will unveil "Boone County in the Twentieth Century" which will set Boone County's history against the backdrop of the world, national and state events. Displays of each decade will contain artifacts, photographs, narratives and audiovisual displays illustrating each decade.

The historical center building is a former Masonic Temple that was built in 1907. More on display inside are extensive military collections dating back to the Civil War, prehistoric and Native American items, a Dragoon Trail exhibit, a recreated slope coal mine, early agricultural equipment exhibits and more. During a stretch of several days in September, the historical center displays quilts from across central Iowa and has quilting demonstrations during the annual Pufferbilly Days celebration.

The community's main celebration, Pufferbilly

Nationally known Elvis performer and soloist Jamie Aaron Kelley of Boone performed as part of the grandstand entertainment at the Boone County Fair.

PUFFERBILLY DAYS CHILDREN'S PARADE

A fisherman tries his luck at a dock on Don Williams Lake northwest of Boone.

Boone Iowa

Boone Speedway

From humble beginnings, the Pufferbilly Days celebration is held the first weekend following Labor Day weekend, becoming one of the largest festivals in the state of Iowa. More than 30,000 visitors come to spend a fun-filled weekend celebrating Boone's railroad heritage, while mixing in some quality entertainment to keep the interest of all ages. In addition to drawing top quality country and rock'n' roll bands and singers, there are lip sync contests, craft markets, an Art Show in McHose Park and numerous games and activities.

The crown in the event is the annual Pufferbilly Days parade Saturday morning featuring more than 90 minutes worth of high school marching bands, floats and performers.

The Pufferbilly Days event falls on the same weekend when race drivers across the nation compete for top dollars and championship status on a dirt oval track at the Boone Speedway.

The I.M.C.A. Super Nationals at the Boone Speedway is an event that has grown from humble beginnings and now draws more than 500 racers to the track to race in a variety of classes. There is also regular Saturday night racing at the Boone Speedway throughout the summer months.

Among the busiest tourism spots in Boone is the Boone & Scenic Valley Railroad, which through efforts of Iowa Railroad Historical Society

Days, pays tribute to the railroad past and present. It, too, pays homage to Kate Shelley with a one-act play "The Legend of the Bridge" which will be staged for the first time ever at this year's event. The play will be performed by members of the Boone Community Theatre, which provides spring and fall productions in addition to a children's theatre and workshop in the summer months.

Small rail cars tour the Boone & Scenic Valley Railroad route in the spring and fall.

Boone Municipal Swimming Pool at McHose Park is a popular summer attraction.

37

Boone IOWA

Railroads

membership and more contributors, brought back to life to a railroad history era when it was common to see passenger trains stopped at the city depot and conductors and engineers all decked out in their uniforms. Those days are gone, but the heritage is preserved through the railroad that now carries an average of 45,000 passengers a year using volunteer crews.

Efforts began more than 20 years ago to purchase 250 acres and more than 12 miles of track, purchasing a small diesel locomotive and a few boxcars to get into the tourist railroad business.

Today the Boone & Scenic Valley Railroad runs electric trolley cars, diesel locomotives and steam locomotives to pull passengers in box cars through scenic views along the Des Moines River valley. The tourist railroad features its 200-ton Chinese-built steam locomotive on the weekends. The special locomotive is the only one of its type running outside China, and the last production locomotive built by the Datong Locomotive Works in 1989.

In addition to passenger rides, which includes a trip across a historic single track high bridge, the railroad company has dinner trains or dessert trains offered in air conditioned comfort.

One television "celebrity" that often visits the Boone & Scenic Valley Railroad is Thomas the Tank Engine. Its arrival in Boone in 2004 will be Sept. 17 through 19 and Sept. 24 through 26 in Boone.

One additional summer regular event occurs Wednesday night, when the Boone Municipal Band conducts its summer series of band concerts and ice cream socials at the Herman Park Pavilion in Boone. The band plays for about one hour, with different songs each week, in an outdoor setting.

The Chinese steam locomotive makes its way across the Boone & Scenic Valley high bridge.

TV personality Thomas the Tank Engine visits Boone often.

Boone IOWA

One major event each year is the Iowa Municipal Band Festival – scheduled for the second Saturday in July.

Guest municipal bands come from across the state and beyond. A municipal band from Germany will be making a guest appearance at the 2004 festival at Herman Park.

Herman Park is one of many fine playground and activity parks spread throughout the city of Boone. The city has about 300 acres dedicated to parks.

The largest is McHose Park, which also

Park Beauty

is the site for Boone's large municipal pool, complete with a 108-foot waterslide. The pool was built in 1993. The park also has three enclosed rental shelters, open shelter, three ball fields, six tennis courts, a sand volleyball court, six playgrounds, nature trails, equestrian area, a fishing pond, a bike trail and more dirt walking paths.

Memorial Park at 19th and Greene streets features one of baseball's historic baseball diamonds currently shared by Babe Ruth, high school and community college baseball teams. One of the city's parks, Miles-Lee Park at West Fifth and Franklin streets, features a World War II Battle of the Bulge Monument.

Cap Erbe Park and Wildlife Preserve at 2001 SE Linn St., features about 3.5 acres of prairie, garden, walking path, three shelters, playground and large open playing field. The park was named after Norman Erbe from Boone, who served as Iowa Governor from 1961 to 1963.

A Little League Park at West Second and Division streets has seven ball fields and numerous practice fields and often hosts Little League State Tournaments.

Outside of Boone drawing thousands of

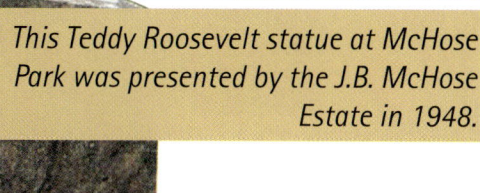

This Teddy Roosevelt statue at McHose Park was presented by the J.B. McHose Estate in 1948.

Car shows are common occurrences during the summer months in Boone and also during Pufferbilly Days.

Boone IOWA

visitors annually is Ledges State Park just south of Boone, which offers a variety of activities including camping, hiking, picnic areas, cross-country skiing, sightseeing trips, bird watching activities and more. The park is named appropriately for its unusual rock formations and ledges and it features 70 acres of restored wildlife habitat including prairie settings, along with about 15 miles of hiking trails.

The Iowa Arboretum south of Boone includes about 40 acres of horticultural collections, about four acres of prairie and more than 300 acres of native Iowa timber with self-guided trails. When visiting the arboretum, don't be surprised to see a wedding taking place in one of the gazebos there, or a bus tour of adults or children on field trips to view the "outdoor library of living plants."

If golf is in your cards, Boone has an 18-hole course at the Boone Golf & Country Club and nearby are the scenic nine-hole public Honey Creek Golf Club and Estates found in a scenic area between Boone and Ledges State Park, and Don Williams Golf Course which also features nine challenging holes. Boone is near at least 10 other golf courses in Woodward, Grand Junction, Dayton, Webster City and Ames to make this area ideal for a golfing vacation.

Don Williams also provides boating and fishing recreation at its lake, camping areas and cabins, picnic areas and shelters, hiking trails and much more.

Seven Oaks Recreation west of Boone provides snow skiing, snowboarding and snow tubing from December to March and during the spring, summer and fall when there's no snow, it offers full service canoe and kayak floats on the Des Moines River from May to October. There is a 4.5 technical single-track mountain bike trail available for daily riding. Seven Oaks hosts mountain bike races each year as well as sanctioned motocross races.

One other big attraction in Boone is the annual Boone County Fair at the county fairgrounds, this year

Flowers are maintained through efforts of garden clubs on the grounds of Ericson Public Library in Boone.

Above: Carl Fritz Henning was instrumental in the establishment of Ledges State Park south of Boone.
Right: The new Boone Business Park in southeast Boone is the home of Patterson Dental.

Boone

scheduled from July 21 through 26. The fair is an event that puts family fun first, with carnival rides, games, parades and a petting zoo. The event matches the best county fairs in the state with its 4-H and open class activities, livestock shows and top-notch entertainment.

One Lincoln Highway monument, right, and a monument dedicated to Co. D 32nd Iowa Infantry, are on the lawn at the historic Boone County Courthouse in west Boone.

One major travel route of historical significance is the Lincoln Highway. The original Lincoln Highway extended from Times Square in New York City and westward for 3,300 miles to the Pacific Ocean in San Francisco. The last of the hard-surfacing on the highway was completed in the late 1930s. The highway entered Iowa at Clinton, passing through 50 communities and 13 Iowa counties along a path that eventually would become U.S. Highway 30. Henry Joy, president of the Packard Motor Car Co., came up with the idea of naming the highway after Abraham Lincoln.

Boone is the home of the Iowa High School Athletic Association, which operates under the auspices of a state Board of Control and administration. The purpose of the association is to promote, develop, direct, protect and regulate amateur interscholastic athletic relationships between member schools and to stimulate fair play, friendly rivalry and good sportsmanship among contestants, schools and communities throughout the state.

Bernie Saggau, Iowa High School Athletic Association executive director for the past 36 years, will be retiring in 2004.

The future looks bright for Boone in the education field, as a new middle school will be built and in operation by 2006, and Des Moines Area Community

This is one of several walking or bicycle trails within the Boone city limits.

An Iowa National Guard unit from Boone returns from action in Afghanistan.

Boone

The Boone County Y outside of Boone runs day camp, summer camp and conference facilities for schools and the public throughout the year.

College Boone Campus is planning classroom expansion to keep up with the demand of enrollment increases.

Expansion is also underway at the Boone National Guard facilities. Soldiers from units based in Boone have been called to duty in the past year or more – some have returned while others continue serving their country as members of the Guard in Afghanistan, Iraq and Kosovo. The new facility, called the Readiness Center, will be instrumental in the training of new Guard members.

Guard members participate in numerous community activities and were instrumental when flood waters ravaged residential areas with the city during the flooding of 1993, when the Des Moines River flooded for extended days over Highway 30.

It was a time when residents pulled together and worked to preserve what they could. It's a trait among Boone residents who show they care – from the story of Kate Shelley's actions to save many from a disastrous train wreck, to those who walk each year in the American Cancer Society Boone County Relay for Life to raise thousands of dollars for cancer research.

The city that is vibrant and growing also has a closet full of history and heritage, and its citizens are those who are reluctant to let it all ride out on the rails.

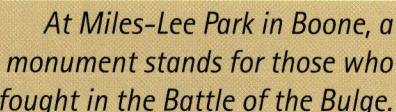

At Miles-Lee Park in Boone, a monument stands for those who fought in the Battle of the Bulge.

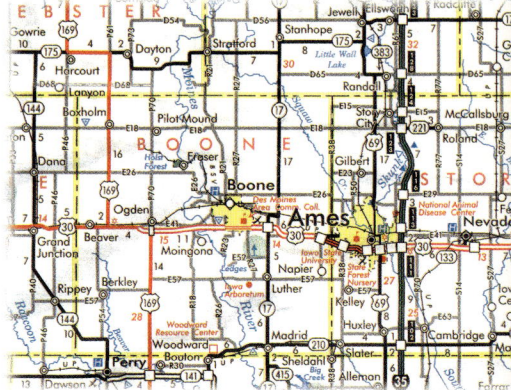

LEARN MORE

The city of Boone is the county seat of Boone County, which is located in the central part of the state. It is about 50 miles north of the state's capital, Des Moines, and about 15 miles west of Ames and Iowa State University, thriving along Highway 30. The city has a population of 12,800

STORY CONTRIBUTOR

Chuck Hackenmiller
Editor of the Boone News-Republican, who has been a resident of Boone since 1991.

Pride In Our Hometowns.

P·O·R·T·R·A·I·T·S
OF
Charles City

"AMERICA'S HOMETOWN."

For a community to stake such a claim it had better have plenty of things with which to back it up. Those familiar with Charles City, Iowa, however, will tell you the nickname is well deserved and perfectly suited.

For this north central town of 7,812 people on the banks of the Cedar River features a little of everything that makes America great, and a whole lot of determination that has helped it thrive with hard-earned success ... and survive some of the worst disasters that nature – and man – could throw at it.

CHARLES CITY

Pride In Our Hometowns.

P·O·R·T·R·A·I·T·S
OF *Charles City*

"America's Hometown."

Since the time it was first discovered by Joseph Kelly in 1851, across the river from a wigwam encampment of Winnebago indians, Charles City has become known as the birthplace of the American tractor, the childhood home of a nationally-known women's rights activist and where the treatment of poultry diseases was revolutionized. On a more infamous note, Charles City also happens to be where the last-known lynching took place in the state of Iowa. It occurred in 1907, after James Cullen was jailed for the brutal murder of his wife and step-son. The recent acquittal of a murder suspect in near-by Nashua fueled fears of a similar happening in this case and resulted in the formation of a lynch mob. They broke Cullen out of jail and strung him up on the iron Main Street bridge, leaving his body hanging there for three days. It was one of the few black marks in the community's otherwise shining history.

A Snapshot

Today, visitors marvel at the community's beauty, with its ample parks and green spaces, well-kept appearance and the scenic Cedar River winding its way through the center of town. A diverse economy provides jobs and business opportunities, with a growing industrial base buoyed by a recent multi-year, multi-million dollar investment by Fortune 500 company Winnebago Industries, Inc. Numerous shopping, dining, cultural and recreational opportunities also provide residents and guests with places to play and enjoy themselves.

It is the community's 'hometown' charm and feeling, though, which has made

Charles City

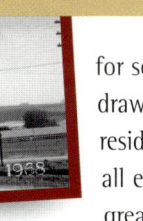

Then-Sheriff L.L. Lane captured this image of the giant tornado in 1968 just before it leveled much of Charles City.

for so many life-long residents and draws back so many other former residents and retiree's. For among all else, Charles City is known as a great place to raise a family. Its biggest asset is its people, its warmth and friendliness. If the town's physical and historical attributes don't leave a lasting impression, then the way people treat you in "America's Hometown" will.

"Charles City is all about 'community.' It's about families and quality of life," remarked Mayor Jim Erb. "We offer the best of both worlds, with modern 'bigger city' conveniences and 'small town' values and friendliness."

Charles City is also known as a survivor. On May 15, 1968, the community was devastated by the largest tornado in Iowa's recorded history, which killed 13 people and leveled half the town. The storm destroyed 256 businesses, 1,250 homes, resulted in damage costs in excess of $20 million and forever changed the face of Charles City. It took a huge rebuilding effort, and a commitment to stay by more than 175 families left homeless by the twister, but Charles City bounced back.

The community endured another major crisis in the 1980s and early '90s – this one a man-made 'disaster.' The farm economy crisis of the '80s dealt a severe blow to Charles City's largest and most successful industry – the White Farm tractor plant.

It was in 1900-01 when Charles Hart and Charles Parr first developed their gasoline traction engine in Charles City. Hart-Parr Company Sales Manager W.H. Williams decided such a name was too big a mouthful, however, and the new invention was called simply a 'tractor.' It was the first production line tractor in the United States, hence giving Charles City the distinction of being the birthplace of the American tractor.

The tractor plant flourished and was eventually purchased by James Oliver, who changed the name to the Oliver Farm Equipment Company and later the Oliver Corporation. In 1960, it was acquired by the White Farm Motor Corporation. In its heyday in the mid-1970s, the tractor plant employed 2,600

This bell tower in Andres Memorial Park serves as a reminder of the school which once stood on that site before it was destroyed in the tornado of 1968, which devastated much of Charles City.

The Floyd County Historical Society Museum features an extensive exhibit on the history of the tractor in general and of the White Farm tractor plant in Charles City in particular.

Charles City, Iowa

people and was among the leading industries in all of north Iowa. With its good-paying jobs and tradition of excellence which all of its workers took pride in, the tractor plant was a place that everyone in the community seemed centered around and where sons wanted to work like their fathers before them.

The plant was forced to declare bankruptcy with the fall of the farm economy in the '80s, and was acquired by Allied Products Corporation as the White-New Idea Equipment Company. The blow from the farm crisis was lasting, however, and eventually fatal, with the announcement in 1993 that the plant would be shutting its doors forever. The loss of over 400 jobs at the time, and just as importantly such a long-time fixture in the community, had some people predicting doom and gloom for Charles City.

As it had before with the tornado, though, this community found a way to survive. Some folks and businesses did leave, but through

What's in a name?

the resiliency and determination of those who remained, Charles City again bounced back. In 2003, it was recognized with the Iowa Department of Economic Developments top tourism award, while in 2004 Charles City was one of only two towns in Iowa to be honored as a 'Capital Community' by the Federal Home Loan Bank for its "innovative financing to attract new businesses, to complete new construction and renovation projects, to increase its housing stock and to initiate city beautification programs to enhance tourism."

Charles City was initially named 'Freeman,' but re-named for Charles Kelly, the 14-year-old son of founder Joseph Kelly, a Wisconsin miller by trade who was first attracted to the site in 1851 by the river's water power, the 'ford' or river crossing, and the ample supply of timber in the area. John Blunt and his family, who also hailed from Wisconsin originally, are actually credited with being the first white settlers to build a home in the area, having moved here in April of 1852.

It is interesting to note that the community actually tried on three other names in addition to 'Freeman' before finding one that fit in 'Charles City.' Joseph Kelly's first choice of 'Charlestown' in 1854 was dropped after the discovery of another town by that name in Iowa. The name was then changed to 'St. Charles,' but again it was found to have already been used in Madison County. Then came 'St. Charles City' in 1857, which was the name used by the state legislature at the time of

Left: Charles City's tractor heritage ranges from Hart-Parr in the early 1900s to the mighty modern marvels of White Farm Equipment. Right: Charles City's Public Arts project combines the beauty of art with the natural beauty of the community's recreational trail

Charles City Iowa

the community's incorporation. However, the town's newspaper at the time, the Republican Intelligencer, successfully campaigned later that same year to shorten the name to 'Charles City.'

The community's right to be the county seat of Floyd County was also anything but simple. Charles City was named the county seat in 1854 by a judge in a highly controversial ruling, since most county seats at that time were traditionally located near the center of the county. The town of Floyd appealed the ruling, and three times the courts decided the judge who had named Charles City as the county seat was not legally entitled to do so. Despite the on-going legal tug-of-war, construction of the first county courthouse was begun in Charles City in 1856. A year later, the courts awarded the county seat claim to Floyd, but in 1859 the Iowa Supreme Court ruled that it should be in Charles City.

ENJOY NATURE'S BEAUTY ON THE COMMUNITY'S RECREATIONAL TRAILS OR WALKING BRIDGES

On a side note, one of the more influential combatants in the county seat drama was Asgrow Benjamin Franklin Hildreth, a state senator and a legislator for the powerful railroad industry at the time. It is said Hildreth kept the railroad away from Floyd because of the courthouse battle, and to this day there is no railroad service in that community.

Hildreth was also instrumental in the creation of Charles City's most famous hotel, which was the scene of one of the community's most spectacular fires as well. The elegant three-story Hildreth Hotel was built in 1893 at a cost of $90,000, and was considered one of the finest in all of Iowa. The adjacent Opera House, also built by Hildreth, was a popular entertainment venue. The Hildreth Hotel was all about elegance and style. On February 5, 1925, however, the building was destroyed by a fire which is believed to have originated in its hamburger shop.

THE LION'S FIELD MUNICIPAL SWIMMING POOL

Today, where the Opera House once stood, is the Charles Theatre. One of only two remaining art deco-style movie houses in the Midwest, the colorful front exterior features real gold in the paint on the leaves, while the interior is being restored to its original splendor by the community theatre group, the Stony Point Players, which

The City Improvement Association of Charles City rescued the old town clock and returned it to Central Park.

Charles City

purchased the building. A live performance stage, modern sound system, outdoor walk-up concession window and other amenities have also been added by the all-volunteer theater staff, and because there are no paid employees, the theatre can charge patrons a mere $2 a night (youth are only $1) to watch first-run movies.

Across the street from where the Hildreth Hotel and Opera House once stood, and smack in the heart of downtown Charles City, is Central Park. Created in 1854 when the town was first established, the block-long, block-wide haven of green grass, trees and park benches has always remained the community's central gathering place. With radios and televisions not yet invented and newspapers at the time afforded only by the wealthy, early settlers in Charles City got their news from word-of-mouth. When there was news of community-wide importance, church bells in town would ring and alert people to gather in Central Park, where the mayor or another town leader would announce such things as the beginning and end of the Civil War and the assassination of President Abraham Lincoln.

> Charles City's first major newspaper was responsible for shortening the community's name from St. Charles City to Charles City.

From the very beginning it was agreed that no buildings would ever spoil the green space of Central Park. To this date, that agreement has been honored and respected. The park continues to serve as the central gathering place for the community, with various activities, outdoor summer concerts and a series of 'Party in the Park' events held there each year.

Across from Central Park on North Jackson Street is the historic Carnegie Library building, donated in 1904 by capitalist Andrew Carnegie.

According to the conditions of the Carnegie gift, the elegant building, with its wooden archways and stained glass windows, can only be used as a public library or public cultural center. The Charles City Public Library moved into its new facility in 1979, and the Charles City Arts Center now occupies the Carnegie building. In addition to hosting exhibits and artistic workshops throughout the year, the Arts Center also sponsors an annual 'Art-A-Fest' in Central Park to allow area artists to spotlight and sell their work.

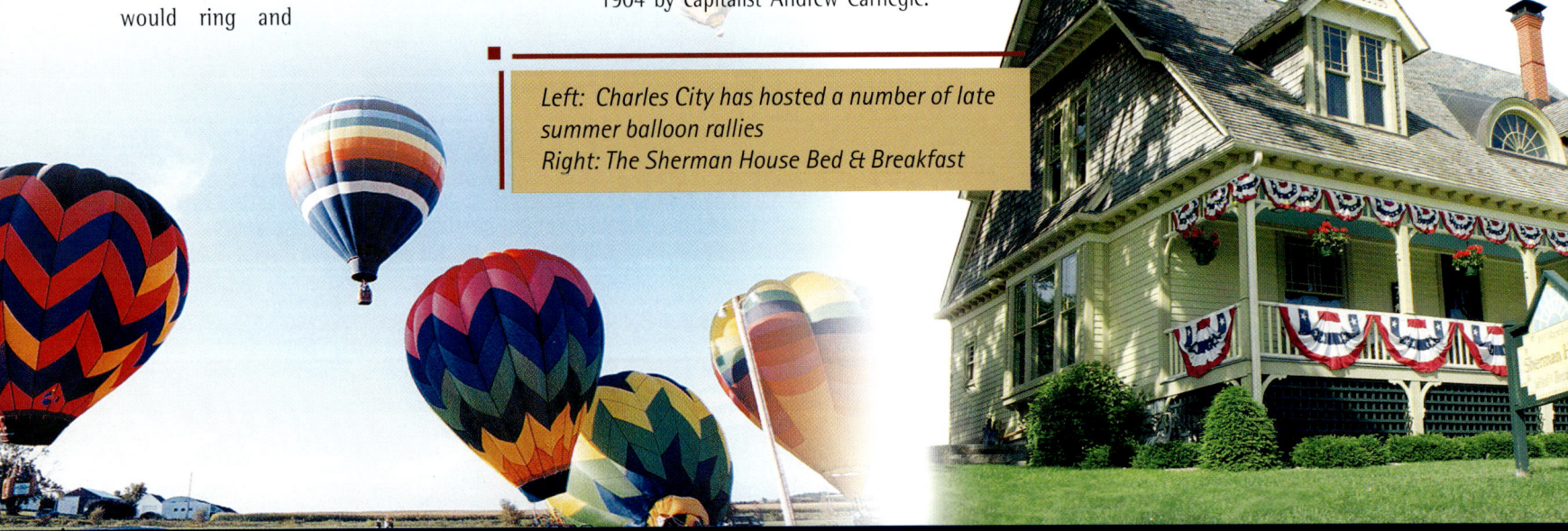

Left: Charles City has hosted a number of late summer balloon rallies
Right: The Sherman House Bed & Breakfast

Charles City IOWA

BEST-KEPT SECRET REVEALED

Speaking of the Public Library, few communities the size of Charles City can boast of a facility such as the one offered here. Modern architecture, public computer use and Internet access, a separate children's library, state-wide sharing system and the scenic Zastrow River Room all make it standout. What is really special, though, is the custom-built art gallery and the treasures within. Few visitors from outside the community can believe what they see when they walk in the doors – works from the likes of Rembrandt, Picasso and Grant Wood. They are all part of the Arthur Mooney Collection, which was donated to the City of Charles City in 1941.

Arthur Mooney grew up in Charles City and turned an interest in photography into a prominent career with the Eastman-Kodak Company. His many travels allowed him to add to his considerable private art collection. Before his death, he decided he wanted his hometown to be able to enjoy the art he so loved. However, the Charles City Public Library didn't quite know what to do with the collection of raw, unframed pieces. So for years it sat locked in the library's basement vault, its existence known by a very few.

In 1996, however, a local fund-raising effort generated enough to get the art pieces framed so they could go out on tour and be enjoyed and appreciated. When the late Katherine Zastrow bequeathed the library a large monetary gift to build a community meeting room in 1997, the library successfully applied for grant money with which to build a permanent home for the Mooney Collection at the same time. The climate-controlled gallery opened its doors in 2001, and Charles City's best-kept secret was a secret no longer.

It's never been a secret the role Charles City played in the birth of the American tractor, but few folks outside of the community realize some of the other major

Left: The Farmers Market attracts local vendors and shoppers alike on Wednesdays and Saturdays throughout the summer and fall months. Top: The Cedar River in Charles City offers a number of recreational opportunities.

Charles City

contributions to society that came from Charles City. Carrie Lane Chapman Catt, for one, was a leading pioneer of the national women's rights movement and a driving force behind both the League of Women Voters and the creation of the United Nations. Her childhood home is just outside of Charles City and is now a tourist attraction.

Carrie Lane Chapman Catt

Joseph E. 'Dr. Joe' Salsbury was another. An immigrant to America from England when he was 21 years old, Salsbury developed an interest in veterinary science and enrolled in the Kansas City Veterinary College in 1911. He spent that summer working as a veterinarian apprentice to Dr. J.H. McLeod in Charles City. Years later, when Dr. McLeod was ready to sell his practice, 'Dr. Joe' returned to Charles City, bringing with him his family and a long-standing passion – to find a cure for poultry diseases. That interest resulted in the development of a number of poultry disease treatments, including chicken worming capsules that proved to be extremely popular with area farmers, as it was discovered a side benefit of the treatment was a growth stimulant that made for larger chickens.

Dr. Salsbury's Poultry Service Company steadily grew into a thriving enterprise with a nationwide sales force. Dr. Joe would go on to pioneer the development of a chicken pox vaccine, as well as initiate a 'Poultry Short Course' that drew poultrymen from all across the U.S. and around the world to Charles City. The business was re-named Dr. Salsbury's Laboratories and in 1937 moved into a new state-of-the-art complex at 500 Gilbert Street – which today is home to the Floyd County Historical Society Museum. The late 1930s and early '40s saw the company move into biologics for other livestock as well, and in 1946 a new pharmaceutical production facility just west of Charles City along Highway 14. A chemical production facility was added to that site in 1948. Over the years, both production facilities were expanded, and eventually the entire Salsbury Laboratories operation relocated to the campus on the west side of town.

In 1979, Salsbury Laboratories was

Re-live history at the Floyd County Historical Society Museum

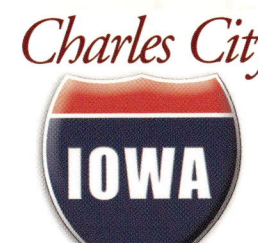

Charles City IOWA

efforts, the community's overall appearance has been greatly enhanced, particularly in the historic downtown district where restoration and preservation are stressed.

Quality of life

All work and no play can make for a dull town. Charles City enjoys playing as hard as it works, with a wide range of recreational opportunities for all ages, a local YMCA, three golf courses within a 10-mile radius, a modern municipal swimming pool and water slide, acres of parkland, ample hunting and fishing opportunities, a scenic riverside recreational trail, and, of course, the river. For over 15 years now, Charles City has played host to the Continental Amateur Baseball Association 9-and-Under Little League World Series tournament that draws teams from all across the U.S., Mexico and Puerto Rico. The many cultural activities are easily accessible to members of the public wishing to join in on the fun.

CAMBREX

purchased by the Soltex Polymer Corporation, a subsidiary of the Belgium-based Solvay S.A., and re-named Solvay Animal Health. Solvay was not interested, however, in the Salsbury feed additive and fine chemical production part of the operation. Those were purchased by the New Jersey-based company Cambrex and operated as Salsbury Chemicals before changing its name to Cambrex-Charles City. Today, both industries are major employers in Charles City. Wyeth bought out the operation in the mid-1990s from Solvay and now operates it as Fort Dodge Animal Health.

Charles City's largest employer is a nationally-recognized company that before 1999 did not have a presence in the community. Winnebago Industries, Inc., recognized what Charles City had to offer in terms of quality workforce and quality of life, though, and between 1999 and 2003 invested in not one, but three separate production facilities, including the largest expansion project in company history. Today, Winnebago Industries employs more than 600 at its Charles City campus.

The overall business climate in Charles City is a fertile one, thanks to the aggressive efforts of the Charles City Area Chamber of Commerce, Community Revitalization and Charles City Area Development Corporation. Charles City is one of 33 'Main Street Iowa' communities in the state, and has taken a pro-active role in business assistance and enhancement through such programs as revolving loans, facade improvement grants and upper story rehabilitation grants. As a result of these

Winnebago Industries, Inc., has invested heavily in Charles City, establishing a three-facility campus and employing over 600 people there.

Charles City IOWA

Charles City also places a premium on education, with a selection of public and private schools in town, as well as a satellite center for North Iowa Area Community College. Local school and club sports are popular with participants and fans alike, while the Charles City High School Music Program earned a coveted Grammy Award, and the highly-acclaimed Drama Department brought home a state championship banner in 2003. The recent addition of TLC: The Learning Center also brings quality child day care and early childhood education to the forefront.

The Floyd County Memorial Hospital offers hometown medical care, and is affiliated with the world-renown Mayo Clinic in near-by Rochester, Minn., which regularly sends specialist to Charles City for local clinical care to supplement the local medical community.

And tourism? Take your pick from among other things the previously mentioned cultural treasures, the Historical Society Museum with its extensive antique tractor collection, the childhood home of Carrie Lane Chapman Catt, the near-by Rockford Fossil and Prairie Park or the Little Brown Church in the Vale made famous by the hymn of the same name. And let's not forget Charles City's most famous landmark – the historic Suspension Bridge built in 1906 which still is in use today and is on the National Register of Historic Places.

Odds are you will need more than one day to take in all of that, and Charles City has you covered with four great motels and one of the best bed & breakfast stops in the Midwest

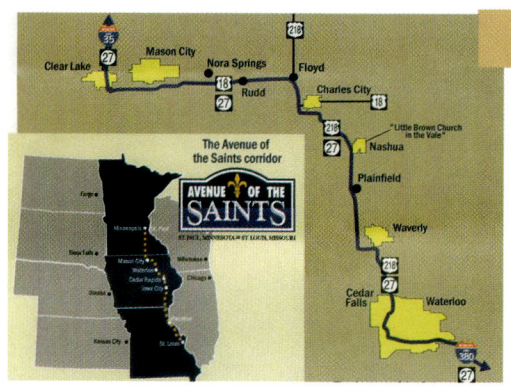

in the Sherman House. Traveling by RV or camper? That's no problem either, thanks to a large campground right in town

Bigger than a small town and smaller than a big town, Charles City has it all ... or is close to it all, thanks to the adjacent four-lane Avenue of the Saints interstate. Local rail and air transportation is also available, making getting to wherever you want to go a snap.

From a Teen Center to the Senior Center; from service clubs to card and car clubs; from nursing homes to independent assisted living; and through the welcoming hand of the Charles City International Fellowship organization, Charles City reaches out to all ages and nationalities. The community catches your eye, but it's the people and how they treat you that captures your heart.

"There's a spirit in that town that is beyond human, and the whole trip home everyone on the bus was in agreement that we don't think we could ever top this trip," remarked one visitor following a community tour. "Out of 22 tours, we've never had a trip like this. Congratulations Charles City! You really made us feel welcome!"

Then again, what else would you expect from America's Hometown?

LEARN MORE

Charles City is located in northeast Iowa, 30 miles east of Mason City and Interstate 35, and just south of the Minnesota border along the Avenue of the Saints (Hwy. 18/27).

For more information, please contact the Charles City Area Chamber of Commerce at (641) 228-4234, or visit
www.charlescitychamber.com
You may also visit the Charles City Press website at:
www.charlescitypress.com

Mark Wicks
Managing Editor, Charles City Press

The story of Charles City is brought to you by Mark Wicks, the managing editor the Charles City Press and a adopted son of America's Hometown. Information contained in the story has been collected by a number individuals throughout the years, with special recogniti to Marilee Monroe and Jeff Sisson, as well as Cameron Hanson and Heather M. Hul who authored, "Past Harves A History of Floyd County to 1996."

Pride In Our Hometowns.

P·O·R·T·R·A·I·T·S
OF
Cherokee

A STRONG AGRICULTURAL AND INDUSTRIAL REGION

Nestled in tree-covered hills surrounded by rich farmland, Cherokee is the center of one of the strongest agricultural and industrial regions in the northwestern part of the state. Whether approaching from the north, south, east, or west, the town, located in a serene river valley, appears over a hill as if out of nowhere and is a welcome sight to travelers.

The city's location was chosen because of its close proximity to the Little Sioux River, the only means of transportation besides prairie schooner during the middle 19th century. Once the railroad was built nearby, the city was able to usurp the opportunities it provided.

CHEROKEE

Pride In Our Hometowns.

P·O·R·T·R·A·I·T·S
OF *Cherokee*

THE CENTER OF ONE OF THE STRONGEST AGRICULTURAL AND INDUSTRIAL REGIONS IN NORTHWESTERN IOWA.

By the mid 20th century, Cherokee - deriving its name from the Cherokee Indian tribe, had grown into a railroad terminal of significant proportions with several tracks leading to the roundhouse where engines were maintained. Today, although a train moves through the community once a day, people from the agriculture community and nearby industrial markets transport their goods by truck along U.S. Highway 59 and Iowa Highway 3, or over well-maintained county highways.

A SNAPSHOT

Cherokee's history begins in the early 1800's when the county was one of 49 sections of land divided from Indian Treaty lands.

Cherokee's water tower sits high and visible to all visitors.

Buildings began to appear as people moved in. One of the new families was Robert & Catherine Perry. Born in Northern Ireland in August 1832, Robert immigrated to the United States at the age of 23. He married an Irish gal named Catherine McDermott in Connecticut and then decided to push farther west. In 1856 they came to Cherokee County.

Robert and Catherine, with all their belongings, arrived at the winding Little Sioux River in June of that year. They saw a country that was untamed but their strong resolve to make a new home for themselves did not diminish even though there were few white people and the Indians were numerous. Robert constructed a primitive log cabin and moved his

Cherokee

History

family's few pieces of furniture inside before winter set in.

It wasn't long before more white settlers joined the new settlement, later known as Old Cherokee. Robert Perry's enthusiastic and very vivid description of his county home, with its valleys, trees and rivers, enticed members of the Milford Massachusetts Emigration Company to choose a site on the west side of the river, northeast of the present city of Cherokee. They were seeking land for their members whose wagons were close behind. Thirteen Milford colonists came in 1856, two of them with families of children, and then another group of men led by George Banister settled several miles south the same summer.

A tribe of Sioux Indians attacked the settlement the next year. After three long days of fighting, the band of Indians left the area and headed for the Iowa Lakes region, about 60 miles to the northeast, where they attacked a settler and his family. When the citizens heard of the massacre at Spirit Lake, some deserted Old Cherokee but many stayed.

When Robert Perry was asked, along with two other men, to pick a site for their courthouse in 1861, he scouted the area thoroughly to determine the best spot. Perry picked a piece of land by the river in Pilot township. A year later, the government built a series of stockades with blockhouses to provide a safe haven for the settlers from nearby Indian problems. Fort Cherokee looked out over the entire Milford Colony.

After Cherokee men returned from the Civil War, the promise of a railroad that would run through the village from Fort Dodge to Sioux City brought countless businesses and professional people. In 1869, Mr. N. T. Burroughs, one of the men who platted the present location for the town, came to Cherokee County to open a real estate office.

In March of 1870 the Dubuque and Sioux City Railroad was finally completed but it did not cross the Little Sioux where expected. Speculators had built up quite a town by then so they had to literally drag their houses and shops, as well as their county courthouse, to the new location.

A picture from the past: Downtown Cherokee as it was in 1929.

Left: Downtown Cherokee, present day.

Cherokee IOWA

Goldbury's Bank was the first to open its doors in New Cherokee in 1871. Mr. Burroughs operated in both real estate and the livestock business until 1873. Then his interests moved to banking and in 1875, Scribner & Burroughs erected an attractive brick building on the corner of Main and Railroad Streets. In 1883, the bank became known as the First National Bank of Cherokee, with Burroughs as president.

Cherokee's early residents did not have to travel far to obtain necessary supplies. Everything they needed was available in town and the same is true today. Attorneys, bankers, school teachers, manufacturers, restaurant owners, and mechanics arrived in the growing community to provide jobs and services for a population that was growing by leaps and bounds.

Senator Guy Gillette was born in Cherokee, February 3, 1879. He attended the public schools, graduated from the law department of Drake University in Des Moines, and was admitted to the bar in 1900. He began a law practice in Cherokee in 1906 and became a member of

SOMETHING FOR EVERYONE

the State senate between 1912 and 1916. During the First World War he served as a captain in the United States Army and upon his release was elected as a Democrat to the Seventy-third Congress. From then until his retirement in 1961, he served in a variety of positions in the U.S. Senate.

Besides grasshoppers, blizzards and prairie fires, the town of Cherokee suffered a massive flood in 1891, leaving about 100 people homeless. But not even a flood could staunch their pioneer spirit. The census figures increased and in 1896, Evangelist Billy Sunday preached his first sermon to the residents. Chautauqua invited

The bells of St. Paul's United Methodist Church ring out every day at 5 p.m. with hymns old and new.

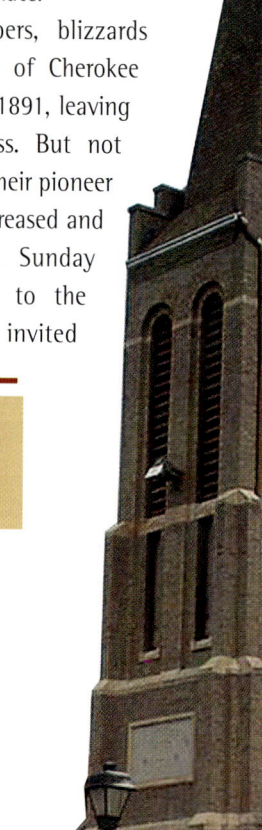

Immacul[ate] Concept[ion] Catholic Chur[ch] has been arou[nd] since the l[ate] 1800s. T[he] building, th[e] current locati[on] was built [in] 19[..]

Cherokee County Courthouse, pictured in 1900.

Democratic candidate William Jennings Bryan to town in 1897. He lost the election to President McKinley that year.

In 1901 the infamous Maple Street buildings caught fire ridding the town of 'these stinking shacks' as the townspeople called them. This section of town, located close to the railroad depot, was filled with bars and houses of prostitution. Like many towns in the Midwest, Cherokee's history is also marked with vigilantes and shoot-outs as well as bank robberies. Steele's Bank was the first one to be robbed.

Manufacturing giants Vernon Lundell and R. J. Thomas, besides providing work for hundreds in the mid 20th century, put Cherokee on the map when people from across the nation began ordering the equipment manufactured in their plants. In 1945, Vernon Lundell's first invention was a two-wheel dumpcart, but Lundell Manufacturing based its reputation on thirty different farm machines. Today, Vernon's idea for a recycling machine helps divert and recycle up to 90 percent of municipal solid waste.

In 1959, R.J. Thomas began manufacturing Pilot Rock Park Equipment, outdoor park, and campground site furnishings. You will find R.J. Thomas Manufacturing Company equipment in use by city, county, state and federal parks, campgrounds, amusement parks, recreation areas, and private individuals throughout the U.S. and in many other countries.

In 1949, another Cherokee resident made the name of Cherokee well known throughout the country. Bob Barnes, owner of Barnes PRCA Rodeo Stock Contractors, is known across the nation as he and his family bring quality bucking horses and bulls to the rodeo arena. Bob is the longest individual PRCA stock contractor in the nation and a member of the ProRodeo Hall of Fame.

In 1958, former president Harry S. Truman stopped by to speak to anyone who wanted to listen and then in 1965, Sir Tyrone Guthrie, an internationally known English stage director, playwright, and writer from the Minnesota Theater Company, opened the new Cherokee Community Center. President Jimmy Carter and President George H. Bush also visited and spoke to residents at Washington High School's auditorium.

The declining farm economy of the mid

Canon at located at Koser-Spring Lake Park. The park is a gathering place for residents and visitors alike.

57

Cherokee IOWA

80's affected everyone in the agriculture industry surrounding Cherokee, which in turn affected everyone in Cherokee including those in the real estate business. Sticking it out though, Cherokee real estate agent and the owner of Miller Mac Agency, Joan Ballantyne, was awarded the Distinguished Service Award in Real Estate, one of only 67 real estate agents across the nation who received that award. She also served as the National President of the Women's Council of Realtors.

Some professional sports stars also called Cherokee their birth place. In the 1930's track star John Graves became the town's hero as he broke records set by those who went before him. Gordon Steele wrestled for Yale University and football player, Adam Timmerman, born in Cherokee in 1971, was drafted by the Green Bay Packers in 1995. He was traded to the St. Louis Rams three years later and is currently fulfilling his second five year contract with the Rams. Ralph Kroger, owner of Victory Gym, was named Mr. America in 1975, the same year he won the Mr. USA title and the Mr. International title.

Commander in Chief of Strategic Air Command, General John D. Ryan graduated from the public school system in Cherokee and was appointed to West Point by Senator Gillette in 1934. His son, 4-star General Michael E. Ryan was also Chief of Staff of the U.S. Air Force until 2001.

While word of mouth enticed many to consider Cherokee as their home in the mid 1800's, culture adds a great deal to the charm of this community and is the modern day drawing card. Since 1951,

Ralph Kroger earned the title of Mr. America, Mr. USA, and Mr. International in 1975. Over his 40 years in competition, he earned several other titles as well

Sioux Valley Memorial Hospital serves the areas needs for healthcare.

Cherokee IOWA

The annual Cherokee Jazz & Blues Festival brings headliners from Kansas City and New York City to Cherokee for a week-end celebrating music.

visitors have been able to enter the doors of the Sanford Museum to view exhibits on a variety of subjects and the Sanford Planetarium was the first in the state of Iowa.

Since 1959, the Cherokee Community Theater presents full-scale productions plus melodramas, musicals, one act plays and readings three times a year. The Cherokee Symphony was co-founded in 1956 and provides the community with high quality musical entertainment. It has been referred to as "the best kept secret in Northwest Iowa."

Each year, the Cherokee Jazz Festival, held in January, brings some very talented people into close proximity with jazz aficionados to celebrate this American tradition. Among those are repeat performer Mark Pender, trumpet player with the Max Weinberg 7, the house band for television's Conan O'Brien Show on NBC. Many well-known and legendary Kansas City area jazz musicians also participate in the three-day gala.

The Cherokee Depot is a renovation in progress and offers a variety of historical opportunities. The annual PRCA Rodeo is held the first weekend of June. This event, as well as the Cherokee County Fair, brings thousands to Cherokee each year.

Floods are a periodic threat to any river valley and continue to occur every now and then, with the most devastating in 1965, 1969 and again in 1993. The 1993 flooding in the United States, part of the torrential rains and raging waters that plagued much of the Midwest, is described as the most significant and damaging natural disaster to ever hit the United States. Once cleanup began, 150 homes were relocated to higher ground or razed by FEMA leaving the flood plain free for wildlife to roam and inhabit.

RESTORED BELL FROM THE ORIGINAL COURTHOUSE BUILT IN 1861

HEROKEE WELLNESS CENTER

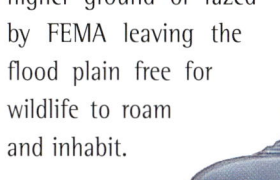

Cherokee IOWA

Cherokee civic groups were and still are a vital part of the community providing support during the floods and for the years before and after. The Cherokee VFW, with members who fought in World Wars 1 and 11, Korea, Granada, Vietnam, and The Golf War, was granted a charter on October 29, 1931. The Kiwanis, the Lions Club, the Knights of Columbus, Cherokee Business and Professional Women, and the Rotary Club are philanthropic organizations that offer one or two scholarships yearly to graduating high school students as well as raise funds for several worthwhile community charities.

Cherokee's health needs are well looked after with a 67 bed hospital, a life line, 4 medical clinics, 4 dentists, 3 chiropractors, 2 optometrists, a

CHEROKEE HIGH SCHOOL, 1906

hearing aid specialist and three extended care facilities, as well as a large mental health facility. Cherokee also has two pharmacies and 2 funeral homes.

Cherokee's Mental Health Institute, built in 1902, housed as many as 1729 patients in 1945. Today, its buildings are home to a small population of mentally handicapped people, and an alcohol treatment facility, as well as other community based programs. In 2003, a Civil Commitment Unit for Sexual Offenders (CCUSO) was established at the MHI facility, bringing dozens of new jobs with it.

Cherokee's retirement community, The Beck, is located in close proximity to the Sioux Valley Memorial Hospital and Wellness Center; where a brand new facility members can enjoy the pool, racquetball courts, and weight training equipment, as

Zylstra Harley Davidson provides Cherokee residents with motorcycles to ride the winding roads of the Loess Hills nearby. Larry Kennelly is the sales manager for Zylstra Harley Davidson in Cherokee.

Above: Cherokee Mental Health Institute in 1911. L Present day Mental Health Institute.

well as other aerobic equipment. Victory Gym, a downtown facility, is also open to those who wish to work out and stay in shape.

Cherokee is home to the current Miss Rodeo Iowa, Megan Wiemold, who makes good use of an expansive new horse arena to ride and train her horses. To provide opportunities for residents to stay in shape, as well as a place for many to participate in a variety of sports, Cherokee has several parks. These parks are used for the Hershey Youth Track & Field Meet, the Outdoor Fun Fair, Braves Flag Football, Fall Youth Soccer, Adult Slow Pitch Softball, and Sand Volleyball Leagues. Fishing, jogging, hiking, biking and disc golf also are offered. Koser-Spring Lake Park is an 18-acre lake with several camping

MUNICIPAL POOL

MISS RODEO IOWA

amenities and a Yacht Club available for group meetings, reunions, weddings, and other gatherings, complete with kitchen facilities.

The Cherokee Golf and Country Club, first built in 1923, is a venerable nine hole, par 36 golf course

open all year round except for February. Cherokee has an active Little League with five ball fields, and the Municipal Pool is the place where the Cherokee Clippers Swim Team works out. The community offers indoor volleyball and basketball leagues, and has six new tennis courts.

Cherokee Washington High School boasts an eight-lane all-weather track, baseball and softball fields, large gymnasium and auditorium, and football stadium, while the new Cherokee Middle School has its own track and adjacent access to the

The Cherokee Depot is a renovation in progress and offers a variety of historical opportunities.

Cherokee

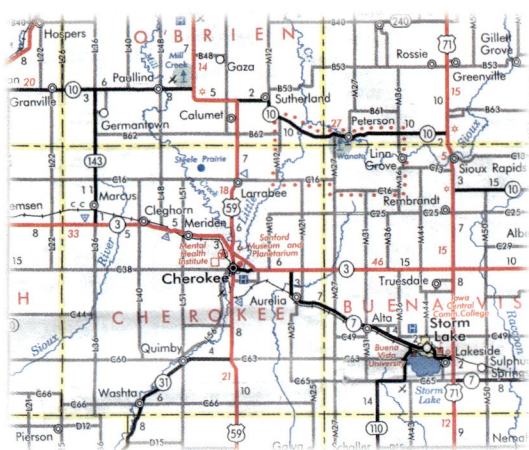

Learn More

Cherokee is located in the Little Sioux River Valley in central Cherokee County, intersected by U.S. Highway 59 and by Highway 3.

For further information contact the Cherokee Chamber of Commerce at 712-225-6414.

Sam Doupe Complex housing all the community ball fields and tennis courts.

Factory owners, veterinarians, and other business people, as well as pleasure pilots, come and go at Cherokee's Airport which has a 4,000 ft. all weather runway. The city's active Economic Development Corporation is always looking for new business opportunities that would be the right fit for the community, making use of the eight construction companies in town to build whatever is needed.

Cherokee contains a history of hard-working families, progressive visionaries, and innovative businesses. Well constructed buildings flank both sides of the Little Sioux River and surround Koser-Spring Lake Park

Cherokee's beauty continues to entice young and old alike, seekers of peace, quiet, and country. New housing stretches boundaries as in the beginning and all are welcome to come, enjoy, and participate.

Story Contributor

Barbara Ann Derksen, a correspondent for The Chronicle Times, began writing about twenty years ago. She has completed two series of children books, a murder mystery titled Mind Trap and is currently working on the first of a murder trilogy. She is also working on collection of war stories.

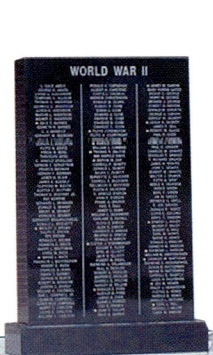

Cherokee County Veterans Memorial

Pride In Our Hometowns.

P·O·R·T·R·A·I·T·S
OF
Clarinda

WHERE THE WORK ETHIC STILL WORKS

For over 150 years the residents of Clarinda have known the value of a fair reward for a fair day's work. Since the earliest settlers first arrived in the area the residents of Clarinda have worked hard to provide a good home and a good way of life for themselves, their families and their neighbors.

With its continuing advances in community development, recreational activities, education and business and industrial ventures, Clarinda continues to prove each day that original work ethic still works.

CLARINDA

Pride In Our Hometowns.

P·O·R·T·R·A·I·T·S
OF *Clarinda*

Where the Work Ethic Still Works

Page County Courthouse

"Through hard work and dedication, the generations before us set the groundwork for the quality of life we all enjoy today. I like to think our city has the vision to do things today that will help keep Clarinda vibrant in the future. I hope what we're doing will continue to attract the same quality of people as we have today who are willing to give of themselves to support our community," Clarinda Mayor Frank Snyder explained.

Clarinda is located in Southwest Iowa, just over 10 miles from the Missouri border and only about two hours from Omaha, Des Moines or Kansas City. Although Page County was surveyed in 1846, the U.S. Supreme Court did not make a decision on the final legal boundary between Iowa and Missouri until 1851. Several settlers were already making their homes in the eastern and southern sections of the county. The county was named in honor of Captain John Page, a hero killed in the Mexican War, by the first Iowa General Assembly in 1847. When a commission was appointed by the Iowa General Assembly to locate a site for the seat of justice for the new county, they chose a site two miles north and west of the busy Nodaway Mill. The name Clarinda was chosen for the new town site in honor of Miss Clarinda Buck, who was visiting her uncle, Alexander Tice, an early pioneer. The story is told that she carried water to the surveyors as they worked. Our town, Clarinda, is the only town in the U.S. with this name. The town was platted in May of 1853, as a square plat of 49 blocks, seven blocks square, centered by a public block. A unique feature of the plat was the wide street laid out in all directions two blocks away from the public block called the North, West, South and East Promenade, and the block outside of this wide street designated the city limits. This Promenade, or Boulevard, is still a unique feature of the city today.

The public block, or town square of Clarinda, is still one of its more popular attractions of the community today. Various restaurants, retail stores and business offices comprise the town square.

A Snapshot

Welcome signs greet visitors at the primary entryways to Clarinda and help create the neighborly atmosphere the community is known for.

64

Clarinda

that surrounds the historic Page County Courthouse.

The laying of the cornerstone for the Page County Courthouse occurred on July 4, 1885. The total cost of this Courthouse was $86,500— which included the building and clock tower, heating, fixtures and furnishings and artwork. On Dec. 11, 1991, a tragic fire nearly destroyed the historic courthouse. On that terrible December night, as the fire raged on, the American and Iowa flags continued to fly on top of the courthouse. It was only when the rotunda roof burned that the flagpole fell, remaining on the burned-out shell of the courthouse until it could be retrieved a few days later. Just as the flags refused to fall, the citizens of Clarinda and Page County refused to give in to the fire as 85 percent of the citizens voted to rebuild the historic building, once again showing the community's strong work ethic and desire to preserve its heritage. Construction began in January of 1993 to restore the courthouse and the county offices were moved back into the Courthouse on March 23 and 24, 1994. On June 5, 1994, a huge crowd attended a rededication ceremony for the Page County Courthouse that featured a special flyover by the Iowa Air National Guard. In 2000, Page County was awarded the "David Archie Award for Historical Preservation" for the restoration of the Courthouse.

An Annual Lighted Christmas Parade is held on the Friday after Thanksgiving to honor the many area fire departments that helped battle the courthouse fire, to celebrate the restoration of the historic building and officially mark the start of the Christmas season in Clarinda. Over the past 150 years many famous people have either lived in or visited Clarinda, but probably none is more famous internationally than its native son, Alton Glenn Miller. The world-renowned Big Band leader was born in Clarinda on March 1, 1904. The home in which Miller and his family lived still stands today at 601 S. 16th Street.

Clarinda first received recognition as the birthplace of Glenn Miller in 1954 when the city was selected to host one of the press premieres of "The Glenn

Goldenrod School was where Jesse Field Shambaugh first introduced the theories that led to the development of the national 4-H movement. The school now stands on the grounds of the Nodaway Valley Historical Museum in Clarinda.

The Clarinda water tower stands along Cardinal Drive near Clarinda High School.

Clarinda, IOWA

CLARINDA PUBLIC LIBRARY

Miller Story". Glenn Miller's mother, Mattie Lou Miller, traveled to Clarinda along with movie star Jimmy Stewart and his wife, Gloria, for the festivities. Ben Zersen who had played in Miller's very first band while in Fort Morgan High School and John Mosbarger of Grant City, Missouri, who gave Miller his first trombone, also attended the movie premiere.

Then, 22 years later, the first Glenn Miller Day was held in Clarinda as part of the community's Bicentennial Celebration on May 13, 1976. The Clarinda Lion's Club led the way for the celebration by providing a plaque that was placed in the yard of the Glenn Miller birthplace home. Soon after the first event, the Glenn Miller Birthplace Society was established to bring together Miller fans from all over the world. This first Glenn Miller Day was the beginning of many festivals with the Glenn Miller Birthplace Society presenting its 29th Glenn Miller Festival in June of 2004. That celebration honored Miller's 100th birthday. Clarinda has a population of approximately 5,800 people for 51 weeks of the year, but during the second week of June each year that population virtually doubles as Glenn Miller enthusiasts from around the world flock to his birthplace to honor the memory of his music and his life. In fact, the Glenn Miller Festival has become so popular it has been expanded from one day in 1976 to a five-day event in 2004.

Among the international guests who have attended the Glenn Miller Festival is Mr. Hideomi Aoki from Japan. As an avid Miller fan and a lover of the town of Clarinda, he searched Japan for a musical group to bring to Clarinda. That group was a Girls High School Band from Tamana, Japan that first appeared at the Festival in 1990. This band has returned in 1993, 1996, 1998, 2000, 2002 and 2004 to entertain the Glenn Miller fans and citizens of Clarinda. While visiting Clarinda, the band members stay in private homes, which has promoted a strong cultural exchange between Clarinda and Tamana, Japan. This relationship has led to establishing a Sister City relationship between the two cities, an exchange program and Sister School relationship between Clarinda High School and Tamana Girls' High School and the creation of the Japan branch of the Glenn Miller Birthplace Society.

Other popular festivals that draw thousands of visitors to Clarinda

The new Lied Public Library is located at the intersection of 16th and Garfield Streets.

Clarinda

each year are the Southwest Iowa Band Jamboree, traditionally held on the first Saturday of October, and two weeks later Clarinda hosts the Annual Clarinda Craft Carnival sponsored by the Clarinda Chamber of Commerce.

Baseball has been a summer tradition in Clarinda since 1954. The Clarinda A's, an amateur league team, have thrilled thousands of fans while introducing them to the National Pastime. Over that time, the most famous player to wear the A's uniform was Hall of Fame shortstop Ozzie Smith of the St. Louis Cardinals.

Known as "The Wizard of Oz" for his acrobatic defensive skills, Smith played for the Clarinda A's during the 1975 and 1976 seasons. Following his playing days in Clarinda, Smith has remained a strong supporter of the Clarinda A's program and regularly returns for the Clarinda A's Hall of Fame Banquet held each year over Thanksgiving weekend. After Smith was inducted into the Major League Baseball Hall of Fame, the city of Clarinda recognized Smith by renaming the street in front of the city baseball stadium in his honor.

Other Clarinda A's players who went on to star in the major leagues included Von Hayes and Bud Black. In all, 28 former A's players have went on to appear in the major leagues as either a player, a coach or an umpire.

A small, one-room school house originally located in rural Page County is also credited as being the birthplace of the 4-H movement and the teacher at the school, Jesse Field Shambaugh, is recognized as "The Mother of 4-H." In 1901 Field Shambaugh started her teaching career at Goldenrod School and it was there that she first introduced her theories on "teaching country children in terms of country life."

HOME OF CLARINDA A'S AND 4-H

While teaching at Goldenrod School, Field Shambaugh developed farm and home related courses for her students and also established the Boys' Corn Club. After leaving Iowa briefly, Field Shambaugh returned to Page County in 1906 as county superintendent of schools. One of her goals as superintendent was to expand the Boys' Corn Club and other programs she had originally started while teaching at Goldenrod School. With the assistance of teachers, who served as leaders for the group, Field Shambaugh was able to introduce these programs to the 130 rural schools in Page County. In the fall of 1906 Field also began preparations for a Junior Exhibit at the Farmers Institute to be held in Clarinda. To encourage participation in the Junior Achievement

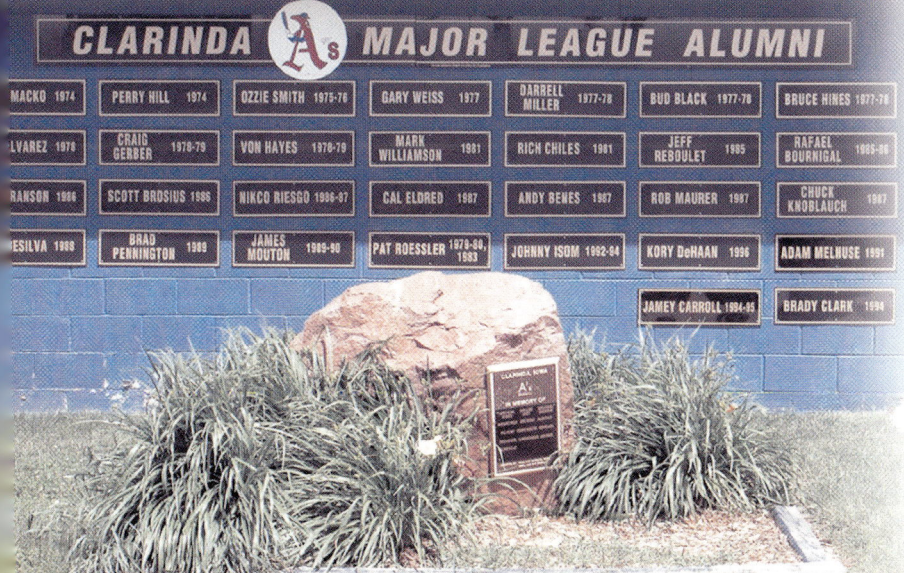

The Wall of Fame at Municipal Stadium honors former Clarinda A's players who have went on to appear in the major leagues.

Lisle Corporation is a family owned manufacturing company that was founded in 1903.

Clarinda, Iowa

Show, Field designed a special pin featuring a three-leaf clover with the letter H on each leaf and a kernel of corn in the center as the symbol of the 3-H program. The three H's stood for Head, Heart and Hands. A fourth leaf was later added to the clover, with an H for health, and remains the symbol of 4-H today. Goldenrod School still stands today on the grounds of the Nodaway Valley Historical Museum in Clarinda and is one of the many exhibits of local history visitors can enjoy.

The Nodaway Valley Historical Society (NVHS) is dedicated to preserving the rich heritage of the Clarinda area by collecting, restoring, cataloging and displaying artifacts, memorabilia and educational information in a protected and controlled environment. The NVHS was organized in 1988 and the Museum was built the following year on a ten-acre site at the south edge of Clarinda near the junction of Highway 71 and Highway 2. The museum is open daily, except for Mondays and holidays. Visitors from near and far have a special interest in many aspects of the local heritage in and around Clarinda, including 4-H, Glenn Miller, a Prisoner of War Camp that was located in Clarinda during World War II, the Orphan Train which stopped in Clarinda, industrial and military history of the area, and genealogical research to name a few.

Three other Clarinda natives have gone on to have successful movie and television careers. Marilyn Maxwell was born in Clarinda on Aug. 3, 1922. A popular movie star of her day, Maxwell toured with Bob Hope during World War II and also sang with the Ted Weems Orchestra. Born and raised in Clarinda, Billy Aaron Brown is currently pursuing an acting career in Hollywood. Brown is best known as "Kyle" on the ABC sitcom "8 Simple Rules for Dating My Teenage Daughter." He also starred in the motion picture "Jeepers Creepers 2" and has appeared in various television movies staring Mary Kate and Ashley Olson. He has also made guest appearances on such television shows as "Touched By An Angel" and "Boston Public." Richard Carson, brother of famed television personality Johnny Carson, was also born in Clarinda. Richard Carson served as Director of "Wheel of Fortune."

The Glenn Miller Festival is held in Clarinda each year during the second week of June.

The Clarinda Lied Center features an indoor swimming pool, gymnasium, weight room and community room.

NSK-AKS Precision Ball Company is a Japanese based company that has been in operation in Clarinda since 1988.

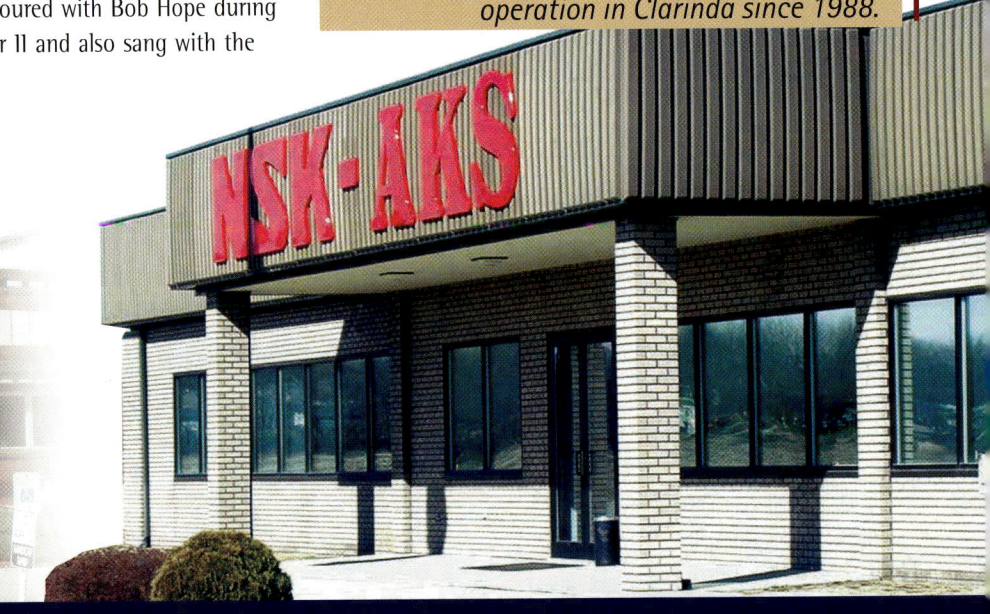

Clarinda, IOWA

In 1903, Clarinda was graced by a visit from President Theodore Roosevelt. While on a tour, President Roosevelt stopped in Clarinda to visit Colonel William Peters Hepburn, who was serving as a United States Senator. Colonel Hepburn was instrumental in the development of the Panama Canal and the passage of the Pure Food and Drug Act. During his overnight stay in Clarinda, President Roosevelt visited the Clarinda High School building then located at the corner of 16th and Garfield streets. To honor the historic visit, the local Daughters of the American Revolution chapter placed a boulder and plaque at the site.

When the lots of the new town plat of Clarinda were sold at auction in September of 1853, a group of men joined together to purchase the southernmost block in the plat opposite the public block for a public school, and built a one-room school of native cottonwood logs ready for the January, 1854 term of school. This "school block" was the site of an active Clarinda school from that time until 2000, and will now be the location of the new Lied Public Library. The Lied Public Library will be a state of the art facility for the community that will feature not only books, but also computer labs and a meeting center. The existing Clarinda Public Library was formally dedicated in April of 1909. The year before, the city of Clarinda had received a $15,000 grant from the Carnegie Foundation to build a Carnegie library.

THE 'SCHOOL BLOCK'

Like with the Lied Public Library, the Lied Foundation was instrumental in helping finance one of the more popular recreational facilities Clarinda has to offer. Christina Hixson, who is a native of Clarinda, oversees the Lied Foundation and committed matching funds for the construction of the facility. The community conducted an extensive fundraising effort to match the funds received from the Lied Foundation that included receiving a donation from Johnny Carson. The Clarinda Lied Center was opened on April 18, 1994. The facility features an indoor swimming pool, aerobic classroom, weight room, racquetball court, a gymnasium, indoor walking track and a community center. While the Lied Center is the jewel of the Clarinda Parks and Recreation Department, the city also features four parks located throughout the city. Clarinda City Park, which the Lied Center is a part of, also features a playground area, shelters, tennis courts, two baseball fields and two softball fields. Visitors to Clarinda can also enjoy a

CLARINDA REGIONAL HEALTH CENTER

The Clarinda Mental Health Institute located at the north edge of Clarinda was opened in 1885.

Clarinda

A mural near the corner of 16th and Main Streets immortalizes the former Hawley Opera House.

round of golf at the Clarinda Country Club. Located at the north edge of the city, the Clarinda Country Club features an 18-hole golf course and a newly constructed clubhouse.

Proof that the work ethic still works in Clarinda is no more evident than in the companies that form the industrial base of the community. Started in 1903, the Lisle Corporation is a family owned manufacturing company that produces parts and specialty tools for the automotive industry, along with lubrication and tire products, and original equipment items. Lisle Corporation traces its start back to a company that produced well boring and drilling machines. During World War II, the company became a defense subcontractor and was awarded the prestigious Army-Navy "E" Award for superior work in making products for the armed forces. In the 1950's, Lisle Corporation extended its production to include one of its more popular items, the mechanics' "creeper." A prime example of the company's willingness to adapt to changing market conditions occurred in 2003 when Lisle Corporation acquired EZ Way. The company, originally based in Minneapolis, Minn., manufactures patient lifting devices used by hospitals and nursing homes.

Besides the Glenn Miller Festival and its Sister City relationship, Clarinda also holds strong industrial ties to Japan. NSK Corporation has operated a bearing plant in Clarinda since 1975, while Clarinda NSK-AKS Precision Ball Company has been in operation since 1988. Another key manufacturing enterprise in Clarinda is H&H Trailer Company.

Over the years, Clarinda and the surrounding area have benefited from the comprehensive protection provided by the Clarinda Police Department, Clarinda Volunteer Fire Department, Clarinda Emergency Medical Services and the Page County Sheriff's Department. Clarinda Regional Health Center has also recently been classified as a critical access hospital and provides quality medical services to patients from throughout the region.

Clarinda is also home to the Clarinda Mental Health Institute. The cornerstone of the Clarinda Asylum for the Insane, as it was originally known, was laid on July 4, 1885. The main building was constructed on 513 acres of land just north of Clarinda. Within two weeks of opening on Dec. 13, 1888, there were 241 patients residing there. By 1949, the population had grown to 1,551 patients. Until the construction of the Pentagon, the Clarinda MHI was the longest building under one roof in the United States. The Clarinda MHI is part of the Clarinda Treatment Complex, which also features a medium security prison, the Clarinda Correctional Facility, and a facility for adjudicated youth, the Clarinda Academy.

Throughout its history Clarinda has depended on its strong work ethic to provide the best quality of life possible for its residents. That same work ethic still works today and will remain the key to the future success of this fine community.

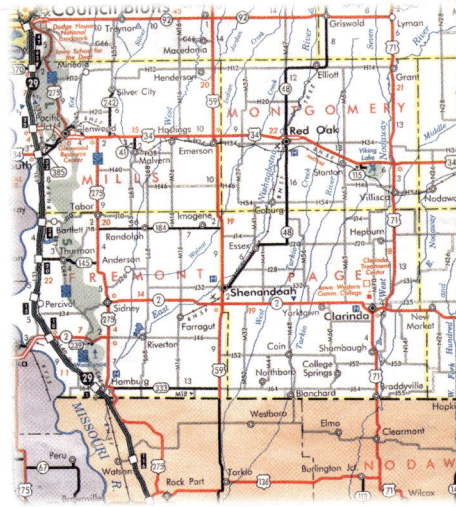

Learn More

Clarinda is located in southwest Iowa the intersection of Highways 2 and 71 community is 10 miles from the Misso border and only about two hours from Omaha, Des Moines or Kansas City.

For more information please feel free call the Clarinda Chamber of Commer 712-542-2166 or visit websites at:
www.clarinda.org

Story Contributors

- Kent Dinnebier
    Editor, Clarinda Herald-Jour
- Steve Snook
    Publisher, Clarinda Herald Jo
- Nodaway Valley Historical Society
- Clarinda Chamber of Commerce

Pride In Our Hometowns.

P·O·R·T·R·A·I·T·S
OF
Clinton

CLINTON

IOWA'S CITY OF GOOD FORTUNE

The city known as Clinton, Iowa, was born near the Mississippi River and christened New York; and from it's conception, it has been a city blessed with good fortune.

Settled around 1834, it later adopted three other cities and included them in a single family. The city's first brush with good fortune came when the original tiny townsite of New York, with one store building owned by J.M. Bartlett, was renamed Clinton after it had been purchased in 1838 by Capt. C. G. Pearce of Cincinnati, Col. Beal Randall of Baltimore and a third person, who is only remembered as "Col. Jennings."

Pride In Our Hometowns.

P·O·R·T·R·A·I·T·S
OF *Clinton*

Iowa's City of Good Fortune

Today, Clinton is the twelfth largest city in Iowa and is well known, in part, for maintaining a network of parks and recreational areas that support a wide varitey of sports that are popular both in the heat of summer and the cool of winter. Sporting opportunities include: swimming, softball, minor league baseball, golf, tennis, hiking, cross-country snow skiing and snowmobiling and a host of others.

The city is also home to an endless number of cultural and community based events ranging from the all-volunteer "River City Band" to a contemporary ballet to civil war reenactments to the art of watching eagles. It also boosts a petting zoo and a riverfront marina featuring boating and other water sports.

A Snapshot

The diversified economy of the area, with a broad spectrum of manufacturing and service industries, government agencies, banks, schools, medical facilities - including one hospital with two sites - a private college and a board range of retail shopping establishments, makes Clinton today the center of commerce not only for its nearly 30,000 residents but also for the surrounding communities as well.

But, Clinton wasn't always the focal point of the area.

By the time Pearce, Randall and Jennings purchased what would become Clinton, a neighboring community known as Lyons, located to the north, already had been established by Elijah Buell. Two other communities also sprouted up nearby – Ringwood and Chancy.

Clinton sought to annex Ringwood as early as 1870, but residents of

Clinton's newly renovated Fifth Avenue South is adorned with statues.

the area objected; and the plan was shelved until 1873 when good fortune once again smiled on Clinton, and a merger agreement was reached.

Chancy had grown rapidly because of the large number of workers attracted to the area by the lumber mills and railroad shops. A movement for the annexation of Chancy had been in progress for several years when a "blue ribbon" committee composed of leaders of both communities worked out the necessary details. A park, a church and a meal site still carry the name Chancy as does the No. 4 fire

HISTORY

station.

Lyons continued to operate as an independent city with its own council, school and fire department until April 20, 1895, when, at a special election, consolidation with Clinton was approved.

Clinton, located on the Lincoln Highway and linked to Illinois by two major bridges, is well-known for building its foundation on the lumber business.

Before the Gay Nineties had even been ushered in, good fortune had once again rained down on Clinton as it gained the reputation for having more millionaires per capita than any other city in the nation. Its wealth was reflected by the numerous mansions concentrated on Fifth, Sixth and Seventh avenues south. While its claim of millionarires on a per capita basis has lessened through the years, the city continues to be known today for its industrial base and its ties to the river.

The city also is looking ahead at progress. Officials are developing the city's river front through the state's Vision Iowa program, casino gaming is available, the community has renovated the city's downtown area and the city is developing a

CARNIVAL FUN

Balloons in June, Clinton's hot-air balloon event, is an annual celebration.

Clinton Iowa

business and technology park.

But, back to the past.

The city of Clinton might still be a small hamlet named New York if it were not for geographical good fortune. Platted as the town of New York in 1836 by its first settler, Joseph Bartlett, the community was one of several that clustered on the west bank of the Mississippi River.

The fledgling settlement had little hope of growth. In 1839, it consisted of a sprinkling of cabins, two stores and a tavern. Lyons, to the north, where a ferry had been established by Elijah Buell, grew at a healthy pace. Lyons was first a mill town with grain and flour mills before being recognized for its lumber potential.

But then, good fortune once again came to Clinton.

Railroad bridge, saw mills set city on a new course

Throughout the 1840's New York – as Clinton was still known – changed little while the communities around it continued to develop. However, in 1855, the Chicago, Iowa and Nebraska Railroad changed its plans and announced it would cross the river at Little Rock Island adjacent to Bartlett's settlement, instead of at Lyons. Things would never be the same.

The Iowa Land Company bought Bartlett's tract and renamed it Clinton, in honor of DeWitt Clinton, governor of New York State. From that date on, Clinton grew, absorbing Ringwood, Chancy and Lyons.

In the early 1800's, not everyone could afford

CLINTON COUNTY COURTHOUSE

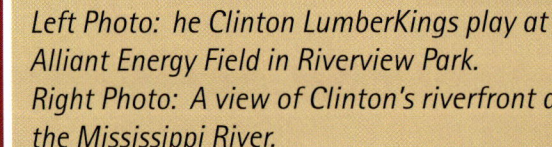

Left Photo: he Clinton LumberKings play at Alliant Energy Field in Riverview Park.
Right Photo: A view of Clinton's riverfront at the Mississippi River.

74

passage on the steamboats which paddled the Mississippi, bringing goods and people to Clinton County. Some came by horse-drawn wagons; others walked the many miles.

Among the walkers in 1835 was Dr. George Peck. When he came upon a high bluff on the west river bank, he thought it ideal for a great city and set about platting it. He named his town after an Indian tribe, but misspelled it. Camanche, with its erroneous "a" was born.

That same year, Martin Dunning arrived from Chicago with a load of general merchandise and became the first businessman to settle in Camanche. Peck's investment was secured when Albany, Illinois, was platted across the river, and a ferry to Camanche was established.

Castle Terrace

Camanche was the first governmental seat when the county was formally organized in 1840 but eventually, with good fortune on its side, lost its county seat status for Clinton County to the city of Clinton.

A bit of Camanche history remains - its old railroad depot has been fully restored and set on the library grounds as an historic museum.

Between the late 1850's and 1900, the Clinton area was regarded as the sawmill capital of the nation. Huge log rafts were floated downriver from Wisconsin and Minnesota, cut into lumber at Clinton, then shipped to growing communities east, west, north and south via the river and the railroads.

In 1865, the sawmills of Clinton, Lyons and Camanche produced 21.5 million board feet of lumber. By 1892, production had risen to more than 195 million board feet, and good fortune smile upon some of the communities' early residents.

Lumbermen W. J. Young, Chancy Lamb and David Joyce were counted among the 13 millionaires residing in Clinton during one period and were among the city's more influential leaders.

These families and others who gained great wealth during the era constructed magnificent mansions along Fifth, Sixth and Seventh avenues in Clinton. That area became the center of elite social life. Elaborate and festive dinner parties, often catered out of Chicago, were frequent.

Once

Riverfront Activity

The Clinton Municipal Transportation Administration's trolley bus can be seen motoring on Clinton's streets.

Clinton IOWA

Modern Day Clinton

again, the good fortune of location aided what would become known as the River City Area.

Today, the railroad and the river continue to provide economic diversity in all directions, attracting manufacturing and heavy industry to the community, plus providing sport and recreational activities and commerce. Since the early years of this century, and continuing forward, the Clinton area has prospered as an industrial center, with a steadily growing list of products and services, which are delivered to all parts of the nation and the world.

Education, culture play major role in modern Clinton

Beyond its economic base, Clinton has had the good fortune to prosper in other areas, including cultural events and educational institutuions .

Founded in 1918 by the Sisters of St. Francis as Mount St. Clara College, the four-year, coeducational, liberal arts school became, in December of 2002, The Franciscan University. The institution has had a long, distinguished history of providing quality education and takes pride in its heritage and commitment to the Franciscan core values of reverence for life, truth, joy through service and the promotion of peace.

Clinton Community College offers a wide variety of academic programs and continuing educational opportunities. Studies in business, agri-business, health, transportation, manufacturing and public service arenas are all offered at the college. Those

Clinton Community College

The Mississippi Belle II provides casino entertainment near Riverview Park.

Curtis Mansion

Clinton

seeking a higher education or the opportunity to expand into new career options are the recepients of individual good fortune.

Educational opportunities beyond those associated with higher education are also a part of modern-day Clinton.

The Discovery Center honors the memory of Clinton Native Frank Adler ("Funny Felix, King of Clowns"), who was a clown with Ringling Brothers and Barnum & Bailey circus for almost 50 years. Best known for his acts with trained pigs, he also performed for three presidents and was known as the White House Clown.

The Discovery Center is a family fun place – a family learning place – a place where children are encouraged to touch and ask why! The Center combines interactive displays with hands-on experiences to promote exploring, discovery and learning about our world – a place where children and adults learn to play (by "playing"????).

The museum also houses some of Adler's costumes and personal memorabilia.

Clinton's resident dance company, Gateway Contemporary Ballet, has been bringing the delight of classical and modern dance to the area for more than 15 years. Whether it's a full-length ballet in spring, free riverfront concerts in summer or a showcase of guest artists in the fall, the ballet company offers something for everyone nearly all year. The ballet also performs with other artistic organizations and for various clubs, festivals and benefits, helping to uphold Iowa's reputation as one of the most culturally aware places in the United States.

The Lillian Russell Theatre is located aboard a restored old river paddle wheeler on the beautiful riverfront in Clinton. There is a professional summer repertory theatre offered from June through mid-August, with great musicals and hilarious comedies. The troupe of talented, young Midwest actors, Broadway professionals and some seasoned, skillful, local actors provide a summer of theatre magic.

The River Arts Center,

BICKELHAUPT ARBORETUM

The Clinton Area Showboat Theatre presents plays and musicals throughout the summer.

77

Clinton

THE FRANCISCAN UNIVERSITY

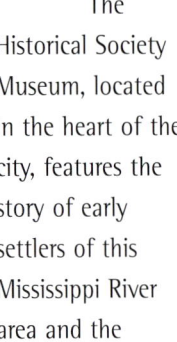

operated by the Clinton Art Association, in downtown Clinton, provides new exhibits in a variety of media every five weeks. The center's gift shop contains unique gift items on consignment that have been created by artists from the Clinton area as well as from all over the United States. During the year, classes and workshops, taught by local teachers and well-known Iowa artists, are held in painting, pottery, calligraphy, ceramics and drawing.

Clinton is one of the smallest cities in the United States to support a full, professional symphony orchestra that performs classical concerts throughout the season. Guest soloists, from near and distant parts of the country are featured regularly.

Museums, events offer both beauty and history

From watching American Eagles along the spectacular bluffs of the wonderful Mississippi, to participating in an amazing Civil War reenactments or simply strolling through the 12-plus acre widelife garden filled with some of Mother Nature's best, outdoor lovers love Clinton.

In 2003, the Bickelhaupt Arboretum was voted as one of the "Top 10 Lawns with a View in the Midwest" by Briggs & Stratton. This 14-acre outdoor museum of select-labeled trees, shrubs, ground covers, perennials and annuals, features one of the top dwarf and rare conifer collections in the country, numbering more than 600 cultivars, prairie grasses and flowers, flowering trees and shrubs, ornamental shrubs, a Stout Medal daylily collection as well as shrub roses, perennials and a reflective herb garden.

The Historical Society Museum, located in the heart of the city, features the story of early settlers of this Mississippi River area and the

VAN ALLEN

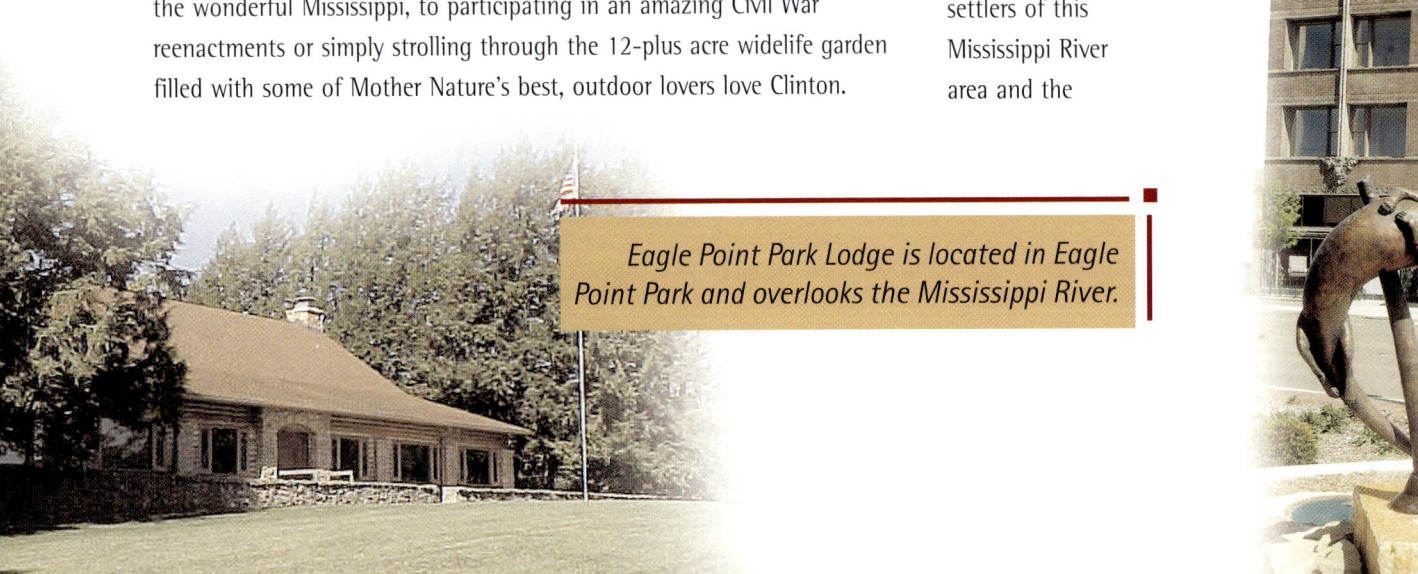

Eagle Point Park Lodge is located in Eagle Point Park and overlooks the Mississippi River.

booming lumber business. Items on display in the permanent collection include old photographs of the area, memorabilia, period furniture, an authentic 1924 kitchen and the 'Resolute,' one of only three manually-powered fire engines on display in the world.

Eagles, America's bird, which have long been a part of Clinton, continue to be an educational and entertainment mainstay in the community.

The annual eagle watch is held the first Saturday in January every year, except in 2005 when it will be held the second Saturday.

The U.S. Army Corps of Engineers, Thomson Park Rangers, U.S. Fish & Wildlife Service and the Soaring Eagle Nature Center co-host a special Eagle Watch Day during peak season on the upper Mississippi. Visitors enjoy outdoor eagle viewing at Lock & Dam 13 and other area viewing sites. Eagle seminars, wildlife exhibits and children's activities are held at Clinton Community College throughout the day.

The community is also home to the Soaring Eagle Nature Center located in the downtown area just south of Eagle Point Park. One part of the center, the Nature Barn, is open for special events throughout the year and during the school term for environmental education classes. Hiking trails, natural prairie, wetlands area and a one-room school are located at the Nature Center.

Eagle Point Park offers great hiking and cross-country skiing, and the 200-acre park features fantastic bluffs along the river in Clinton. A 1937 Stone Tower provides a spectacular view of the Mississippi River and surrounding area. Children's playgrounds are situated throughout the park. The North End Overlook provides a panoramic view of the widest part of the entire Mississippi River.

CIVIL WAR MEMORIES

CLINTON 8 THEATRE

A statue greets visitors to Eagle Point Park.

Clinton IOWA

An incredible Civil War re-enactment unfolds every year during the third weekend in May in beautiful Eagle Point Park. On Friday, hundreds of eighth grade students learn first-hand about the Civil War. Friday night, President Lincoln addresses the citizens of Clinton. Saturday, visitors are allowed to tour the armies "at the front" as they engage in skirmishes and probe defenses. During the mid-afternoon the area is surrounded by the sights, sounds and smells of the Civil War. Later in the evening, spectators are invited to join the re-enactors for a good ole' fashioned barn dance at the Main Lodge overlooking the river and on Sunday witness the period church service mid-morning., see a parade review by President Lincoln at noon and a full-scale battle in the afternoon.

Holiday Lights are special in Clinton

While Clinton offers year-around happenings covering a wide array of events, including guided tours of restored Victorian homes; craft events with a myriad of imaginative art objects, including pottery and hand-loomed rugs; a Father's Day balloon fest that sets the night aglow; and Iowa's largest Fourth of July Festival, it is the community's love of holiday lights that brings thousands pouring into the city.

The "Fantasy of Lights" event is held the weekend before Thanksgiving. The annual spectical features decorated trees, wreaths, stockings and centerpieces boldly displayed at Eagle Point Park Lodge.

The fantasy opens with a gala and auction on Friday night. Saturday morning is a Teddy Bear Tea with Santa for the

Clinton County Courthouse

Lodging Opportunities

Clinton Public Library

children. On Saturday night, area middle school students are invited to a teen dance with many door prizes given away. On Sunday, the last day of the event, a brunch is served, featuring a wide variety of tempting cuisines while a luncheon and style show round out the affair.

On the Sunday before Thanksgiving, the city also holds its annual "Home for the Holidays" open house in downtown Clinton. Those attending the event can enjoy shopping in antique and specialty shops, dining in unique restaurants, riding in a horse-drawn carriage and visits with Santa Claus.

One of the community's main holiday happenings is the "Symphony of Lights" festival that encompasses a variety of events and begins the day before Thanksgiving and ends on New Year's Eve.

The annual event opens on the Wednesday prior to Thanksgiving and features the "Symphony of Lights Walk." This one-mile course is entirely within Eagle Point Park and takes place over the rolling, paved park roads. The entire mile is lighted by the spectacular "Symphony of Lights" display. It is the one opportunity every year to leisurely enjoy this unbelievable lighting display on foot.

The "Symphony of Lights" program continues Thanksgiving Day thru December 30, when visitors to the park can drive through the Christmas lighting

A look inside Clinton brings historical buildings and railways.

Clinton IOWA

extravaganza which is set on the hillsides of Eagle Point Park and includes over 300,000 lights in 10 major displays.

On the Saturday after Thanksgiving a 3.1-mile foot race takes place on the paved, rolling roads within the park. The entire "Symphony of Lights" display is toured twice during the course of the race. Prizes are awarded to division winners, and the park is open to racers for one hour after the race.

The annual lighted extravagansa ends on New Year's Eve with

City Of Good Fortune

an evening of finery at the scenic Lodge at Eagle Point Park. This event features dancing to a live band, food, libations, corsages for the ladies, boutonnieres for the gentlemen, a memento picture of attendess and a follow-up breakfast.

While the small hamlet originally named New York never grew in size to equal that of the better-known metropolitan city on the east coast with of the same name, the renamed, once-struggling settlement that became Clinton has flourished into a community filled with all the necessities needed to make life worth living. As the waters of the mighty Mississippi continue their constant flow beneath its bridges, Clinton will continue its never-ending course of being Iowa's city of good fortune.

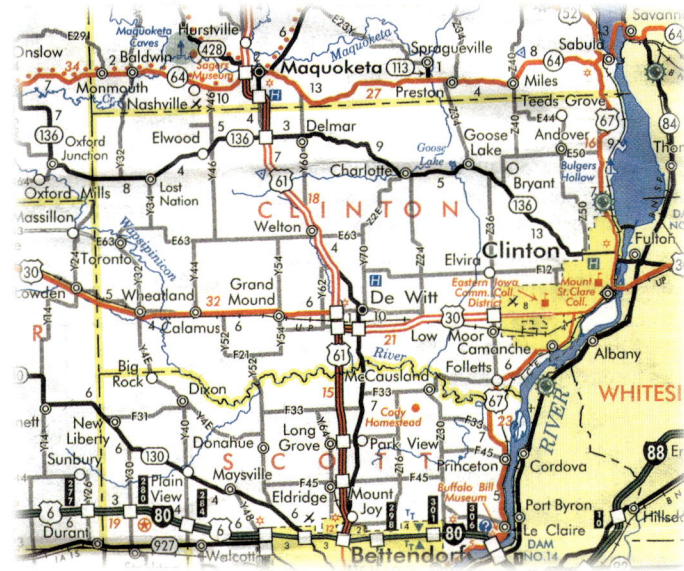

Learn More

Clinton is located in eastern Iowa at U.S. 67 and U.S. 30.

Contact the Clinton Area Chamber of Commerce at (563) 242-5702.

Story Contributors

Charlene Bielema
Cllinton Herald Editor

Clinton Convention and Visitors Bureau

Pride In Our Hometowns.

P·O·R·T·R·A·I·T·S
OF
Council Bluffs

IOWA'S JUMPING OFF POINT

With river, rails and trails that became roads, in its early days Council Bluffs was known as a "jumping off" point to futures filled with promises of bigger and better things to come. Today, the city is once again itself on the move and has become one of Iowa's best places to visit, run a business and/or raise a family.

Council Bluffs has clearly returned to its roots as a "jumping off" point for those wanting a brighter future.

 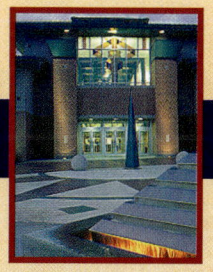  

COUNCIL BLUFFS

Pride In Our Hometowns.

P·O·R·T·R·A·I·T·S
OF
Council Bluffs

Rarely seen in most Iowa communities, the black squirrel, found here in large numbers, has become a symbol of Council Bluffs.

Iowa's Jumping Off Point

A Snapshot

THIS CITY—nestled between a rare range of Loess Hills and the longest river in the country, the mighty Missouri—yields dramatic stories of heroism, sacrifice, vision and perseverance. Its legacy illuminates the spirit of this heartland city on the edge of the great American West. Its people are indebted to the pioneers who settled this special place and those who followed, through the ages, who have nurtured and loved Council Bluffs. Stretching back to its beginnings in the 1820s, the city had several names, including Hart's Bluffs, Camp Kearney, Miller's Hollow and Kanesville. In 1853, by legislative action, the village became Council Bluffs.

Today, Council Bluffs is a city alive with the excitement of growth – growth that is driven by various factors and that is coming in a variety of forms. Business expansion is at an all-time high with both local and outside developers making major financial investments. Numerous new residential developments are under way to even better serve the housing needs of more and more people who are coming to the general area and discovering the benefits of living in a city committed to being one of America's best places to raise a family. In addition, Council

Council Bluffs is a city rich in history and historic beauty. The clock (at left) was installed as part of a downtown Streetscape that also included brick sidewalk sections, Victorian-style street lights and the elimination of all overhead utility wires and their poles. The fountain iwas a highlight of Bayliss Park, a downtown park that serves as the core of a host of Council Bluffs' activities. The community is in the midst of replacing the current fountain, so that a more than 100 year tradition conitinues.

Council Bluffs

Bluffs is expanding its reputation as a tourism destination point. From being a part of the Omaha metro area, rich with entertainment and cultural opportunities, to its own historic monuments and museums filled with rich artifacts, to the city's modern-day casinos, art centers and semi-professional sporting events, today's visitor to Council Bluffs can find something for almost any interest or taste.

Tom Hanafan is keenly aware of the community's revitalized spirit of pride and determination. Now in his fourth term as the city's first popularly elected mayor, Hanafan speaks enthusiastically about the renewed excitement the citizens of Council Bluffs have for their city. "People are proud to claim Council Bluffs as their hometown and are infinitely more aware of the rich history and heritage created by those who sacrificed, toiled and dreamed of a beautiful city. It is within this present perspective that I express my gratitude to each and every citizen for the rare opportunity you have afforded me to lead our great community."

> Brigham Young was selected to lead the Mormon Church during a ceremony held in a tabernacle in the town the Mormons named Kanesville, which later became Council Bluffs. A replica of the tabernacle has been constructed where the original stood.

The History

Years before the country ripped itself apart with civil war, Council Bluffs became identified with those seeking a better life further west. Looking to get rich quick, some 10,000 gold seekers ferried the river at Council Bluffs headed for California in 1849. The Mormon migration, which began in 1846, moved west to Utah by 1852 and, in

Saint Francis Catholic Church at Sixth Street and Fifth Avenue in 1910.

> Council Bluffs' St. Peters Catholic Church is listed on the National Register of Historic Places.

Council Bluffs

The Illinois Central passenger depot at 1216 West Broadway as it appeared in 1910.

1853, the Mormon name, Kanesville, was changed to Council Bluffs. Over the next two decades the city became the preferred "jumping off" point for thousands of overland travelers bound for the Pacific Coast.

When Abraham Lincoln came to Council Bluffs in 1859, he spoke with General Grenville Mellen Dodge concerning the construction of a railroad to the Pacific. Following the general's service in the Civil War, Lincoln named Dodge chief engineer for the Union Pacific Railroad and its move westward. Even in those early years, General Dodge was often heard to predict that Council Bluffs would be the eastern terminus of the transcontinental railroad. Enabling legislation and President Lincoln's executive orders in November 1863 and in March 1864 directed that the eastern terminus of the road be within the township in Iowa opposite the Town of Omaha, Nebraska. In 1869, the transcontinental railroad ensured the city's enduring importance to American travel, and commerce was ensured when the transcontinental railroad crossed the Missouri at Council Bluffs.

General Dodge's efforts paid off for the city. With the railroad operating fully, Council Bluffs became a major rail center, linking the industrial east with the emerging west. The largest mail distribution point in the United States was at a Council Bluffs facility known as The Transfer. With eight main rail lines, Council Bluffs was the fifth largest rail center in the nation in the 1930s and 1940s and, in proportion to its population, was the leading railroad community in the world. As Council Bluffs' most distinguished citizen, General Dodge's contributions still remain an important part of the community he loved, fought for and helped to build.

Rail Center

Famed Council Bluffs minister, orator and author, the Rev. J. R. Perkins, pastor of the First

President Abraham Lincoln named Gen. Grenville M. Dodge, who had served with the Union Army in the Civil War, as the chief engineer for the Union Pacific Railroad and its move westward. Dodge's home in Council Bluffs remains an historic landmark and prime tourist destination. Dodge's daughters commissioned Daniel Chester French, renowned sculptor of the Lincoln Memorial in Washington and the Minute Man in Concord, Mass., to create the bronze sculpture in honor of their mother, Ruth Anne Dodge. Because of its aging process the sculpture is known today as "The Black Angel."

Council Bluffs Iowa

Congregational Church, was one of a number of General Dodge biographers. Perkins wrote: "When he (Dodge) died...on January 3, 1916, he was placed in a stone mausoleum on a high hill in a cemetery at Council Bluffs, Iowa —a mausoleum that faces the West, overlooking the broad floodplain of the Missouri River, now a network of great railroads whose beginning he knew."

Another remarkable Council Bluffs' citizen was Nathan M. Pusey, the first non-New Englander to serve as president of Harvard University from 1953 to 1971. Born and raised in Council Bluffs, Pusey graduated from Abraham Lincoln High School in 1924, where he earned a scholarship to Harvard University in Cambridge, Massachusetts. He even married Council Bluffs native, Ann Woodward, in 1936. After serving as president of several prestigious, small universities, Pusey was selected in 1953 by the Overseers of Harvard University as its president. The mission of Pusey Elementary School in Council Bluffs is to facilitate the educational goals expressed by the outstanding educator for whom it is named.

> While Council Bluffs is a city steeped in history, it continues to add modern attractions for visitors and residents alike. The Western Historic Trails Center (below left) provides visitors with an overview of the many trails that originated in Council Bluffs and allowed pioneers to open up the western half of the nation. Four lighted towers greet those entering Council Bluffs from the west on Interstate 480.

A Welcoming Site

Famous Visitors

Ernie Pyle, a Pulitzer Prize winning syndicated columnist, visited the city in July, 1941 to interview the Albert and Kathleen McGinn family and Rev. J. R. Perkins. Pyle had asked a friend of his, local newspaper man Harry Mauck Jr., to identify colorful people in the city he might interview for his syndicated column, with the possibility of mention in his national newspaper's publication. The

Western Heritage Museum

Council Bluffs

McGinn family story, which appeared in some 50 newspapers, triggered a host of letters from around the country praising the parents and their 10 children for their love and togetherness and saying they enjoyed the account of the McGinn family circus with trapeze stunts and a sideshow featuring the strongest thing on earth—an onion.

Presidents Lincoln, Taft, Eisenhower, George W. Bush and Vice President Dick Cheney have been visitors to Council Bluffs. Stephen Ambrose, David Halberstam and Hugh Sidey are among the noted authors to visit this area. Ambrose, a well-known national historian, wrote extensively about the railroads. Halberstam, a Pulitzer Prize winner at age 30 for his reporting on Vietnam, was the featured speaker when the new library opened. Sidey, famed White House correspondent for Time magazine, who actually started his journalistic career at Council Bluffs' nearly 150-year-old newspaper, The Daily Nonpareil, was a key speaker at a community event in 2003.

THE BIG FLOOD

In 1952, the Missouri River, which gave the city its birth, threatened to take away its life. In April the greatest flood ever to roll down the valley pounded at the 19-mile protective levee around Council Bluffs.

Fear gripped the city as authorities issued warnings that the flood could become the worst in the city's history. In less than four days, more than 30,000 residents sought safety in the higher eastern part of the city. Some 500 trucks shuttled evacuees from the west end of the city to higher groundt. Furniture from the empty homes was stored in locked railroad cars that were also moved to higher ground.

Men and materials that flowed into the besieged city from nearly 100 other communities aided the efforts of the local volunteers. Three hundred experienced flood fighters were called from engineering districts as far away as Memphis, Tennessee; Vicksburg, Mississippi and Kansas City, Missouri. For days, thousands of volunteers stacked sandbags and built levees and flashboards, that kept the river contained north of the city. It was perhaps the biggest news event in the city's history covered by national and international news media.

Council Bluffs IOWA

Throughout its more than 150-year existence, Council Bluffs has witnessed tornadoes, blizzards, heat waves, business recessions and boom times. Today, the city is home to riverboat casinos, historic restoration, new parks and athletic complexes, a marvelous tribute to veterans in Bayliss Park and stunningly designed streetscapes and entrances to the city at both the east and west ends of the community. Sidewalks laced with multi-colored bricks, Victorian-styled lampposts and ceramic medallions depicting the history of Council Bluffs provide visitors with a sense of the community's rich heritage. Visitors entering from the west are greeted by four uniquely designed artistic lighted structures that are computer driven to allow the light within the structures to mirror the changing seasons.

In recent years, the city built an outstanding new library that remains one of the most technologically advanced in the state. The new library is home to much more than books. Included within its walls are an advanced computer lab and a community meeting center that brings people from all walks of life into the library.

Present Day Council Bluffs

Once the pride of the community, the old library was abandoned and left unused for several years. When it was replaced by the city's new $12-million dollar modern facility, one of the few remaining Carnegie libraries in Iowa was restored following a community wide effort to raise the necessary funds to make it the home of the new Union Pacific Historic Railroad Museum. Within a month of becoming president, George W. Bush visited the Carnegie structure to help kick off the building's restoration. Today, railroad buffs and visitors from around the world visit the museum not only to see railroad relics but to also view a collection of historic documents and artifacts that are related to one of the most expansive periods in the nation's history.

Ten million visitors and tourists come to Council Bluffs annually to view his-

The Lewis and Clark Monument at 19962 Monument Road, seen below as it appeared in 1939, was extensively renovated and expanded before the 200th anniversary of the Lewis and Clark Expedition.

Lewis and Clark Monument—Today

Council Bluffs

General Dodge House

The original fountain from Bayliss Park now stands at the intersection of West Broadway and Pearl Street, greeting those entering the downtown area.

toric sites, landmarks and classic homes of another era and to enjoy the entertainment, cultural activities, sporting events and the community's three first-class casinos: Harrah's, Ameristar and Bluffs Run—all boasting banquet, convention and hotel accommodations on site or nearby.

These aspects of the community have made Council Bluffs a convention mecca. Yet another recent addition to the community is a state-of-the-art convention center and sports arena that is home to the River City Lancers, a semi-professional hockey team.

The area is witnessing retail and commercial growth beyond all expectations. Among opportunities for shoppers are the huge Mall of the Bluffs, the impressive Manawa Power Center and The Plaza at the Mid-America Center.

Council Bluffs takes great pride in its many modern sports complexes that include numerous soccer, baseball and softball fields and four golf courses. In addition, residents enjoy two colorful neighborhood water parks. The new public Dodge Riverside Golf Club and Restaurant offer a scenic view of the Missouri River. More than more 25 miles of bike trails and hiking paths run through and around the community. Combined, these facilities make up an advanced network of fitness opportunities.

Some businesses, dating back to the beginnings of the city in the mid-

Squirrel Cage Jail

Looking north from the Bayliss Park fountain around 1915.

Council Bluffs' three-story Squirrel Cage Jail is one of a handful of rotary jails re— ing in the United States.

Council Bluffs

> Council Bluffs' three casinos are but some of the attractions that draw millions of visitors to the city every year. The Mid-America Convention Center provides space for concerts and conventions and is the home to the River City Lancers hockey team.

1850s, are still thriving in what has become a diverse, commerce-friendly community. Others, that have become a part of the community more recently, have also found Council Bluffs to be a great place to do business.

A number of businesses have recently expanded their products and services:

- **The Council Bluffs Energy Center,** located just south of the city, was selected by MidAmerican Energy for a $1.2 billion expansion that will double the plant's output and leave the facility one of the top ten performing power plants in the nation.

- **Plumrose USA,** a food processor that supplies luncheon meats and bacon products to grocers nationwide, recently invested in a $14 million in an expansion that created 154 new jobs.

- **ConAgra Frozen Food** completed a $12 million, 160,000-square-foot expansion of its Council Bluffs plant that produces, among other products, frozen dinners for the Marie Calendar and Healthy Choice labels.

Business that are new to the area include:

- **Automated Concepts** offers design and manufactures robotic equipment for a nationwide client base.

- **Mastercraft Furniture** invested in a 66,000-squre-foot facility for the manufacture of hand-crafted, upholster furniture.

- **The Manawa Commerce Center,** a 175,000-square-foot, that opened in mid-2004, provides high-cube distribution/warehouse space for metro companies.

These firms represent but the tip of the commercial iceberg that is rapidly growing in the community now being referred to as **"Iowa's Leading Edge."** The city's original business district from the 1850s on West Broadway is still an active part of the downtown area and is listed on the National Register of Historic Places. A preservation plan is in place to

Growing Commerce

Sports-Convention Center

91

Council Bluffs

ensure the future of this part of the community.

The old downtown section of Council Bluffs is experiencing a major facelift and has turned into a major attraction for business and professional service and sales firms. A recent addition is The American Republic Insurance Company that will provide more than 120 high-paying jobs.

Those moving to Council Bluffs do so because they feel welcomed and know the city's amenities. The city is a mosaic of vibrant neighborhoods, ranging from historic, century-old homes and mansions to modern, upscale houses dotting the hills and linear terrain reaching to the river. It offers charming town homes, condominiums and smart apartment complexes. Senior living accommodations are plentiful, attractive and utilitarian. Newcomers realize that their families will be well served, with early childhood centers and choices in elementary, middle and high school education.

COMMUNITIES

In addition to public schools, a variety of faith-based schools are an option for families.

A new, state of-the-art complex, "The Center" for people 50 years old and older offers an outstanding physical fitness center, a heated swimming pool an array of social activities.

A key partner with K-12 schools, Iowa Western Community College is one of the nation's leading community colleges. Their programs offer high school students the opportunity to earn college credits in the arts and sciences. Others may choose from numerous vocational courses.

The Iowa West Foundation, a community enhancement non-profit corporation, funds a wide variety of community and regional projects, including a substantial college scholarship program. As of 2003, more than 140 graduating seniors from southwest Iowa and eastern Nebraska had received four-year $20,000 awards.

The earliest church in the city was established in 1838 by

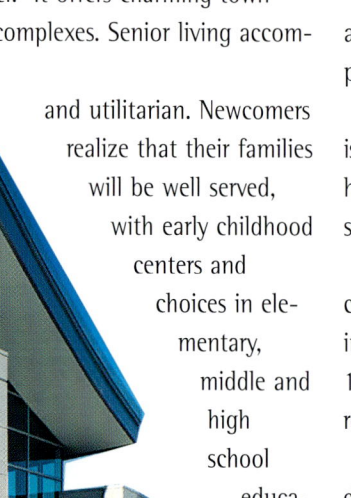

IWCC ART CENTER

LAKE MANAWA

St. Louis Jesuit missionaries, Pierre-Jean De Smet and Felix Verreydt. This mission, St. Joseph's/St. Mary, served the Potawatomie Indians – who were some of the very early inhabitants of the area and who had invited the missionaries into the territory. Today, more than 60 places of worship attract congregations of all faiths.

The entire region has benefited from the comprehensive protection provided by the Council Bluffs Fire and Police Department and the Pottawattamie County Sheriff's office. The city's two hospitals have advanced facilities, engage in ongoing medical research and serve patients from throughout southwest Iowa.

Two institutions noted for outstanding educational, social and value-oriented services are Iowa School for the Deaf (ISD) and Children's Square, USA.

ISD serves deaf and hard-of-hearing students at the school along with adults in the wider community. In the past 150 years, ISD has become a major educational force for special-needs students. The most dramatic single addition to the ISD campus recently was the Lied Regional Multi-Purpose complex that is a physical fitness facility for both ISD students and the community. The school's existing strong leadership will help ensure the vision and promise of this institution for years to come.

A Baptist minister, Rev. J. G. Lemen, established Children's Square as the Christian Home Association in the 1880s. Longtime president Carol Wood explains the impact of Children's Square on Council Bluffs: "Thousands of children and their families have been served across these years. While programs and services have changed to meet new and emerging community needs, the core purpose for which we were founded remains

Children's Square

Iowa School for the Deaf

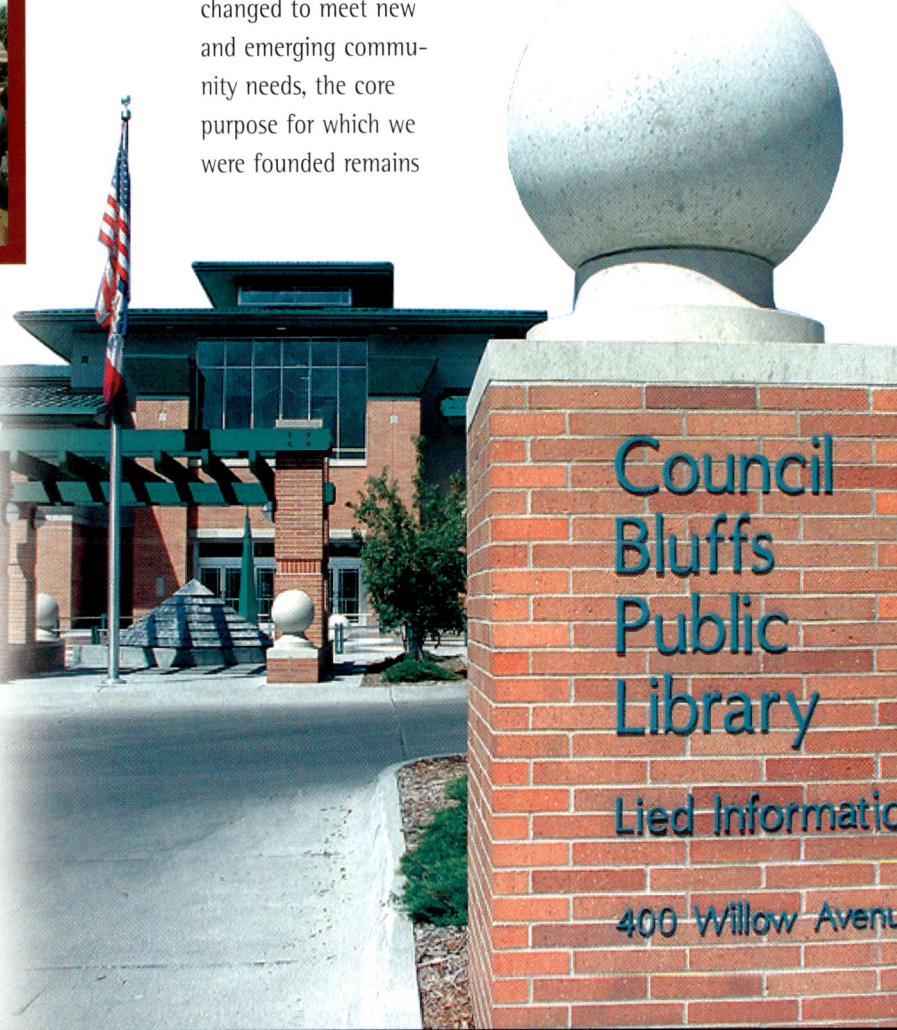

Council Bluffs

Council Bluffs is located in the southwest corner of Iowa along the Nebraska and Iowa border, at the intersection of I-80 and I-29.

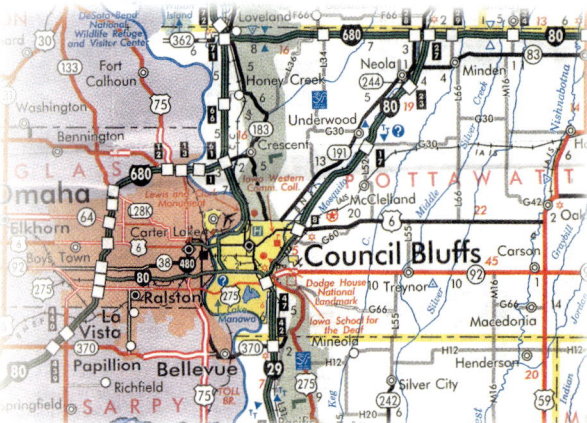

Learn More

For more information please feel free to call the Council Bluffs Visitors Convention Bureau at 712-325-1000 or visit websites at:
www.councilbluffsiowa.com
www.nonpareilonline.com

Story Contributors

Bill Ramsey and Betty Shrier
Local Historians

Jon Leu
Managing Editor, The Daily Nonpareil

Veterans Plaza, located on the east side of Council Bluffs' downtown Bayliss Park, was dedicated on July 4, 2003 as a tribute to Pottawattamie County residents killed while serving in every war since the Civil War.

steadfast. We are a place of refuge, hope and healing for our most vulnerable citizens."

For more than 40 years, the Vocational Development Center, or VODEC, has provided vocational training to persons with primarily developmental disabilities.

Modern-day Council Bluffs is a community that is clearly on the move, growing and expanding to meet the ever-changing and increasing needs of its citizens and the world, while at the same time remaining dedicated to the core principals upon which it was established - principles related to not only the economic needs of its citizenry but also social, educational and spiritual desires as well. These principles nurtured the city's past and will protect the city's future development as well. Those principles have continuously been based upon hard work, sacrifice and imagination.

When asked, "What will the future bring?", John Nelson, native, resident and community leader, said the future would be determined by the values we instill in those who follow us. There's no doubt that people who knew great hardship and sacrifice made possible the bounty the community experiences and enjoys today.

Regardless of what the future brings, with key rail opportunities, the intersection of two Interstate Highways and the city's soon to be extended 5,000 foot airport runway, Council Bluffs has clearly positioned itself in a manner that will ensure the city will be a key "jumping off" point for the future and all it holds.

Veteran's Plaza

Pride In Our Hometowns.

P·O·R·T·R·A·I·T·S
OF
Denison

IT'S A WONDERFUL LIFE

Strategically located at the confluence of the East Boyer and Boyer rivers, this city has provided the "wonderful life" for nearly 140 years, even before hometown celebrity Donna Reed starred with Jimmy Stewart in Frank Capra's classic movie, "It's A Wonderful Life," providing the community with its present-day theme.

Founded in 1865 by Baptist minister and land company agent, Jesse W. Denison, the county seat of Crawford County immediately provided opportunities for people to make a good living. People came to Denison through the westward migration of the nation, the Mormon migration to the west and through the promotion of land by the Providence Western Land Company of Providence, Rhode Island, the land company with which Jesse Denison was associated with. The latter included an influx of German immigrants in the 1870s.

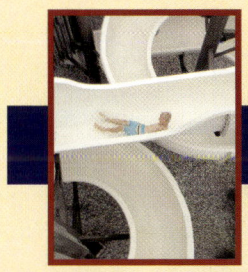   

Pride In Our Hometowns.

P·O·R·T·R·A·I·T·S
OF
Denison

The hills surrounding Denison provide residents visitors with many beautiful rural sce[nes]

IT'S A WONDERFUL LIFE

Today, Denison continues to provide opportunities to its residents and to a new wave of immigrants – Latinos seeking to improve the standard of living for their families. Drawn to the community primarily by jobs at meat-processing plants, the Latino population has begun to put down roots.

Latinos are purchasing houses and property, and Denison's business community boasts several Latino-owned establishments. A Cultural Diversity Committee meets monthly to address issues relating to cultural diversity.

Denison is changing in other ways too, with a focus on regenerating its downtown business area through a streetscape project with ties to the era of the movie, "It's A Wonderful Life." The city government is implementing elements of a long-range plan, or road map to community development, called "Denison 2020." The Denison Chamber of Commerce and countywide economic development group, Crawford County Development Corporation, have initiated a new program designed to help individuals start and build their own businesses – Support Entrepreneurial Endeavors in Denison (SEED).

A SNAPSHOT

Denison's mayor, Ken Livingston, said the community is in a metamorphosis. "At this time, there is more than $80 million in development in various stages, either occurring or about to start," Livingston said. "In two years, many of our projects will either reach fruition or be well on their way to conclusion. Our focus for now is to try to bring some of these projects to a successful close before taking on many more issues.

With this much development in our immediate area, this community is on the threshold of tremendous change which positions us

One of the community's water towers proclaims Denison's theme – "It's A Wonderful Life," taken from the 1946 classic film of the same name. The movie starred Donna Reed, a native of Denison.

where we need to be as we prepare to address our future."

Mike Pardun also sees Denison as being proactive in shaping its future. As the public school district's elementary principal for five years, the district's superintendent beginning in June 2004 and the chairperson of the Denison 2020 Executive Committee, Pardun has a good grasp on the pulse of the community. He described the community as a hard-working, meatpacking town that is not ashamed of that designation.

Pardun sees opportunities for business and industry expansion to tie into the industries that already exist in the community, such as Farmland Foods, Tyson Fresh Meats, and Premium Protein Products.

"I'm excited where we are headed," said Pardun, pointing to the plans the community is implementing. "What is exciting about Denison is that it is trying to be the master of its own fate, not fall into the trap that so many rural communities have, that others control their destiny."

The founders of Denison similarly had the desire to make the community the master of its own future when they picked out the location for the city. The site at the forks of the Boyer River was selected because of the available lumber for fuel and building, and because it was within one mile of the center of the county. The location was also in line with a proposed railroad. And because of its distance from larger cities (65 miles from Council Bluffs, 75 miles from Fort Dodge, 90 miles from Sioux City and 125 miles from Des Moines), the community was seen as developing into a trade center.

The Vison

The vision of the founding fathers was on target. Not only did the railroad come (both the Union Pacific and Canadian National/Illinois Central railroad lines serve Denison today), but Denison grew rapidly in the early years. According to Anna Marie Schneller's history of Crawford County, by 1870 immigrants were coming into Crawford County in much larger numbers than anyone had expected. The population that had been about 250 people in 1860 had grown to 961 according to an 1875 a village census done for the Iowa Railroad Land Company.

Denison's roots are tied to agriculture, and early on, Denison became known as home to the meat empire when W.A. and Morris McHenry brought their herd of imported Aberdeen Angus cattle to the area. The meat empire is a designation that has continued through today. In the 1950s local businessmen had a

Left: A soldiers' monument was erected on the southeast corner of the Crawford County Courthouse lawn in 1917-1918.
Right: The Denison Hillside Sign welcomes visitors and residents alike to the community. The Hillside Sign is located at the junction of Highway 30 and Highway 59 on the west side of the community.

Denison, IOWA

goal to add labor to the area's agricultural products, and a pork slaughtering plant was started in 1959. This plant was sold to Consumers Cooperative Association in Kansas City (now called Farmland Industries) and became Farmland Foods, purchased in October 2003 by Smithfield Foods.

Business leaders in the community also promoted an effort to raise $1,200,000 to build a beef slaughtering plant west of Denison. That plant opened for operation in 1961 and became the first Iowa Beef Processors plant (later called IBP and now Tyson Fresh Meats). Denison is also home to other food industries, including Premium Protein Products.

Set against this background of opportunity, industry and a good work ethic, Denison became the hometown of a number of celebrities.

Actress Donna Reed grew up on a farm southeast of Denison and attended Denison High School. She was born Donnabelle Mullenger on January 21, 1921. At age 16, she left Denison by train for Los Angeles to complete her formal education and to pursue her dream of becoming an actress. She had

> *The stage at the Denison High School Fine Arts Center, constructed in 1990, plays host to school and community concerts, plays and a number of other school and community events.*

roles in more than 40 movies, including "It's A Wonderful Life" and "From Here to Eternity," for which she won the Academy Award for Best Supporting Actress. Reed is also well known for her television series, "The Donna Reed Show" which aired from 1958-1966. Reed often returned to her hometown and following her death in 1986 her Academy Award was left to the City of Denison and is on display at the historic W.A. McHenry House. The Donna Reed Foundation for the Performing Arts was established, and the Donna Reed Performing Arts Festival and Workshops marked its 19th year in 2004. The Festival attracts professionals in the entertainment

DONNA REED

industry, including those from Hollywood, who volunteer their time and talents to teach students who come to Denison from across the nation.

Clarence Chamberlin, the son of a Denison jeweler, flew across the Atlantic Ocean June 4-6, 1927, two weeks after Charles Lindbergh's historic flight from New York to Paris.

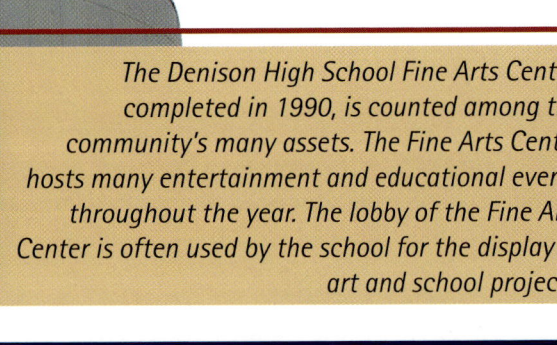

The Denison High School Fine Arts Center, completed in 1990, is counted among the community's many assets. The Fine Arts Center hosts many entertainment and educational events throughout the year. The lobby of the Fine Arts Center is often used by the school for the display of art and school projects

Denison IOWA

Although Chamberlin was not the first to fly across the Atlantic, he did established two records. One was for distance; the 26-foot-long Wright-Bellanca monoplane traveled 3,911 miles, 295 miles farther than Lindbergh's flight. Chamberlin was just 43 miles short of his goal to reach Berlin, Germany, before his plane ran out of fuel. The second record was being the first person to fly a passenger across the Atlantic. Charles A. Levine paid $10,000 to accompany Chamberlin. The trip took 42 hours and 31 minutes. A month before his flight, Chamberlin had set an endurance record for flying by circling New York City for 51 hours and 11 minutes, with a flying partner, Bert Acosta. Chamberlin was also the first pilot to make a ship-to-shore flight by flying a mail plane to New York City from the deck of a ship 120 miles at sea; this was done in 1927. Chamberlin graduated from Denison High School.

Another noted Denison aviator was Chuck Fink, the youngest B-24 bomber pilot in the European theater in World War II. Fink was the commander of the "Lonesome George" (a B-52), which made the first non-stop jet flight around the world in 45 hours and 19 minutes on January 16-18, 1957.

Probably due to Chamberlin's influence, Other notable people who hail from Denison include:

The cornerstone for the Crawford County Courthouse, located on Broadway in Denison, was laid July 30, 1904. Builders used Port Wing Sandstone on the exterior of the first floor and Bedford White Stone on the exterior of the second and third stories. A dome that had been on top of the courthouse was removed in 1946.

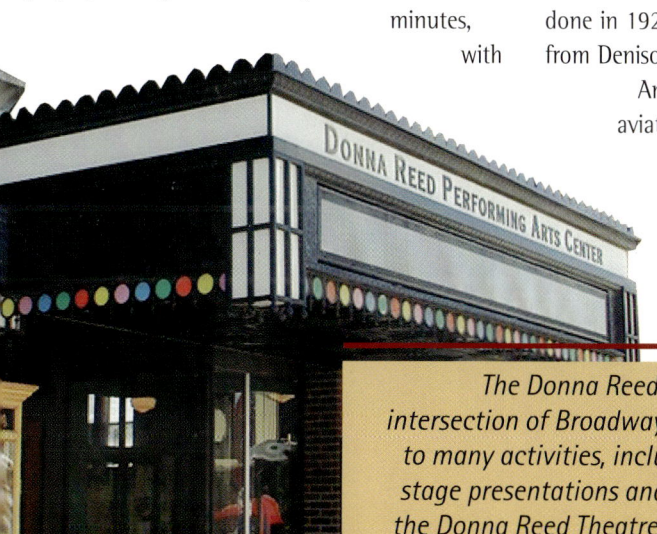

CONNERS CORNER BED AND BREAKFAST

The Donna Reed Center, located at the intersection of Broadway and Main, is the host to many activities, including first-run movies, stage presentations and community events in the Donna Reed Theatre. It is also the home to the Donna Reed Foundation for the Performing Arts, Reiney's Soda Fountain and the Denison Chamber of Commerce office.

99

Denison IOWA

Governor Leslie M. Shaw, governor of Iowa from 1898-1902 (terms were for two years then) and served as United States Secretary of the Treasury in President Teddy Roosevelt's administration. A picture of Shaw signing the check to purchase the land for the Panama Canal is displayed in the Norelius Community Library and the McHenry House.

- Judge Leon Powers, who made national news by writing the dissenting opinion at the Nuremberg Trials.
- Robert Saggau, whose football jersey, number 34, was retired at Notre Dame. At the beginning of World War II, following the All-Star football game in Chicago, he was sworn into the Navy.
- Jack Saggau, Robert's brother, a star athlete at Denison, became a sports announcer on WHO Radio in Des Moines and was known as "TIP" on the radio, held the sports announcer's position prior to Ronald Reagan.
- Bernie Saggau has served as executive director of the Iowa High School Athletic Association for 36 years. Saggau, 75, has stated he plans on retiring the fall of 2004 when the Iowa High School Hall of Pride is completed.
- Gordon Locke, captain of the University of Iowa's undefeated football team of 1922, was named on Walter Camps' 1922 All-American first team at quarterback, although he actually played fullback at the University from 1920-1922.
- Bob Leahy, an Iowa Masters golf champion in 1953 and 1957.

While the founders of Denison might have envisioned the confluence of the East Boyer and Boyer rivers as a good location, they could not have envisioned the problems that would occur some 137 years later. Fed by a torrential rainfall on July 8 and 9, 1993, both rivers rushed out of their banks,

The outdoor pool at the Denison Aquatic Fun Center is a popular destination on a hot summer day. During the summer the two 150-foot waterslides adjacent to the outdoor pool at the Denison Aquatic Fun Center give youth, and some daring older people, hours of just that – aquatic fun. The aquatic center includes an outdoor children's activity pool, a mini-golf course and an indoor pool with adjacent hot tub and sauna.

The signs at the bottom of Opportunity Drive, loca(ted) east of Denison on Highway 30, designate the entrance to the Job Corps Center. There, youth between the ages of 16 and 24, can receive traini(ng in) carpentry, welding, business technologies, unarme(d) security, painting, health occupations, brick maso(nry), culinary arts, facilities maintenance and auto mechanics (through the nearby Western Iowa Tec(h) Community College campus). Students can also receive their high school diploma or GED.

Denison IOWA

causing $10 million in documented damage and an undetermined amount of undocumented damage. The flood hit many businesses, including the community's largest employer, Farmland Foods. Eric Skoog, chairperson of the Project Impact Steering Committee, an organization formed to help implement flood-mitigation projects, said that 72 percent of the people in Denison were affected by the flood, either by where they worked or where they lived.

This was not the first flood experienced by the community in recent history. There were the infamous Father's Day floods in 1990 and 1991. Another flood in July 1996 mobilized business owners and citizens to form the Project Impact Steering Committee. The community received $500,000 of Project Impact and FEMA funds, which were used to leverage millions of other dollars in funding for flood-mitigation projects. Even before the community received the Project Impact and FEMA funding, $100,000 was committed locally to leverage state and federal money for the first flood-mitigation project, clearing debris from the banks and the channel of the East Boyer River. "We took the attitude that we had to do something," stated Paul Assman, Project Impact Manager for Denison.

Projects have been ongoing to reduce the threat of flooding. The East Boyer Watershed Project constructs detention dams to slow the flow of water into the East Boyer River. And for many years the Project Impact Steering Committee has been working in cooperation with the Army Corps of Engineers Office in Omaha, Nebraska, to construct a levee along the East Boyer River. The construction of the levee is anticipated in the near future, if all goes according to plan. The levee would not only protect property from flooding but would also beautify the river corridor.

Denison has weathered other storms in recent history, including economic storms that could have been devastating. On May 31, 2002, Farmland Industries, the parent company at that time of Farmland Foods, the major employer in Denison, filed Chapter 11 bankruptcy. The bankruptcy caused uncertainty up

Bottom: Constructed along the historic Lincoln Highway in 1929 by L.J. Cronk, Cronk's Café enjoys the designation as the oldest restaurant in Western Iowa that has been operated continuously at the same location.
Right: A replica of the famous Earl Marshall Black Angus Bull is located at the entrance to the Crawford County Fair Grounds.

Denison IOWA

and down main street and throughout the community until Farmland Foods was sold to Smithfield Foods in October 2003. Denison's IBP plant also went though a change of ownership when IBP was purchased by Tyson Foods in 2001.

Denison's priority for education can be seen in the number of educational facilities and the quality of the education offered. The community boasts two parochial schools – the K-6 St. Rose of Lima Catholic School and the Preschool-8 Zion Lutheran School. Denison Community Schools will add a transitional kindergarten program in the fall of 2004 to its K-5 elementary building on 20th Street. The public school district's 6-8 middle school is housed in a well-maintained, vine-covered 1936 vintage school building located near uptown Denison. The public high school, with its attached Fine Arts Center is situated on the north side of the community. The high school is the host of the State Academic Decathlon competition in March.

Western Iowa Tech Community College's Denison campus, located east of the community on Highway 30, expanded and remodeled its building in 2003; the building is also home to Buena Vista University's Midwestern Campus.

The community recognizes the importance of early childhood development. The Crawford County Childcare Center opened in March 2002 and houses two Head Start classrooms operated by West Central Development Corporation, the public school's early childhood special education program and five rooms for Children's Imagination Station day-care program which in June of 2004 transitioned from a county-run program to a non-profit operation. Other preschools include Our Savior Lutheran Church's Open Arms Preschool and Community Preschool.

The campus of Midwestern College, which opened in 1968 and closed in the early 1970s, provided another opportunity. The campus is now the home to the Denison Job Corps Center, which provides

Dancers in colorful Hispanic-style dresses entertain an audience at the band shell in Washington Park. The cultural diversity in Denison is recognized through a number of events and celebrations.

Constructed on the south side of the community, the 18-hole Denison Community Golf Course features beautiful views of Denison and the surrounding countryside.

Kids' Kastle, located in Washington Park, is a popular playground, constructed through volunteer labor in 1997.

training to youth ages 16-24 at no cost. Job Corps is funded by the U.S. Department of Labor, and in Denison, the Job Corps Center is operated by MTC Corporation. Students can received their GED or high school diploma or training in one of the several vocations offered by the center. The Job Corps Center also houses Head Start and day-care programs for the young children of its students.

Education is just one part of Denison's high quality of life, although an important one. Other factors that add to the quality of life are – The Donna Reed Performing Arts Festival and Workshops, which takes place annually during the third full week of June. Donna Reed Heritage Museum, which was dedicated June 25, 2004.
- Donna Reed Center, which was constructed in 1914 as the Deutsche Operahaus (German Operahouse) by the Deutsche Operahaus Gesellschaft (German Operahouse Company). It is currently used for showing first-run films, discounted and free movies, stage presentations and community activities, and it hosts the Donna Reed Film Society. The Donna Reed Center includes Reiney's Soda Fountain, a restored turn-of-the-century soda fountain.
- Crawford County Speedway, located at the Crawford County Fair Grounds, which features IMCA racing on Sunday nights.

DENISON MIDDLE SCHOOL

- Crawford County Fair, conducted annually during the last full week of July.
- Yellow Smoke Park, a 358-acre recreational area with campgrounds, a lake for fishing and swimming and a nature center, located east of Denison. People can be seen walking, roller-blading or riding bicycles to and from Yellow Smoke Park on the "Wheels to Heels" trail. Parks play an integral part in the life of Denison residents.

Concentration on housing with work being done on new housing developments. There is a renewed interest in historic homes, through the Restoration Renaissance, a program that recognizes people who have made improvements to their houses or have kept their houses in good condition. And there is interest in historic buildings, including the Crawford County Courthouse building and the Norelius Community Library, both of which are celebrating centennials in 2004.
- More than 10 parks and recreational complexes. Northside Rec includes soccer

The Crawford County Childcare Center was constructed through the effort of the county board of supervisors, the City of Denison and the Denison Community Schools. It houses two Head Start classes, an early special education classroom and five day-care rooms.

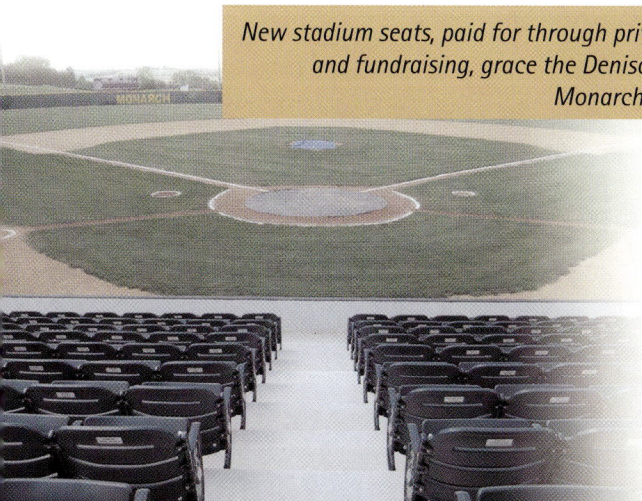

New stadium seats, paid for through private donations and fundraising, grace the Denison High School Monarch baseball field.

Denison

Learn More

From Sioux City, Iowa, take Interstate 29 South, exit onto Iowa 141 (exit 127) toward Sloan. Turn left onto Iowa 141/330th Street/county road K-42; continue to follow Iowa 141. Turn slightly right onto U.S. 59/Iowa 141 East. Turn left onto Iowa 39.

From Omaha, Nebraska, take Interstate 80 East, exit onto U.S. 59 at the Avoca/Harlan exit (Exit 40). Take U.S. 59 North to Denison.

From Des Moines, Iowa, take Interstate 80 West, exit onto U.S. 59 at the Avoca/Harlan exit (Exit 40). Take U.S. 59 north to Denison.

City of Denison, 712-263-3143

Denison Chamber of Commerce, 712-263-5621

Donna Reed Foundation, 712-263

Story Contributor

Gordon Wolf
Editor, Denison Bulletin and Rev
Historical contributions by Mearl L
Photos by Bruce A. Binning

fields, softball diamonds and a baseball diamond. The Denison Aquatic Fun Center has both an indoor and an outdoor pool with water slides and a toddler's pool. The Denison Community Golf Course features 18 holes surrounded by the beautiful hills in the Denison area. The community also boasts Little League and Senior League baseball diamonds, a flag football field and an adult softball league diamond.

- Employment and business diversity through Farmland Foods, Tyson Fresh Meats, Professional Computer Systems, Premium Protein Products, Petersen Manufacturing, Bohlmann, Inc. and Amaizing Energy, which has begun constructing a 40-million-gallon-a-year ethanol plant.
- The Crawford County Senior Center and, on the other end of the age spectrum, a youth council established by the mayor.
- People wanting to become involved in a civic organization have many choices, including, but not limited to, the Jaycees, Rotary, Kiwanis, Golden K Kiwanis and Optimist Club.
- Medical services, which include Crawford County Memorial Hospital, Family Practice & Surgical Specialists, Denison Medical Surgical Associates, P.C., and Crawford County Clinic, P.C.
- The religious community which includes 15 churches.

Another quality of life issue for Denison is the diversity that the Latino population is bringing to the community. Pardun said this is an exciting change he sees in Denison.

"This is relatively new for Denison, but in reality this is what the nation looks like. Diversity is just new to rural areas. Our diversity gives us a leg up in some ways, a head start on what many other communities are going to experience," he stated.

While the community is currently finding ways to recognize this new diversity, through such events as an annual cultural diversity picnic, he hopes in the future that the community in general recognizes all ethnic groups as part of the same melting pot.

"As I look down the road, there are some unique things I hope to see us progress with. I hope the streetscape project will attract some specialty shops that play off the 1940s theme. We have the Highway 30 or Lincoln Highway corridor for which there has already been some conversation about enhancements. Denison is planning a community conference center; there are some growing pains occurring with that, but I believe these are the right kinds of cogs to put in place that are ultimately going to complement what we have," said Pardun.

During national holidays the grounds of the Crawford County Courthouse are ablaze with the colors of red, white and blue from the many flags that are flown. During the spring, summer and fall, flowers contribute their colors to the scene.

Pride In Our Hometowns.

P·O·R·T·R·A·I·T·S
OF
Indianola

COME SEE WHAT'S UP!

Indianola is a town in touch with its history. Old buildings that no longer serve their original purpose are rarely destroyed. Instead, they are repurposed. Old families that have long lived in the community rarely leave. Instead, new generations step forward with new visions for the future of the community. This strong sense of its roots gives Indianola a firm foundation as it grows into the future.

Pride In Our Hometowns.

P·O·R·T·R·A·I·T·S
OF *Indianola*

COME SEE WHAT'S UP!

George Washington Carver, at the far right, attended Simpson College in the early 1890s after he had been denied admission to other colleges because of his race. later said that people at Simpson "made me believe I w human being."

The story of Indianola can't be easily separated from the story of Simpson College, the Methodist-based school located in Indianola. While the college has an impact of almost $60 million on the community, Robert Downing, a 25-year member of the Board of Trustees, fourth generation Simpson alumnus, and an Indianola resident, says its impact on the community should be measured in more than dollars and cents.

"It sets us apart from all the other fast growing suburbs," he said. "It gives a heritage and a history that the other communities don't have."

And Simpson has been a part of Indianola's heritage since almost the very beginning. The Methodist mission began in the city in 1850, a year after the city was organized, and in 1855 they built their first church building. While Presbyterians and Baptists soon followed, it was mostly the Methodists who gathered during the summer of 1860 to organize the Indianola Male and Female Seminary. Organizers of the new institution had hopes that the school would sometime become a college, but since there were no public high schools in the entire state at the time, it was thought best to take one step at a time.

A SNAPSHOT

By 1867 the school had achieved collegiate status, and had been renamed the Simpson Centenary College, in honor of the abolitionist Methodist Bishop Matthew Simpson, who had preached at Abraham Lincoln's funeral. In 1869, College Hall was finished, housing classes for the new college-level students. Today, the building serves as a gracious

The National Balloon Museum was designed to look like two inverted balloons. The entrance arches also suggest walking into a balloon. The structure is trimmed in blue and yellow ceramic tile to represents the serenity and gracefulness associated with ballooning.

Indianola IOWA

A plaque on the campus at Simpson College commemorates George Washington Carver's attendance at the college in the early 1890s, a time when African Americans rarely had the opportunity to attend college.

centerpiece for the college, welcoming students as they arrive at the admissions office for tours or to enroll, and providing an elegant site for the college to host receptions for notables who visit the campus.

Those notables have included nationally known speakers such as Jeanne Kirkpatrick, former United Nations ambassador, South African bishop and Nobel Prize winner Desmond Tutu, presidential candidate Jesse Jackson and former British prime minister, Harold Wilson. Many of the speakers come to deliver one of the endowed lectures the college offers free of charge to community residents as well as Simpson faculty, staff and students.

Today, the college enrolls 1,353 full-time students and more than 600 part-time students, including a number of adults who are finishing degrees or continuing their education in Simpson's night and weekend program.

The campus is a beautiful 75-acre expanse that features 34 buildings. The oldest buildings on campus, such as College Hall, built in 1869; Ladies Hall, now Mary Berry, built in 1891 and Hopper Gymnasium, dedicated in 1912; have had significant renovations and stand proudly beside newer additions to the campus, such as the Thomas H. McNeill Hall and the Amy Robertson Music Hall.

The George Washington Carver Science Center also was recently renovated, and pays homage to Simpson's most famous alumnus. Carver, who was born into slavery in Missouri, entered Simpson in 1890, financing his education by taking in laundry in a shack across the street from the college. He studied art and painting at the school before going on to Iowa State University where he studied horticulture, launching a career in science that eventually would take him to the Tuskegee Institute in Alabama. In 1941, Carver

Corner Sundry is one of the longest running businesses in Indianola. The old-fashioned soda shop opened in 1949. The business is still serving green rivers and other treats on Indianola's square.

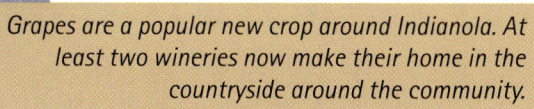

Grapes are a popular new crop around Indianola. At least two wineries now make their home in the countryside around the community.

Indianola IOWA

College Hall was built at Simpson in 1869. The building served in a number of capacities before being restored to house the school's admissions offices, among others.

returned to Simpson to deliver the baccalaureate address to an audience of almost 2,000 people. A year earlier, he told the college president that "At Simpson College, the kind of people there made me believe I was a human being."

The college has been a foundation for Indianola's reputation as a cultural center. In addition to the many speakers the college hosts, the theater department presents several productions a year and combines with the music department to present lush musical theater or operatic productions. Student and faculty recitals, lectures and performances also are open to the community.

But Simpson isn't the only artistic outlet. Carousel Community Theater, founded in 1965, stages everything from children's theater to musicals up to three times per year. The group performs anywhere it can find a suitable location, whether it's at the fairgrounds, in the library or at the high school auditorium. The Indianola Concert Association also offers a yearly series of concerts at the high school auditorium.

Visual arts find ample display space in Indianola, with various exhibits of local and national artists at Farnham Gallery at Simpson College. The Indianola School's Gallery of Art features work by artists from the Midwest, as well as international displays from Germany, Kuwait and China.

But perhaps the granddaddy of all the artistic offerings in Indianola is the Des Moines Metro Opera. Although the company bears the name of the better known capital city, its business offices are housed in Indianola's Carnegie Library, built for $10,000 in 1906, and refurbished as a home for the opera company when the city built a new library in 1984. Blank Performing Arts Center, on the Simpson College campus, is the company's performance venue.

The company brings singers from across the country to Indianola, where they produce three elaborate

Don Berry, publisher, editor and owner of The Record-Herald and Indianola Tribune, was both an accomplished newspaper operator, and a talented photographer. His images of Warren County capture the county's social, industrial and business history. Berry took this picture at Lake Ahquabi, a 770-acre state park south of Indianola. Dedicated in 1936, many of the park structures were built by the Civilan Conservation Corps.

Don Berry shot this image, which shows the old R[ ] office, where the paper was located until the 199[0]

Indianola IOWA

main stage productions in repertory each summer. Traditional operas, such as "Madama Butterfly," "La Boheme" and "Carmen" are interspersed with more cutting edge fare such as the operatic version of Tennessee William's "Summer and Smoke" and the world premiere of "The Tempest" by Lee Hoiby.

The company was founded in 1973 by Simpson College alumnus Robert L. Larsen who hoped the company would give young American singers a stage, and Midwestern audiences a chance to see opera.

It does much more.

Each year, more than 400 young singers audition for about 40 spots in the company's apprentice artist program. The apprentice artists sing in the choruses and cover the leading roles of the main stage productions and work with a team of music coaches, stage directors and conductors to improve their professional skills. Professional singers from around the world fill most major roles in the main stage productions.

An educational arm of the company, OPERA Iowa, has introduced almost 500,000 students and adults to opera through its appearances in communities and schools in Iowa, Michigan, Minnesota, Wisconsin, Arkansas, Illinois, Kansas, Missouri, Montana, Japan and China.

In addition to its artistic success, the company also is a very real financial engine, bringing about 175 staff members, orchestra members and singers to the community for close to three months each summer. The company's intimate 488-seat theater is filled every night, usually with visitors from around Iowa and the nation outnumbering the locals at the performances.

Once the opera's last encore has died away, the Warren County Fair takes center stage. The fair occupies 40 acres in the heart of the city. During the week-long fair at the end of July, close to 1,000 livestock exhibits sit side-by-side with a carnival full of rides and games, tractor pulls and bull rides, and homemade meals

CREATIVITY

Douglas Duncan not only helped establish the Des Moines Metro Opera, but he also was its first business manager and performed in several productions, such as "The Magic Flute," which the company first presented in 1975. Duncan died in 1988.

Berry's photos captured the faces of the people of Warren County. Today, the photo collection is at Simpson College, which has received a grant to preserve the existing photos. Photos that Berry took before 1920 were destroyed in a fire.

Indianola

from the Warren County Beef and Pork Producers, to say nothing of the pie and other delights to be found at other booths.

The fairgrounds also is home to the Warren County Historical Museum and Library, which houses a collection of memorabilia from the county's early days. Nearby is the burial site for one of Indianola's more famous residents, the racehorse Allerton. Allerton's owner, Harry Hopper, was a Warren County entrepreneur who purchased the fairgrounds in 1912 so he would have space to train and run his horses. In 1909 he bought one of the world's best trotting horses, a stallion named Allerton. The horse died in 1912 and in 1919 Hopper sold the fairgrounds back to the Warren County Fair Association.

Hard on the heels of the county fair follows the National Balloon Classic. The Classic was launched in 1970, when a group of balloonists moved their event from the state fairgrounds in Des Moines to the Simpson campus in Indianola. From 1970 until 1988, the National Balloon Championship made its home, first on the Simpson College campus, and later on a 35- to 40-acre piece of property east of Indianola that the balloon board purchased in 1987. When the Balloon Federation of America, which sponsored the championship, decided to move the event, Indianola decided to keep its eyes on the sky and created the Classic. Each year, more than 90 balloons compete in events as varied as the hare and the hound and the annual outhouse tip. The first weekend of the balloon event also features an arts-and-crafts fair on the downtown square with a number of area artisans displaying their work.

Skys The Limit

The Classic's offices are located in the National Balloon Museum, established by the Balloon Federation of America in 1973. After years of moving

Buxton Park, north of Simpson College, is two full blocks of beauty at almost every season. The land was donated in 1906 by William Buxton Jr., whose family operated Peoples Trust and Savings Bank in Indianola for many years.

About 100 balloons regularly come to Indianola for the National Balloon Classic in August. Indianola has been home to a national level ballooning event since the early 1970s.

Indianola IOWA

Dean and Dolly Ruther are in the midst of restoring this old home on one of Indianola's original streets, Salem. The home was the Indianola hospital until 1952 when it was no longer able to meet state standards.

from temporary location to temporary location, the museum settled in 1988 in a permanent location on the north side of Indianola. There almost 24,000 visitors a year inspect the museum's archives tracking 200 years of hot air balloon history. In 2003 an addition to the original facility was dedicated, and named for Chuck Laverty and his wife, Irene, long-time supporters of the Classic, and a descendant of John Laverty, who did the original survey of Warren County back in 1849.

The museum alone relies on almost 2,000 hours of volunteer labor a year to operate, but that's just the beginning. In addition to the hundreds of volunteers who bring off the Classic and the fair, volunteer organizations like the Elks Club and the Warren County Historical Society provide labor for the Log Cabin Days celebration, a toast to Warren County's history held each September.

The Warren County pork and beef producers cook up great meals in the shadow of the Ferris wheel at the Warren County Fair each year.

All of these events draw an enthusiastic audience from the 13,044 residents of the city, as well as many visitors from surrounding communities. Located at the intersection of north-south U.S. Highway 65/69 and east-west connector Iowa Highway 92, Indianola is easy to get to, with particularly easy access offered to the state capital and its airport, 17 miles to the north.

In 1871, more than 200 of Indianola's finest citizens crowded into three railroad cars and made the trip to Des Moines in only 50 minutes to celebrate the completion of the first railroad with an evening of dining and dancing. Today, a new highway bypass around the south side of Des Moines connecting to Hwy. 65/69, makes the trip from the Des Moines International Airport to Indianola a 15-minute drive for the cream of America's politicians. From the days in early 1975 when an

Old Bluebird, built in the early 1860s, was the first building on the Simpson College campus. It was painted a lead color, leading to the appellation, "Blue Bird Seminary." The building was destroyed in a windstorm in 1871.

Indianola IOWA

Notables

unknown Jimmy Carter first met with supporters in Simpson historian Joe Walt's Indianola living room, politicians have found Indianola a fertile place to campaign.

President Bill Clinton visited Indianola in 1996 and 2003 to speak at the Harkin Steak Fry, hosted by Iowa's fiery populist Senator Tom Harkin, who hails from Cumming, just a few miles to the north. Sen. Hillary Clinton drew hundreds of people to a campaign stop for her husband on a frigid winter night. Other notables from Vice President Al Gore and presidential hopefuls senators Joe Lieberman, John Edwards and John Kerry, along with Representative Dick Gephardt, Secretary of Education Lamar Alexander and eventual President George W. Bush, all wooed Indianola's voters.

While the road brings notables to Indianola, it also gives residents an easy commute to lucrative jobs in the nearby city. Almost half of Indianola's work force drives north to work in Des Moines and its suburbs each day.

The community also is working to provide more jobs within the city itself. Several groups help attract new business to the community, including the Indianola Chamber of Commerce and the Indianola Development Corporation, which are combined in the Indianola Development Alliance. The development corporation is an investment based group that provides initial development of land in the community's industrial park, before selling it at affordable rates to existing businesses that want to expand and to new industries that relocate to the community.

While the community works to bring new businesses to town, it already draws a significant number of older residents. The Village, a retirement community associated with Wesley Retirement Services, offers town homes, apartments and long-term nursing options to residents over the age of 55. Opened in 1990, the community is home to more than 180 residents from 19 states today. In 2003, Wesley Services began major construction to add 12 one-bedroom apartments and two studio apartments for individuals who need assisted living,

The Village today boasts a pond with a gazebo for the community's 180 residents to enjoy.

Former President ;Bill Clinton and Missouri Representative Dick Gephardt are among the many national politicians to campaign in Indianola. During an event in 1996, former president Clinton drew more than 11,000 people."

Indianola IOWA

Classic operas, such as Puccini's "Madama Butterfly", are regulars on the Metro Opera's stage at Blank Performing Arts Center in Indianola. In 2004, the company staged its third presentation of this audience favorite.

along with 18 private rooms and a secure courtyard area for individuals with dementia.

Wesley isn't the only option for retirement age residents. Windsor Manor, an assisted living facility, now under construction on the east side of Indianola, will soon offer housing in 26 apartments and 10 units in a special memory care wing.

With all of its attention on the older members of the community, the youth also receive quality services. The Indianola Community School District serves more than 3,200 students from pre-kindergarten through 12th grade in its six attendance centers.

Young & Old

In addition to its traditional programs, the school district also offers innovative programs at both the elementary and senior high level. Students in kindergarten through fifth grade have the option of attending year-round classes. Housed at Irving Elementary, one of three elementary schools in the district, year-round students attend classes the same 180-days as traditional-year students, but classes begin in July and continue until a three-week fall break. At Christmas, students enjoy a slightly extended holiday break before returning to class until a three-week spring break. Students may attend optional intercession classes during their breaks. Classes end at the same time as the traditional year classes.

At the high school level, students in grades nine through 12 may attend the Learning Center, an alternative high school that focuses on academic, vocational and personal social skills. The school serves students from six Warren County school districts and offers individualized instruction.

While the school district focuses primarily on academics, the district also has had its fair share of athletic successes, including a string of state team track titles in the 1970s, a state wrestling title in 1994, and a boys' state basketball title in 2001. Individuals from Indianola High School also have gone on to athletic success, most poignantly Chris Street, who graduated from Indianola High School in 1990 after leading Indianola to the state basketball tournament for three consecutive years. After graduation, Street went on to the University of Iowa, where he became a much-loved member of the Iowa basketball family before

The Indianola boys' basketball team captured their first state title in 2001. Players said they were motivated by the memory of Chris Street, who led the team to three state tournaments before going on to play for the University of Iowa.

Indianola

his tragic death in a car accident in 1993.

Currently, Indianola residents are paying close attention to Casey Blake, an Indianola graduate who is living out a dream as third baseman for the Cleveland Indians, batting .271.

Indianola's wide variety of activities and offerings is continually growing. Efforts are being made to try to construct a YMCA athletic facility to offer entertainment for families. A thriving Indianola Parks and Recreation Department provides crafts, sports and other activities for kids through senior citizens and an assortment of Warren County parks provide a plethora of nearby outdoor recreation. Indianola residents are well contented with their lot.

"Indianola has a lot of advantages," says Frank Rasko, a long-time resident and builder. "Quality of life is one of the issues I touch on pretty heavily. It's pretty diverse and it offers a lot of opportunity for personal, and hopefully financial growth."

Some residents are pursuing their financial growth through farming a new kind of crop for the area, grapes. New vineyards and wineries are springing up around the county. A new strip mall is under construction on the north side of town and the community country club is expanding to 18 holes. Rasko said that he hopes businesses look at Indianola not just for industrial growth, but for commercial growth. With more than half of the community driving to Des Moines, he would like to see companies locate a portion of their work forces in town.

The new highway bypass around the south side of Des Moines makes access to Indianola even easier for city businesses and residents, pointed out Bob Downing. "I don't think we know yet the impact that will have," he said. "With more rooftops, we'll be able to support more service and retail businesses. We have a lot to sell, but we're going to have to sell ourselves."

Indianola is a community on the grow, with a rich past and a promising future. Come see what's up!

Rich Past-Promising Future

Summerset Inn and Winery offers tours of its vineyards to visitors. Summerset uses many of its own grapes in the wines it produces.

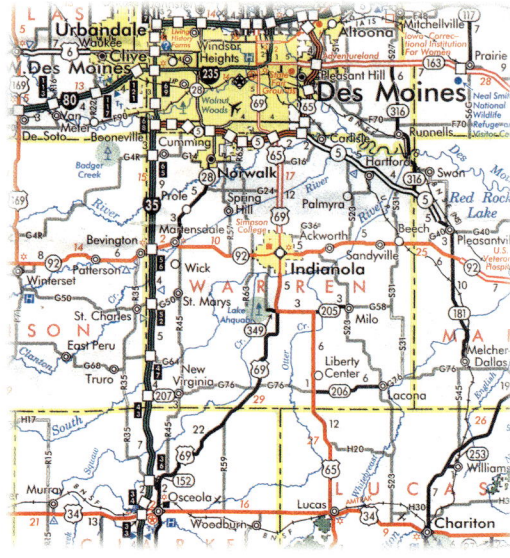

Learn More

Indianola is located at the intersection of U.S. Highway 65/69 and Iowa Highway 92.

For more information, contact the Indianola Chamber Alliance at 515-961-6269 or visit
www.indianolachamber.com

Story Contributors

Amy Duncan
Publisher, Record-Herald and Indianola

Joseph Walt
Senior Professor Emeritus of at Simpson College

Pride In Our Hometowns.

P·O·R·T·R·A·I·T·S
OF
Le Mars

CITY OF GROWTH AND SUCCESS STORIES

Enter the City of Le Mars from any direction, and one will experience vistas of tree-lined streets and avenues. Tree-filled parks and recreational facilities are prominent features of the quality of life in Le Mars.

Le Mars is a city of dynamic growth, and nature's wonders of lavish growth in its tree-filled parks, streets and recreational facilities are reflected in the development of some of the best businesses, educational facilities, churches and societal entities in the midwestern United States.

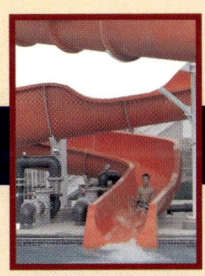

LE MARS

Pride In Our Hometowns.

P·O·R·T·R·A·I·T·S
OF
Le Mars

CITY OF GROWTH AND SUCCESS STORIES

Increasingly Le Mars is attracting new businesses and people with skills and talents who find Le Mars "just right" for their needs and aspirations. It's a great place to live from every perspective – and, of course, Le Mars is truly "The Ice Cream Capital of the World."

In the fall of 1999, "The Ice Cream Capital of the World Visitor Center" opened – and every July "Ice Cream Days" offer special events to celebrate this unique feature of Le Mars.

BEGINNINGS

As it is with so many Iowa communities, Le Mars got its start as a railroad town. It was without a name until the wives of six railroad officials came for a visit. They put together the first letters of their names, and came up with "Le Mars" – which sounds "French," but isn't.

The Le Mars website informs us: "Situated in the northwest corner of Iowa, Le Mars is 25 miles north of Sioux City, 85 miles southeast of Sioux Falls, 120 miles north of Omaha and 205 miles west of Des Moines. U.S. Highway 75 along with state highways 3 and 60 offer an excellent transportation network to nearby interstates as well as venues such as the Iowa Great Lakes.

"Le Mars features a municipal airport with a 4000 foot runway, and rail service provided by Canadian National, Union Pacific and Burlington Northern Santa Fe

A SNAPSHOT

WELCOME CENTER

Le Mars, Iowa

> Fred Close (pictured) and his brother, William, bought large parcels of land in Northwest Iowa and subdivided it into farms that were sold to the "second sons" of British landowners.

railroads."

The city's beauty is enhanced by the meandering Floyd River, which flows along the western side.

The website continues: "The history of Le Mars dates back as early as the 1850s when white settlers arrived to the region now known as Plymouth County. The county of Plymouth was organized in 1853 and started with two townships. "Within two decades the tiny town would grow to a city of 4,000 residents. In the United States census of 1890, Le Mars was listed as the 4th fastest growing city in the state." (from the Community of Le Mars website)

PARKS FOR PEOPLE

Parks are scattered throughout Le Mars, and they testify to the city's concern for leisure and recreational facilities for its citizens. The twelve parks are varied in their offerings. Its 5.9 acres Cleveland Park, located at 2nd St & 6th Ave S.E., includes a $100,000 community constructed playground built in 1998, lighted skating rinks, restrooms, picnic shelter, horseshoe pits, and basketball court.

Municipal Park is just northwest of Hwy 3 and Park Lane, and offers 3.5 miles of recreational trails, a 3.6 acre spring fed pond for unsupervised swimming and fishing, and there are two docks. There also are: an enclosed shelter house, picnic shelters and tables, two sand volleyball courts, restrooms, cooking grills, frisbee golf, playground equipment and tennis courts.

Swimming Pool Park on 12th Street SE has a 25 meter pool, with two body slides, a plunge pool, bathhouse with restrooms, concession stand, playground equipment and skateboard park. Year round swimming opportunities are available at the olympic-size pool in the Le Mars Community Middle School.

West Floyd Park offers 47.7 acres with seven regulation Little League ball diamonds, playground equipment, restrooms, picnic shelters and tables;

Willow Creek Campground is located at Le Mars Municipal Park, and offers the swimming pond with two fishing docks, easy access to golf course,

> The county courthouse was completed in 1902. For 40 years, a Memorial Day ceremony honors the fallen veterans from the county with a display of flags.

> Foster Park, created in 1903, hosts concerts by the Le Mars Municipal Band during the summer.

Le Mars

recreation trail and tennis courts, 26 cement pads with water and electricity, six grass sites with electric only, restrooms and showers.

Le Mars could also be called "The City of Ball Diamonds," with nine locations for softball and baseball. The Le Mars Little League was the fourth to organize west of the Mississippi River, and typically more than 700 youth, ages 7 to 15, signed up to participate.

The site for summertime Municipal Band Concerts is the gazebo or carousel in Foster Park, located in the 600 block of tree-lined Central Avenue.

One of the most recent additions to Le Mars is the Olson Cultural Center in downtown Le Mars. This outdoor concert facility was erected in memory of Paul and Patti Olson, who owned and operated the radio stations that continue to broadcast to northwest Iowa.

"Ice Cream Capital of the World"® is the trademark of Le Mars, where the Wells' Blue Bunny® facilities manufacture and ship out more ice cream than from any other city in the world.

Ice Cream Capital of the World

The Wells' Blue Bunny® Quality Dairy Foods is a magnificent American success story – and it all started with one man, Fred H. Wells, and his delivery route of milk products.

The following information appears in the Wells' Blue Bunny® website at www.bluebunny.com.

"As the world's largest manufacturer of ice cream in one location, Wells' Dairy, Inc., has made Le Mars, Iowa, the 'Ice Cream Capital of the World.' BLUE BUNNY® branded items are distributed across the nation and in many foreign

The fairgrounds in Le Mars has always been busy. This trio of photos from 1897 and 1898 show some of the activities at the fairgrounds. Yes, those are "trotting" ostriches.

Foster Park is home to this statue of the Trumpeter, commemorating the relationship between Jazz musician Clark Terry and Westmar University.

Le Mars is also home to Wells' Dairy's milk plant. The company manufactures and packages over 2,000 products in almost every size, shape, style, and flavor imaginable — from ice cream and frozen novelties to fresh dairy products like milk, yogurt, and sour cream.

Le Mars Iowa

countries. The company operates two ice cream plants and a milk plant in Le Mars, an ice cream plant in St. George, Utah, a milk plant and freezer in Omaha, Nebraska, and distribution centers in El Paso, Texas and Phoenix, Arizona. Over 2,300 production, sales, office, and support personnel make up the Wells' Dairy family." (quoted from the Blue Bunny® website by permission of Wells' Blue Bunny®, Inc. Le Mars, Iowa.)

It is awesome that this huge enterprise was begun by one man.

• Another company started by one man is Gus Pech Manufacturing Company, a builder of drilling rigs. The company was founded by an immigrant from Germany, who died in 1900 – and the company was bought out by a salesman, W.O. Collins, who in turn passed it on to his sons, Wayne and Robert. Wayne died in 1957 and Robert purchased the entire business.

A lighted Christmas parade winds its way through downtown Le Mars and to the fairgrounds.

The Round Barn, located at the Plymouth County Fairgrounds in Le Mars, was built in 1918. It is 68' high, contains 5200 sq/ft and was built for raising and showing cattle. It was previously located on the farm that Herman and Clara Lang purchased in 1928. The barn was donated to the Plymouth County Fair Board in 1981 and moved to its present location. It was listed on the National Registry of Historical Places in 1986.

In 1986 Robert's sons, Cris and Gregg Collins, purchased the company from their father. Cris is now president and Gregg is vice president.

Gus Pech sells drilling equipment throughout the United States, Canada and Mexico, as well as worldwide – including Taiwan, Thailand, South America, Ethiopia, Algeria, Italy, France and England

• Harkers, Inc. was also founded by one man, Jack Harker, who began delivering meat to area institutions On his retirement the food delivery complex was purchased by a group of Le Mars employees, and Harkers Distribution, Inc. came into being.

• Rowe's Millwright Services and Rowe's Equipment Company are two separate businesses, but owned and operated by the same family members.

Le Mars IOWA

This postcard from 1916 shows the German American Savings Bank. Many German immigrants came to Le Mars in the late 1800s. The building is still standing today at the corner of Plymouth and Central.

Jim Rowe and his son Kerry founded the firms in 1980 for the manufacturing and installation of custom designed, stainless steel meat processing equipment, which is sold all over the United States, and occasionally abroad.

The firms include two other family members: Brian Rowe heads the manufacturing operations, and Scott Rowe is in charge of installations.

• Plymouth Life, Inc., is just one indication of the caring spirit of the Le Mars citizenry. More than a hundred employees are engaged in serving individuals who are diagnosed as having disabilities. Richard Porter heads this human services venture.

The expressed mission is "to help the individuals we serve achieve an excellent quality of life within the least restrictive setting possible."

A BUSINESS-FRIENDLY COMMUNITY

Le Mars has been a business-friendly city from its beginnings. That community spirit is supported aggressively and wisely by the Le Mars Business Initiative Corporation (LBIC) – an organization of leaders from government, business, the Le Mars Area Chamber of Commerce and the community at large. From its beginning in 1998 it has been dedicated to the promotion of a healthy business climate not only within the city, but reaching out to all of Plymouth County – one of the largest in the State of Iowa.

Bill Bomgaars, senior vice-president of First Federal Bank, has been a member of LBIC and its predecessors for many years, and was an active participant in the successful efforts to keep the Wells' Dairy corporate headquarters in Le Mars.

Bomgaars spoke of the crisis that developed over the need for better facilities for Wells' corporate headquarters – which had been split up all over town, locating offices wherever facilities were

Trains hauled most everything that came in or out of Plymouth County. Here is a train taking materials from Gus Pech Manufacturing on the first leg of their journey to Africa.

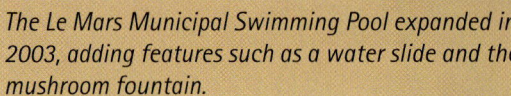

The Le Mars Municipal Swimming Pool expanded in 2003, adding features such as a water slide and the mushroom fountain.

Le Mars

The former Le Mars Central High School now is home to the Plymouth County Museum. The structure is one of six buildings in Le Mars listed on the National Register of Historic Places.

available. Consideration was being given to relocating the headquarters to another city. "Keeping Wells' Corporate headquarters in Le Mars will generate 150 new jobs in their new campus," Bomgaars said, "and if they reach the goal of being the third largest producer of dairy products in the nation, that will require additional production facilities and employees. So it is quite likely that within ten to fifteen years the population of the City of Le Mars will expand to 13,000 or even 15,000."

Bomgaars describes the Le Mars Business Initiative Corporation as having two thrusts. One is to pave the way for new businesses, big and small — and the other is to hold on to present industry and facilitate expansion and growth.

LBIC played an active role in the expansion and and new locations for Cloverleaf Cold Storage, Benkins Warehouse, Bodean's Baking Company, McCormack Distributing, Nor-Am's Cold Storage, Le Mars Public Storage and others.

All this leads to the assessment that the business climate in Le Mars is highly favorable to incoming businesses as well as to those now in existence.

• The educational facilities serving the citizens of Le Mars are excellent, and include the Le Mars Community Schools and Gehlen Catholic Schools. Gehlen's campus is located near St. Joseph Catholic Church on Plymouth Street, NE, and offers elementary through high school education. The Middle School and High School of Le Mars Community Schools are adjacent facilities, located on 3rd Avenue S.W. There also is a Trades and Industries facility on 4th St. SE, and a Vocational Ag Center.

There are four elementary facilities: Clark, on 2nd Avenue NW; Franklin, on 3rd Avenue SE;

EDUCATIONAL & OTHER RESOURCES

Kissinger, located in nearby Merrill; and Kluckhohn, located on Central Avenue S.E.
• The Le Mars Beauty College is a long time

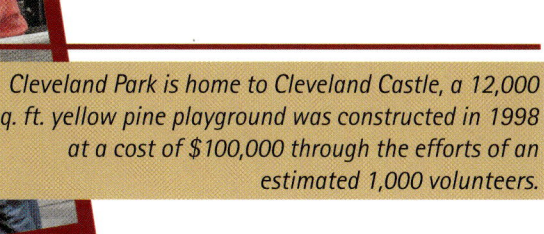

Cleveland Park is home to Cleveland Castle, a 12,000 sq. ft. yellow pine playground was constructed in 1998 at a cost of $100,000 through the efforts of an estimated 1,000 volunteers.

institution in Le Mars. It was founded in 1963, and since then has graduated hundreds of licensed beauticians.

The college is owned and operated by Rod and Sheila Anderson. and draws students from all over Northwest Iowa.

• Le Mars experienced a difficult loss when Westmar University closed its doors in 1997. Larry Schmitz, long time News Director of the two radio stations that then served Le Mars shared his views: "It was a large blow to the city but our citizens responded with a solution. The city passed, with a vote of more than 90% in favor, a resolution to purchase the college campus."

The city is putting the property to good use. The local YMCA, with more than 2500 members, uses the physical education buildings along with the Wellness Center – and the City of Le Mars has created a Convention Center in the former university commons.

A significant number of community agencies rent or have purchased space to house their offices and programs on the campus site – including Buena Vista University Center, Western Iowa Tech Community College, Rejoice Community Church and Plains Area Mental Health Center.

Le Mars' Union Depot displays much of the Victorian and British influences of the early days of Plymouth County.

• Le Mars area churches include all the major denominations, two Roman Catholic parishes and several independent or community churches

• The Le Mars Community Theater presents its dramas and musicals in a facility that once served as the post office – so it also is referred to as "The Postal Playhouse

• Le Mars and Plymouth County are served by excellent and well staffed police and sheriff's departments, and a new state of the art law enforcemer center was opened in 2003 on the east side of the city near the National Guard Armory.

The Le Mars Volunteer Fire Department and ambulance services a provided with the best equipment and training. New locations have been b on east and west sides of the railroad tracks. assuring fast response to al emergencies.

• In this age of communication the people of Le Mars and the surrounding area are served by a local AM radio station, KLEM. Another prominent resource for the Le Mars area and beyond is the Le Mars Daily Sentinel – an award-winning newspaper.

• The annual Plymouth County Fair is held in late July, and draws hug crowds to its exhibitions, contests, food offerings, carnival rides and grandstand entertainment. The Fair is especially attractive because of t large size of Plymouth County, and its diverse economics in businesses and agriculture.

St. George's Episcopal Church, founded in the late 1800s during the high water mark of British immigration, is also listed on the National Register of Historic Places.

Le Mars

Central Avenue, which divides Le Mars and is the city's "Main Street" has several blocks framed with beautiful trees.

- There are three care facilities in Le Mars: Brentwood Good Samaritan Center, Plymouth Manor and The Abbey. Park Place Estates is an assisted living complex, located adjacent to Floyd Valley Hospital.
- The Le Mars Art Center nurtures the cultural scene in Le Mars, and serves to highlight local writers, musicians and artists.

On display in a special center at Trinity Heights in Sioux City are the life-sized figures of a wood carving tableau of The Last Supper, created by local artist Gerald Trauffler. The works of Bud Bolser are well known, as well as those of Jane Schultz. Artist Glenda Drennen teaches classes at the Arts Center.

HOUSING AND CONSTRUCTION

Rich Magnuson of American Bank is one of the most knowledgeable persons in Le Mars

- The expanding Floyd Valley Hospital complex, affiliated with regional Avera Health, serves the entire area. The community is also served by the Medical Associates Clinic, and has easy access to the surgeons of Northwest Surgery P.C. Le Mars also offers the services of chiropractic physicians, dental clinics, the Plains Area Mental Health Center and several optometry clinics.

Late July is county fair time, and some of the best livestock in the state is exhibited at the Plymouth County Fairgrounds.

GP RED RIG

123

Le Mars

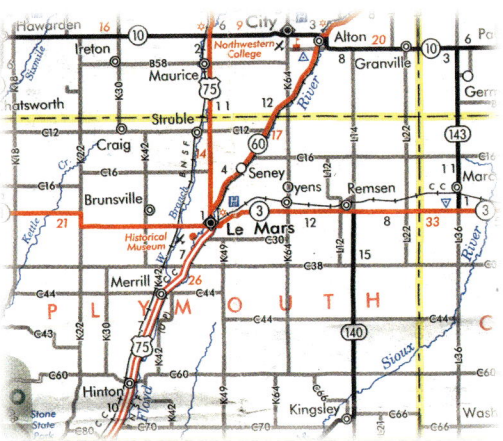

Learn More

Le Mars is located at the intersection of U.S. Highways 60 and 75, just 25 miles north of Sioux City, Iowa.

For more information please feel free to call the Le Mars Area Chamber of Commerce at 712-546-8821 or visit the le Mars website at:
www.lemarsiowa.com
or visit the Daily Sentinel's website at:
www.lemarssentinel.com

Story Contributor

Robert L. Grupp

---

in relation to housing projects and availability. His bank is the number one home, business and farm mortgage filer in Plymouth County.

Magnuson referred to some comments he made about four years ago, indicating that what he said then is still applicable: "I've been in Le Mars for nearly three years. When we moved to town, housing was a real issue and the market was pretty tight. In recent years developers have come forward to meet the housing challenge and we now have a wide choice of price ranges and our market is quite good."

Magnuson stated that compared to Sioux City and other locations Le Mars has reasonably priced housing.

Neal Adler serves as Executive Director of the Le Mars Area Chamber of Commerce as well as Executive Director of the Le Mars Business Initiative Corporation.

"Le Mars has seen continuing growth," Adler stated, "and in the last three years we've had about 27 million dollars in new construction in Industrial Park, and over 200 new jobs created."

Adler predicts that future growth and expansion will be along the Highway 75 bypass, with completion expected in 2006. Wells' new corporate headquarters is the first to locate in that area – on high ground, very visible to highway traffic.

When asked about the features of Le Mars that tend to attract businesses as well as employees, Adler pointed first to the work ethic

FUTURING BUSINESS IN LE MARS

among the people of Le Mars. There are the quality of life factors, offering families enormous cultural, educational, spiritual and recreational resources.

"The city and its officials are very progressive minded – especially for a community this size – and are willing to 'step outside the box' to assist in making things happen. Our location in the central United States certainly is a key factor, with great highways and rail access for nationwide distribution purposes."

There are plans to extend the runway of the Le Mars airport, which will make it more accessible for most of today's corporate jets. Because of the new Sioux City bypass there is easier access to the Sioux City Gateway Airport. In visiting with people of Le Mars, one cannot help but sense the confident anticipation and excitement of significant future growth and improvements in this wonderful city.

Virgil Van Beek has been the mayor of Le Mars for the past seven years of challenge and growth. Van Beek is a former implement dealer, and is now vice president of American Bank in Le Mars.

Van Beek stated that Le Mars is attracting more young families, and the reasons are clear: good schools, churches, recreational facilities and cultural resources – plus employment opportunities and availability of a wide range housing.

"Le Mars, Iowa, is a good place to live," he said. "And I'm glad our children were raised here "

Pride In Our Hometowns.

P·O·R·T·R·A·I·T·S
OF
Logan

BRIDGING THE OLD AND THE NEW

Towns like Logan, Iowa, are often referred to as "bedroom communities" – retreats for individuals to retire to after a full day of work in the city.

But to think of Logan as merely a bedroom community is to dismiss its uniqueness among the small towns that pepper the area. Logan seems to embody its geographical situation. Located just on the cusp of the Omaha-Council Bluffs metropolitan area, Logan is equal parts urban outgrowth and small-town tradition.

 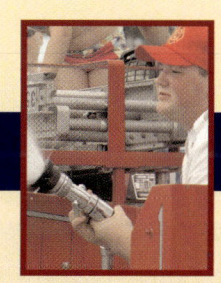  

LOGAN

Pride In Our Hometowns.

P·O·R·T·R·A·I·T·S
OF *Logan*

BRIDGING THE OLD AND THE NEW

A large crowd gathers to witness the start of construction on the second story of the current Harrison County Courthouse in Logan, which was built between 1910 and 1911.

A SNAPSHOT

Though it began as a sort of outpost of the metro area, Logan has quickly adapted to serve as an ideal location for those seeking a delicate balance between the big city and the old-fashioned community.

Although established as a mill site about ten years before the outbreak of the Civil War, Logan is no stranger to battle. From struggling to get the trains to stop, to fighting to become the county seat for Harrison County, to raising more than a half-million dollars for the construction of a new community center, the citizens of Logan have repeatedly shown a "can-do" attitude when it comes to battling to improve their community.

Today, Logan is a place ideally designed to raise a family and enjoy life, as life should be. But, like being successful in battle, quality family life is no stranger to Logan, for it was the basis for the community's beginning. "Uncle" Henry Reel was born in Montgomery County, Virginia, in 1803.

By 1822, Reel relocated, along with his brother John, to Reelsville, Indiana, a community named after members of his own family.

As Indiana welcomed more and more settlers, though, Reel chose to move his

Joe H. Smith, in 1888's "History of Harrison County," sought to dispel the many rumors and hearsay surrounding the relocation of the Harrison County courthouse from Magnolia to Logan.

family – including his wife and three sons – further west. The party traversed the Midwest before finally settling along the west banks of the Boyer River.

By fall 1852, Reel had erected a log cabin along the riverbanks. Between 1854 and 1856, he began construction

Logan IOWA

The Harrison County Courthouse in Logan has stood for nearly 100 years and is one of the area's most recognizable structures.

The History

of a grist and sawmill on the opposite side of the river. High water and other uncontrollable factors slowed Reel's progress, though by November 1856 the mill was ready for production of grain, flour and corn.

In 1864, the C&NW Railroad laid tracks along the Boyer Valley, though through some now-forgotten misunderstanding, the railroad refused to stop at the area around Reel's mill, which had now been unofficially dubbed Boyer Falls.

In 1867, Reel petitioned the Department of Interior for construction of a post office near his mill. His application was granted and a post office constructed, requiring the railroad to now stop for mail exchanges.

Soon after, Reel platted the town and named it Logan, after General John A. Logan, a favorite U.S. Army officer and founder of what we today call Memorial Day.

Logan, however, would never have the chance to carry the lineage of its founding father. All three of Reel's sons lost their lives in the Civil War. Just two years after platting Logan, Reel sold his mill and dedicated his time to minor agriculture and gardening on a parcel of land located where Logan-Magnolia Community School now stands. Mrs. Reel died in 1882 and Reel himself in 1890.

Becoming the county seat

Perhaps Logan's greatest point of pride – and controversy – is the Harrison County Courthouse.

Traditional courthouses don't typically inspire controversy, but there's hardly anything typical about the history of Harrison County's house of government.

Even today, Magnolians will tell you how Logan "stole" the courthouse in 1875.

Theft of a courthouse may seem rather implausible, but there is some truth behind Magnolia's grievance. Their courthouse was, in fact, "stolen," though not in the fashion so many believe.

The "why" is simple: In the late 1800s, being the county seat was a

The band shell in Logan City Park has survived vandalism and the elements but recent renovations, paid mostly through donations, improved the structure for its September 2004 rededication as the Veterans Memorial Band Shell.

Logan

highly desirable designation. It meant a steady and sure flow of citizens through the town. Increased commerce and more settlers were natural and desired byproducts of having a county courthouse in town.

It was also a matter of convenience: Locals – lacking fast transportation – could expect to expedite their legal affairs by not having to travel 10 or more miles to another town.

The "how" is a gray area, though. What is a matter of record is this:

Upon Harrison County's formation in 1853, a county seat locating committee composed of one representative each from Pottawattamie, Fremont and Mills counties chose Magnolia as the ideal location for the county seat.

The following year, construction began on a courthouse, paid for with funds from the sale of town lots.

According to the 1891 "Harrison County History," the courthouse in Magnolia was a "small frame structure, but met the requirements of the day in which it was fashioned; however as the years rolled on, the elements caused this pioneer landmark of public work to decay."

Before the courthouse was even 10 years old, though, the people of Calhoun, who at the time included the area that would later become Logan, challenged for the county seat.

In 1864 a group of citizens from Calhoun, which had been Magnolia's chief rival for the county seat a decade earlier, presented the Harrison County Board of Supervisors with a petition requesting a

Towering crosses adorn the lawns near the Museum of Religious Arts, which welcomes upwards of 10,000 visitors each year. The museum, which is located just west of Logan, houses a variety of relics and items from the world's many religions.

Logan, IOWA

public vote on whether the county seat should remain in Magnolia.

The people of Magnolia countered with a remonstrance requesting a denial of Calhoun's petition, and with more petitioner names than Calhoun, won out. But, the battle wasn't to end.

In 1870, Magnolia was challenged again, this time by upstart Missouri Valley, which had been a town for a mere six years. Petitions supporting a vote on the county seat's move from Magnolia to Missouri Valley were "thick as the leaves at autumn time," according to the 1891 county history.

When the issue went to vote later that year, Magnolia again won out, with 991 votes against a move to Missouri Valley and 935 votes supporting a move. But, the battle still wasn't over. Just three years later, in 1873, Missouri Valley residents again petitioned for a vote on the matter. But Magnolia prevailed this time as well. Though superstition holds that the "third time is the charm," Missouri Valley was unsuccessful in a third bid later that same year. But, the real battle was just about to begin.

With Logan's entrance into the battle over the county seat the story gets a bit murkier. Six-year-old Logan, the so-called "new railroad town," petitioned the Board of Supervisors in 1873 with 1,202 names supporting a county seat move from Magnolia to Logan. But Missouri Valley residents, perhaps resigned to the prospect of never becoming the county seat, sided with Magnolia; and together the two towns countered Logan with a remonstrance listing 1,405 names.

RENEWED CONFIDENCE

With renewed confidence, ever-growing Logan took another shot at the county seat in 1875. Loganites "had the forethought to spring the question at just the right time," and 1,269 residents voted for the county seat's relocation to Logan, beating the 1,267 opponents by just two votes. The results were controversial, though. According to the 1891 county history:

"On the ground of illegal voting, the Magnolia faction filed papers in a contested election case, but through the turning over of some prominent men from Magnolia, who had seen it for their financial interest to move to Logan, unbeknown to the masses at Magnolia, the case was dismissed and without a real order of the court and a little out of due time, the records and effects of the courthouse at Magnolia were all removed to Logan, to the utter amazement of the Magnolia faction, who claim to this day they were sold out by their supposed friends."

Though the official story merely hints at an unseemly nature to the relocation, a number of present-day Magnolians insist a group of Loganites snuck into town in the dead of night and whisked all the court records and books back to Logan, essentially stealing the county seat before due process could be had in the contested vote.

The issue didn't die with the 1875 relocation to Logan, however. Residents of Missouri Valley again petitioned the Board of Supervisors for a county seat change in 1886. The petition was successfully countered by a Logan remonstrance, but with 5,600 petitioners between Missouri Valley and Logan's remonstrance, some surmised that "Missouri Valleyites were possessed of the names of all the voters between that point and Chadron, Nebraska, and as a return to this compliment Logan is

The Logan-Magnolia wrestling squad earned its first-ever Iowa state dual championship in 2003. The wrestling program at Logan-Magnolia has long been a source of pride amid Iowa's highly competitive high school wrestling circuit.

charged with visiting all the graveyards in the county and furnishing names from the remonstrances from the tombstones and monuments therein."

Yet another vote, this time in 1887, resulted in 2,439 voters opposing a relocation to Magnolia and 1,480 supporting it. Though petitions for a change of county seat are nearly unheard of these days, many Magnolians continue to lament the "theft" of the county seat. If the county courthouse has a rival as Logan's source of pride, it would undoubtedly be the town's Fourth of July festivities.

"Logan must celebrate," read the local paper in 1892. "It seems to be a popular demand that it should."

And for more than 100 years, it has been just so.

Present Day Logan

Each year the streets along the Fourth of July parade route are flanked by hundreds of visitors, many of whom don't even live in the area.

Full of floats, cars, bands, clowns, kids, horses, tractors and many surprises, the hour-long parade is merely the kickoff to many activities planned for the day, including a carnival located in the city park, kids' games and water fights among area fire departments.

It all culminates with a huge fireworks display at the school's athletic field that evening.

Logan staked itself as the place to be on July 4 starting in 1892, when the first event was held.

"Logan celebrated the good old-fashioned way," the local newspaper announced. "Home talent provided music and oratory and a large crowd estimated at 6,000 to 8,000 persons attended."

Basket dinners were the trend back then; the park, courthouse lawn, house yards and grassy areas throughout town were covered with families. There were stands, merry-go-rounds, can racks and dancehalls for the "young folks."

In 1902, the fireworks display was the "principle feature" and remained so for many years. It was estimated at least 4,000 people in Logan participated in that year's celebration.

By 1950, a carnival had been added to the park grounds and brought in a number of rides, concessions and shows. The fireworks display was moved to the school's athletic field. The parade had many new entries and covered

$2.6 million in renovations and additions to Logan-Magnolia Community School will undoubtedly improve the school, which was already one of southwest Iowa's most impressive.

four or five blocks. Baseball games were on the schedule, with Logan and Magnolia town teams scheduled to clash on the diamond. Dances were held July 3 and 4 with music provided by Ray Backman's orchestra.

In 1960 the S.O.S. Club was in charge of lining up the parade. Organizational duties were eventually taken over by the local Kiwanis Club.

A 24-team slow-pitch softball tournament was introduced during 1980's Fourth of July festivities.

The 1990s brought a few changes to the event. Blues Amusement was now the carnival of choice and expanded into the street west of the city park. Water fights continued to draw crowds. The parade route was changed in 1999 to accommodate the expansion of the carnival and it has continued as one of the highlights of the celebration.

Entries in the parade have included the Stepping Saints out of Omaha, classic cars, a bicycle club, English foxhounds and the 2nd Maryland Regiment of Omaha.

4TH OF JULY

At least one portion of Logan's Fourth of July festivities seems destined to never change, at least in the foreseeable future.

Along with his crew, LeRoy Bosworth, who has been in charge of fireworks since 1958, continues to paint the sky with fireworks, much to the delight of crowds.

Bridging the old with the new has long been Logan's domain. That spirit has manifested itself in the Logan Community Center.

Built between 1999 and 2000 – a fitting metaphor for Logan's link between old and new – the Logan Community Center seeks to provide the comfort of traditional small-town government while at the same time meeting the needs an ever-growing community requires.

As such, the community center houses not only the town's governing body and police force, but also plays host to a wide variety of public events, including wedding receptions, retirement ceremonies and other social gatherings.

Clinton and Charlene Keay, owners of nearby Perfection Press, initiated the effort to give Logan a new

Logan's Fourth of July parade is a time for people of all ages to participate in national pride.

Logan has a close link to Memorial Day. The town was named after General John A. Logan, the U.S. Army officer who founded the holiday.

Logan

Learn More

Logan is located at the intersection of Highways 30 and 127, about 8 miles northeast of Missouri Valley in the heart of the Loess Hills.

For more information, call Logan City Hall at (712) 644-2425.

Story Contributors

TJ Accola and Mary Darling of the Logan Herald-Observer

---

community center. Their $100,000 contribution, which paid for the land on which to situate the center, was complemented by Jim and Helen Wood's $50,000 donation. The Woods promised an additional $50,000 if local residents and organizations could raise $50,000 of their own money for the campaign.

The crowning contribution, though, came from none other than retired late night talk show host Johnny Carson.

Carson's grandfather, C.N. "Kit" Carson, served as the mayor of Logan from 1944 to 1946. He had run against Clyde Larsen, grandfather of present mayor Mike Foutch. Foutch and City Administrator Nedra Fliehe, along with Foutch's wife, Shelley, had composed a letter that was sent to Carson via Foutch's sister-in-law, an administrative assistant director of the Carson Cancer Center in Norfolk, Neb.

In September 1998, Foutch received a phone call from Carson. Carson's opening words were, "Sorry about the 1944 election." During their conversation, Carson told Foutch he wished to donate $150,000 to the community center project.

Later that month, it was decided that a brand-new facility would be more cost-effective than simply remodeling the existing facilities on the grounds.

An additional $99,200 was received via a grant from the Department of Natural Resources. This was added to a RACI grant to construct the senior citizen room in the facility. Other grants received included $25,000 from the Iowa West Founcation, $104,500 from the Peter Kiewit Foundation, $15,000 from Union Pacific Railroad and another $50,000 – on top of their earlier $100,000 pledge – from Jim and Helen Wood. A

Famous Grandson Helps Community

grand total of $658,700 was received in grants alone.

Alumni, citizens and businesses contributed another $188,110.25 toward the new facility. No tax money was used to pay for the construction. Instead, the new building was funded entirely through grants and donations – quite an accomplishment for a community of just 1,545.

Groundbreaking ceremonies were held June 14, 1999, with move-in day on March 15, 2000.

With the ability to accommodate 400 people, the center is quite versatile. In 2002 alone, the community center was used 249 days, including five wedding receptions, five fundraisers, four graduations and 33 dinners for family reunions, anniversaries, appreciation and retirement events. Use of the center brought in a total of $6,155 to the city.

Local residents are not the only ones who benefit from Logan's many assets.

The Museum of Religious Arts, a facility dedicated to expanding people's knowledge of religion, recently welcomed visitors from Rhode Island, completing the museum's quest to greet guests from each and every state in the nation. Fourth of July visitors are also afforded the opportunity to attend "Movies in the Park," at which local businesses screen a family film in the city's park each Friday night for several weeks.

A new pool is in the works and a recreation center, rare among towns of such size, has been proposed.

Logan will undoubtedly continue to grow – welcoming new residents who wish to escape the trappings of the big city yet retain all the services they want and need. The ability to do just that strikes a perfect balance with Logan's respect for tradition and its craving for a close-knit community. It's the perfect bridge between old and new.

Pride In Our Hometowns.

P·O·R·T·R·A·I·T·S
OF
Mason City

MASON CITY

AMERICA'S "RIVER CITY"

Mason City officially became "River City" in 1958, when favorite son, Meredith Willson, immortalized the community in his hit Broadway musical, "The Music Man."

But the city that was founded around the time of the Civil War has always been associated with a river that settlers originally called Lime Creek – the Winnebago River.

Pride In Our Hometowns.

P·O·R·T·R·A·I·T·S
OF
Mason City

AMERICA'S "RIVER CITY"

Downtown Mason City

A SNAPSHOT

Located midway between Minneapolis and Des Moines, Mason City boasts the first skyscraper west of the Mississippi (the First National Bank Building, built in 1911), the last remaining hotel in the world designed by Frank Lloyd Wright (the Park Inn); the first accredited public two-year college in the state (Mason City Junior College, in 1918); the largest nursing home in the state (Good Shepherd Health Center), and a high school music program that rates among the nation's finest.

Mason Cityans have long been proud of their community, the retail hub of North Central Iowa, and are working to expand business and industry, revitalize their downtown and develop the community's tourism potential.

Mayor Jean Marinos, the city's first woman mayor, observed, "We have incredible assets. We have a good educational base. Our hospital, parks and recreation give Mason City a high quality-of-life index."

The first settlers arrived in what is now Mason City in 1853, soon after the area was opened up for settlement. They chose a site where two rivers converged, Lime Creek and Calmus Creek.

Named for the Masonic leanings of its first settlers, the community was originally called Masonic Grove, then Shibboleth and Masonville, before the name Mason City was adopted in 1855. Phenomenal growth occurred in 1869 with the coming of the railroad.

The years between 1890 and 1920 have been called the "First Golden Age" of Mason City, when the city's industrial economy was at its zenith. The city grew from a population of 6,747 in 1900 to 17,152 in 1915.

Five rail lines and five banks served the city. Mason City achieved its

Two Railroads serve Mason City.

Masonic Grove, along the Winnebago River north of Mason City, was the site of Mason City's first settlement.

maximum population, 30,000, in the 1960 census. It has remained at or near that level ever since.

In 1908, Mason City attorneys James Blythe and J.E. Markley hired Wright, an emerging young architect from Chicago, to design an avant-garde building for their law offices. He designed the City National Bank and Park Inn hotel building, completed in 1910.

CITY NATIONAL BANK AND PARK INN

The Park Inn, now being restored, is "a world treasure," in the words of retired Mason City orthopedic surgeon, Dr. Robert McCoy, a member of the national Frank Lloyd Wright Building Conservancy. Plans are to re-open the hotel pretty much as it existed in 1910 to mark its 100th anniversary in 2010.

Blythe and Markley also commissioned Wright's associates, most notably, Walter Burley Griffin, to design a residential development in a grassy area they had purchased along a winding stream, Willow Creek.

Now known as Rock Glen-Rock Crest, the development is the largest planned group of Prairie School homes (nine were built) in the world unified by a common natural site. Most of the homes were built with Denison hollow clay tile, manufactured in Mason City, and covered with stone.

The George Stockman House, built in 1908, was based upon a design by Frank Lloyd Wright featured in "The Ladies Home Journal."

"Prairie School architecture was the first truly American architectural style to emerge in our country," McCoy said. "Mason City is the largest and most compact focus of this

STOCKMAN HOUSE

Left: The Stockman House was designed by Frank Lloyd Wright.
Right: Horse shows are very popular in Mason City.

Mason City
IOWA

135

Mason City

type of architecture in the state."

During its "Golden Age," Mason City supported several important industries: the railroad, Northwestern States Portland Cement Co., Lehigh Portland Cement Co., Jacob E. Decker & Sons Meat Packing Co., nine brick and tile companies, the Colby Motor Co., Northern Sugar Company (later American Crystal Sugar), and several sand and gravel companies.

These industries actively encouraged immigration from eastern and southern Europe and Mexico to provide an adequate workforce. A large Greek community was established that gave rise to numerous popular eating establishments. An African-American community also developed, many of whom worked on the railroad.

Mason City became known as a melting pot of nationalities.

In the 1925 census, 53 countries were listed as points of origin for foreign-born residents of Cerro Gordo County. Grant Elementary School — one of nine elementary schools in Mason City — reported children of 21 nationalities, many the children of immigrants, in 1930. There were also Jewish and African-American children.

Mason City has had two families that were especially prominent.

One was the Willson family, consisting of John, an attorney and businessman, and Rosalie, a piano teacher, kindergarten teacher and Sunday school superintendent, and their precocious children — Lucile, called "Dixie," Cedric and Meredith. Dixie Willson went on to become a well-known author and children's writer on the East and West coasts. Cedric was an early musician who made a successful career as an engineer and was a vice president of Texas

The Charles H. MacNider Museum in Mason City. A 1949 portrait of General Hanford MacNider hangs in the Charles H. MacNider Museum.

Industries. Composer-songwriter Meredith, a 1919 graduate of Mason City High School, is the one most often associated with Mason City.

Another family that has been synonymous with Mason City since the early 20th century is the McNider/MacNider family.

In 1875, Charles McNider was hired as a messenger boy and janitor at what later became the First National Bank. He rose through the ranks to become president of the bank in about 1908. McNider also became president and general manager of Northwestern States Portland Cement Co. He played an important role in the industrial expansion of Mason City and built a family fortune.

Charles' wife, May, a native of New York, canvassed Mason City at the turn of the century to raise money for the city's first public library building, a Carnegie library built in 1904. When the library became too

Mercy Medical Center

small, she and her family donated the seven-acre site where the city's current library, built in 1939, stands.

The family also donated several tracts of land around Mason City to be used as public parks and, in 1964, purchased and donated a grand 1921 Tudor-style house to the city for an art museum.

Gen. Hanford MacNider, son of Charles and May, who changed the spelling of the family name, is known as Iowa's greatest soldier. He rose to the rank of general and was a nationally known political leader. His list of medals from World War I was exceeded only by those of Gen. John J. Pershing. He served as assistant secretary of war under President Calvin Coolidge. Under President Herbert Hoover, he served as minister to Canada and negotiated the treaty establishing the St. Lawrence Seaway. He became a commanding general during World War II and was promoted to lieutenant general in 1956.

One other Mason City resident who stands out is world-famous puppeteer William "Bil" Baird, a 1922 graduate of Mason City High School. He began making puppets at the age of 14 on a stage he created in the attic of his family's Mason City home. He founded the Bil Baird Marionettes in New York City in 1934. Baird gained national attention in 1965 with the release of "The Sound of Music" motion picture. He and his wife, Cora, created and manipulated the marionettes featured in one scene of the movie.

Other notable Mason City citizens have included: Suffragist Carrie Chapman Catt, then Carrie Lane, who was Mason City school superintendent in 1881 and later, wife of Leo Chapman, editor of a Mason City newspaper; Professional golfer Ann Casey Johnstone; Influential Globe Gazette Editor W. Earl Hall; Joe Lillard, an all-around athlete who played basketball for the Savoy Big Five (the forerunner of the Harlem Globetrotters), professional baseball for the Negro League's Chicago

Notable People

Puppeteer Bil Baird visited the Charles H. MacNider museum on occasion and there is a gallery of his puppets there. He is shown during a visit in the 1970s.

The Colby car was once made in Mason City. This 1911 model is now on display at the Kinney Pioneer Museum.

PAPPAJOHN BUSINESS CENTER

Mason City IOWA

BILL CLINTON VISIT

American Giants and professional football for the Chicago Cardinals; George Baird, younger brother of Bil Baird, the only Olympic gold medal winner from Mason City. He was a member of the 1600-meter relay team in the 1928 Olympics.

Many celebrities have visited Mason City over the years. Among them are:

Charles A. Lindbergh, who, on Aug. 28, 1927, dedicated the Mason City airfield.

President William Howard Taft, who dedicated the Modern Brotherhood of America (Brick and Tile) Building in 1917.

Former President Herbert Hoover, who attended the dedication of Mason City's Hoover Elementary School in 1954.

President Bill Clinton, who announced his intention to run for a second term in Mason City on Feb. 10, 1996. He was the first sitting president to visit Mason City.

In 1960, Amanda Blake, Milburn Stone and Dennis Weaver, "Kitty, Doc and Chester" of the "Gunsmoke" TV series, appeared at the North Iowa Fair.

Television personality Arthur Godfrey, gossip columnist Hedda Hopper and "The Music Man" stars Shirley Jones, Robert Preston, the Buffalo Bills and Ronnie Howard and "Music Man" director Morton Da Costa attended the press premiere of "The Music Man" film in 1962.

Other celebrities who came to Mason City are Sarah Bernhardt, Tom Mix, Jack Benny, Duke Ellington, Count Basie, Louis Bellson, Les Brown, Marian Anderson, Clark Gable, Prince Phillip, Dr. Norman Vincent Peale, Gene Autry, child star Jimmy Hawkins, Spike Jones, Jack Dempsey and Jesse Owens.

Mason City has been the scene of devastating fires and floods, a memorable ice storm in 1936 and grand celebrations. But two events stand out.

One is the robbery of the First National Bank on March 13, 1934, by John Dillinger, George "Baby Face" Nelson and four others. They pulled up in a car toting machine guns just as a

The City Center in downtown Mason City was formerly the 1st National Bank which was robbed by John Dillinger in 1934

Mason City IOWA

crowd had gathered to watch a local man, H.C. Kunkleman, shoot newsreel footage of the bank. The Chicago gang made off with $52,000, shot and wounded two people, and took at least a dozen others to shield their getaway car.

Another memorable day in Mason City's history was the press premiere of "The Music Man" June 19, 1962. Key members of the cast and the Hollywood press corps attended.

One hundred twenty-one bands from 34 states marched in the parade. Warner Brothers contributed $175,000 to enhance float construction and other aspects of the celebration. Meredith Willson led the Mason City High School Band down Federal Avenue.

One of the most important developments impacting Mason City's economy in recent years was the routing of the Avenue of the Saints highway, between St. Louis, Mo., and St. Paul, Minn., through North Central Iowa.

The highway, the first stretch of which opened in North Iowa in 1999, provides a diagonal four-lane to the Chicago market, a key economic development tool, said Dan Culhane, executive director of the Mason City Economic Development Corp.

"Down the road, people will look at the Avenue of the Saints and say it had a tremendous impact on the city," Culhane said.

The city's downtown, which is anchored by Southbridge Mall on the south and the Northbridge development on the north, is also undergoing subtle changes, such as the addition of vintage lighting, to make it more visually pleasing and pedestrian-friendly, City Administrator Tim Moerman said.

With the city's recent designation as a Main Street Iowa community, plans are also being made to improve

A statue of Meredith Willson outside The Music Man Square.

MEREDITH WILLSON

The Mason City High School Band marches in the annual Band Festival Parade in Mason City.

Mason City, Iowa

Lehigh Cement Co.

Alliant Energy's Emery Generating Station

building facades on Federal Avenue. City leaders are also working on plans to improve and enhance Central Park.

The city's largest employers are Mercy Medical Center-North Iowa; Curries and Graham, a manufacturer of doors, windows and frames, and the Principal Financial Group Pension Center.

Other key businesses are Kraft Foods; the $400 million Emery Generating Plant, a new 565-megawatt generating plant of Alliant Energy; the Golden Grain Energy station, an ethanol plant now under construction that will produce up to 50 million gallons of ethanol a year; Sunny Fresh Foods, a $13 million egg-processing facility; Woodharbor Doors & Cabinetry, Inc., manufacturer of interior kitchen and bathroom cabinets, wood interior doors, molding and millwork, and ConAgra Foods, Inc., producer of processed meat products under the Armour, Eckrich and Healthy Choice brands.

More than 469,000 tourists visited Mason City during 2002-2003. They came to visit attractions such as:

The Charles H. MacNider Art Museum, which features a permanent collection of American art, temporary exhibits and the popular Bil Baird marionette collection.

The Kinney Pioneer Museum, depicting life on the Iowa frontier through vintage exhibits and living history.

The Music Man Square, featuring a 1912 streetscape with an

Bottom: The Music Man Square. Right: The Streetscape in The Music Man Square.

The Good Shepherd Health Center is the largest nursing home in the state of Iowa.

ice cream parlor/soda fountain and gift shop in set designs recreated from "The Music Man" motion picture. A Meredith Willson Museum, housing Willson's memorabilia and music-related exhibits, and a children's exploratorium are among other features of this new state-of-the-art facility.

THE MASON CITY PUBLIC LIBRARY

The Mason City Public Library, which features a library garden along Willow Creek and a gallery of framed photographs and signatures of authors dating back to Washington Irving.

The Meredith Willson Boyhood Home. A restored 1895 modified Queen Ann house, it is the birthplace and boyhood home of Meredith Willson.

A trail system provides areas for walking and biking around Mason City.

For those seeking the peace and tranquility of nature, Mason City offers many public parks and a city campground, Margaret MacNider Campground. There is also a new state-of-the-art Mason City Family Aquatic Center, a YMCA built in 2001, and an ice arena.

The city's recreational trails are continually being expanded and include the River City Trail, River City Greenbelt and Trail System, a Trolley Trail connecting Mason City and Clear Lake, and the Winnebago Trail to the Lime Creek Nature Center.

The nature center, a public conservation facility with displays about wildlife and natural resources of North Iowa, includes an outdoor amphitheater and more than nine miles of trails through prairie, woodland and wetland habitat.

The city also offers three golf courses, including a par-three course, and a fairgrounds where activities are held year-round.

Among the city's annual events are the Midstates Hunter/Jumper Show at the fairgrounds, I-35 Speedway stock car races, MacNider Museum Arts Festival, a Civil War re-enactment, the North

Mason City's Family Aquatic Center opened last summer.

Mason City
IOWA

Mason City

Iowa Band Festival and the Greek Festival.

Cultural opportunities abound in Mason City for those seeking live theater or musical entertainment.

The Mason City Community Theatre, Stebens Children's Theatre and the Studio for the Performing Arts stage frequent performances throughout the year. The North Iowa Community Auditorium, on the North Iowa Area Community College campus, is the scene of an annual performing arts series sponsored by NIACC and local businesses.

Concerts are also presented throughout the year by the North Iowa Concert Band, North Iowa Symphony Orchestra and Mason City Municipal Band.

Mason City also provides several interesting educational opportunities.

North Iowa Area Community College, a public two-year college formed in 1966 out of the former Mason City Junior College, is located east of town on a 500-acre campus. It includes the Muse-Norris Conference Center, Murphy Manufacturing Technology Center and Pappajohn Entrepreneurial Center.

DECKER HOUSE-BED AND BREAKFAST

Buena Vista University, a liberal arts college, offers classes and degree programs from its center in Mason City.

Hamilton College, founded in 1900 in Mason City, is the oldest business college continually operating in Iowa. The college recently moved to a new location on the west edge of the city.

La James College of Cosmetology, a long-established cosmetology school in downtown Mason City, specializes in massage therapy, hairstyling, cosmetology and nail technology.

The World Wide College of Auctioneering, the third largest school of auctioneering in the world, was founded in Mason City in 1933. It attracts students from all over the world.

Mason City also has a strong public

Left: Aerial photo of the North Iowa Area Community College campus on the east edge of Mason City. Top: The Decker House is now a Bed and Breakfast.

Mason City

The Robert McCoy residence in Mason City in Rock Glen.

located in the newly renovated former YMCA building, and City Center, upscale apartments in the remodeled First National Bank building. The Decker House Bed & Breakfast, housed in a restored 1894 Neoclassical home and Mason City landmark, opened in 2002.

Mason City has more than 50 churches of numerous denominations. It has more than 100 clubs and organizations.

The city is also well-known in the state for its health care services.

Mercy Medical Center-North Iowa, formerly St. Joseph Mercy Hospital, is a major medical center serving a 14-county area. It was established in 1916. The hospital was recently named one of the 100 top hospitals in the country by

school system that includes a high school and public alternative high school, two middle schools and six elementary schools. The city also has two private schools, Newman Catholic School System — grades preschool through 12th — and the North Iowa Christian School — kindergarten through eighth grade.

A variety of housing styles are available in Mason City, located in established neighborhoods and new upscale housing developments in each quadrant of the city.

Other housing opportunities are River City Apartments,

"The Castle" in Rock Crest in Mason City was designed by Walter Burley Griffin, an associate of Frank Lloyd Wright.

Former Brick and Tile structures remain in a west Mason City neighborhood.

Mason City

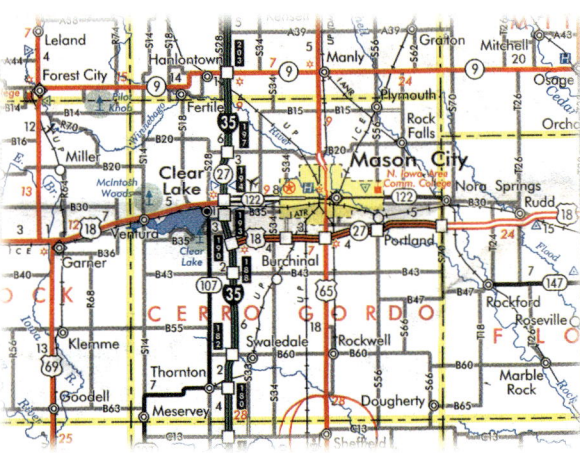

Mason City is located in North Central Iowa, 24 miles south of the Minnesota border. It is eight miles east of Interstate 35, on Iowa Highway 122, and a mile north of the Avenue of the Saints.

Story Contributor

*Kristin Buehner
Reporter, The Globe Gazette*

The Meredith Willson footbridge spans Willow Creek in Mason City.

Solucient, a leading source of health care information, for the third year in a row.

Bright Future

Mason City Clinic, a physician-owned, professional corporation of multi-specialists, provides quality care throughout a 14-county region. Mason City also has a Veterans Administration Clinic.

The prospects for Mason City's continued growth and development are excellent right now, Culhane said.

"When I look at all the pieces that are coming together at just the right time, we're seeing really nice activity," he said. "It's hard not to be excited about Mason City's future." Mayor Marinos added, "We're going to make sure that our community prospers — not just grows."

A young deer stands in the roadway near the entrance to Lime Creek Nature Center on the north edge of Mason City.

Pride In Our Hometowns.

P·O·R·T·R·A·I·T·S
OF
Mt. Pleasant

GROWTH, PROSPERITY AND CONTENTMENT

A visitor's first impression of Mt. Pleasant is, appropriately, a pleasant one: New highway bypasses overlook shiny subdivisions, shopping areas and industrial plants. Stately Victorian homes flank a tree-lined thoroughfare. A lovely fountain splashes in a grassy central park. Children climb on a giant steam engine opposite a well-kept courthouse, where flags ripple in the breeze above the veterans memorial. Townspeople greet one another as they transact their business around a busy square filled with shops, restaurants and offices.

It's a picture of growth, prosperity and contentment, but it doesn't begin to tell the whole story of this dynamic Southeast Iowa community long known as home to the Old Threshers Reunion and Iowa Wesleyan College. Mt. Pleasant is a town where economic, educational and recreational opportunities come together with old-fashioned neighborliness to provide a quality of life most Americans can no longer imagine.

  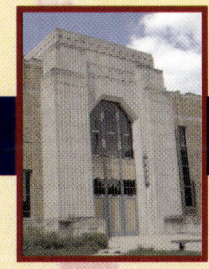 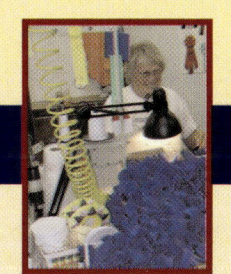

MT. PLEASANT

Pride In Our Hometowns.

P·O·R·T·R·A·I·T·S
OF
Mt. Pleasant

GROWTH, PROSPERITY AND CONTENTMENT

Don't look for the mountain–the altitude is just 734 feet above sea level–but you will find an attitude that is high on small-town living at its Midwestern best.

MT. PLEASANT FIRST SETTLED IN 1835

In the spring of 1835, Presley Saunders put up a cabin and laid out a 41-block town with a public square on this fertile, high prairie near the Skunk River. Henry County was established in 1837 while the area was still part of the Wisconsin Territory. The county's first board of supervisors convened on Jan. 16, 1837, in a log cabin. The first Henry County Courthouse was completed in 1839, the first building constructed as a courthouse in Iowa. The town of Mt. Pleasant was incorporated on Jan. 25, 1842.

Early Mt. Pleasant was known as "the Athens of Iowa." Citizens started a subscription school in a log cabin in 1837. Howe's Academy opened in 1845. St. Alphonsus Catholic Church operated a school and a Female Seminary offered a program for girls. In May 1849, the first public school district was organized.

Members of the Methodist congregation and the community petitioned the legislature repeatedly for an educational institution, resulting in the 1842 establishment of Mt. Pleasant Collegiate Institute. The community gave land north of downtown and a fund drive was begun to erect a building, now

EDUCATION A CONTINUING PRIORITY

known as Pioneer Hall, which still stands at the center of the Iowa Wesleyan campus. At one time, three four-year colleges operated in the county.

Iowa Wesleyan was early associated with human rights efforts. Iowa Wesleyan graduated four African-American women by 1898. Alumna Arabella Babb Mansfield became the first female U.S. citizen to pass the bar examination in 1869. The first state Women's Rights Convention was held in Mt. Pleasant in 1870. Coach Olan Ruble organized the first women's intercollegiate basketball team in Iowa in 1943. Ruble went on to coach several All-American women basketball players in his 21-year tenure.

James Harlan, a key figure

A towering figure in Mt. Pleasant, Iowa and United States history is James Harlan, who came here in 1853 as president of the Mt. Pleasant Collegiate Institute. During his presidency, he gained substantial Methodist Church support for the college, obtained a

Joshua Eberhardt makes his afternoon rounds for the Mt. Pleasant News, published daily since 1878.

Mt. Pleasant

James Harlan

new state charter as Iowa Wesleyan University and completed the Old Main Building (now home to the music department).

In 1855, Harlan became the first Republican U.S. Senator from Iowa, holding office through the Civil War. He was a close friend of President Lincoln, who, shortly before his assassination, appointed him Secretary of the Interior. Harlan served President Andrew Johnson's administration from May 15, 1865, to July 27, 1866, then resigned to reassume the senatorship. He is one of two Iowans whose statues stand in the Hall of Fame in the nation's Capitol.

The 1868 marriage of Harlan's daughter, Mary, to Robert Todd Lincoln, the President's son, brought the Lincoln family into long association with Mt Pleasant. The couple had only begun seriously courting when Lincoln was shot. Sen. Harlan retired to Mt. Pleasant in 1873, living in a frame house at the end of Main Street, which later served as a secondary residence for the Robert Todd Lincolns. The house is maintained by the college and the Harlan-Lincoln House Renovation Committee, both of which raise funds for its restoration. Among the memorabilia is a framed piece of cloth from the suit Lincoln wore at the time of his death, a mourning veil worn by Mrs. Lincoln, Harlan items and period furnishings. Tours are available.

Ill-provisioned volunteers in the Iowa Fourth Cavalry and 25th Regiment of Infantry trained at Camp Harlan, just east of the present Mt. Pleasant Golf & Country Club. Townspeople rallied and made them comfortable, as did Senator Harlan who brought supplies to the soldiers in his buggy. The regiment went to war in February 1862, serving with Sherman on his march from Vicksburg.

The Iowa Hospital for the Insane opened its doors on March 1, 1865, the second state hospital in the U.S. to be built west of the Mississippi River. The campus, known today as Mt. Pleasant Treatment Center, includes the Mental Health Institute, operated by the Department of Health and Human Services, and the Mt. Pleasant Correctional Facility, operated by the Department of Corrections, which includes a large medium security prison for men and a smaller women's prison.

Antique steam engine enthusiasts return to Mt. Pleasant annually for the Old Threshers Reunion.

The Harlan Lincoln House at 601 N. Main was home to Sen. James Harlan and the Robert Todd Lincolns.

Mt. Pleasant

Religious life important.

Religious life has been a strong part of the community from the beginning. The Methodist congregation was first organized in the home of Presley Saunders in 1836. Episcopalians and Baptists met for regular worship as early as 1843. The current First Congregational-Universalist Church is a federation of two of the oldest Christian fellowships in the community- the Congregational Church, organized 1841, and Universalist Church, organized 1848. St. Alphonsus Catholic Parish dates back to 1858 when Father Peter Magney conducted services in various homes. Regular Christian Science services began in Mt. Pleasant in 1899 in rooms owned by Sen. Harlan. The Mt. Pleasant Presbyterian Church, sixth in the Territory of Iowa, was organized in 1840. All these congregations and many more continue to be a vital part of community life.

Women's groups, P.E.O., T.T.T. founded here

On Jan. 21, 1869, the P.E.O Sisterhood was founded by seven female students at Iowa Wesleyan University. Today this organization is international in scope, supporting educational opportunities for women. In 1927, the sisterhood provided funds for the erection of the P.E.O. building, which served as the college library and P.E.O. headquarters for many years. It is now the administration building for the campus. P.E.O. members from across the nation are frequent campus visitors. Chapter Original A maintains a display of memorabilia from the early days.

On June 30, 1911, six

Mental Health Institute

The P.E.O. Building, built in 1927, serves as the administration building for the Iowa Wesleyan College Campus

St. Alphonsus Catholic Church

148

Mt. Pleasant

young Mt. Pleasant women became founders of the T.T.T. Society, which supported charitable works and Red Cross projects, and, by 1917, had grown to six chapters in Iowa. It is now national in scope. Tri-T, as it is known, adopted a national charter in 1931 and identified camping opportunities for disadvantaged girls as its major project. The national office has long been in Mt. Pleasant.

Industrial development took off in the 1960s

Early industry in Mt. Pleasant included brick-making, wagon works, canning, and scale and velocipede manufacturing, but the community was not known as a manufacturing center until the 1960s, when E.A. "Ernie" Hayes and other far-sighted citizens pulled off a remarkable economic turnaround.

Facing declining population and the loss of young people, community leaders dug from their own pockets and collected coins from school children to create the Henry County Industrial Development Corporation. HCIDC bought potential plant sites on the east and west ends of town, then set out to recruit industries to fill them.

Blue Bird Bus Co. was an early victory, opening its plant in 1962 on the west side. Blue Bird produced thousands of school buses here over a 40-year period.

In 1964, Mt. Pleasant voters backed the first industrial revenue bond issue in Iowa to bring in Vega Industries, a manufacturer of Heatilator free-standing fireplaces. The plant is now owned by Hearth & Home Technologies, a subsidiary of HNI Corporation, and continues to be a major Mt. Pleasant employer.

O.E. McIntyre selected Mt. Pleasant for its Midwest plant in 1963 to distribute advertising mail for major magazines and industries. Later known as Metromail, and now as MetroGroup, the plant mails millions of pieces per year and is known for the diversity of its workforce.

Motorola was recruited in 1971 to build two-way radios. The facility was sold to Celestica in 2002, continuing the same type of product.

Wal-Mart founder Sam Walton came to town Sept. 20, 1983, to announce the construction of a 653,000-square-foot Wal-Mart distribution center to serve the company's retail centers in the upper Midwest. It was the first distribution center built outside of Bentonville, Ark. Wal-Mart recently invested $30 million to expand the distribution center to 1.3 million square feet.

Industrial recruitment is now handled by the Mt. Pleasant Area Development Commission, supported financially by the county and city, and operated

MT. PLEASANT MUNICIPAL AIRPORT

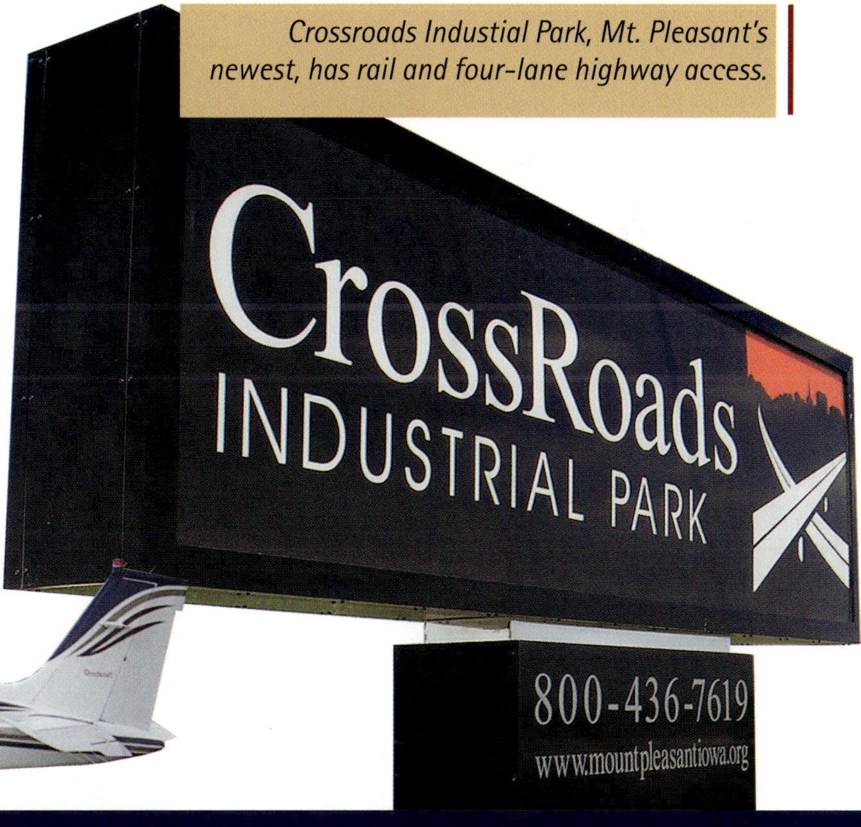

Crossroads Industial Park, Mt. Pleasant's newest, has rail and four-lane highway access.

Mt. Pleasant

under the Mount Pleasant Area Chamber Alliance.

Newest to join the community's industrial line-up are Mt. Pleasant Foods, a state-of-the-art turkey slicing and packaging operation; Millard Refrigerated Services, a cold storage warehouse; Riverside Paper, a Wisconsin-based paper converting company occupying the former Blue Bird property; and Momentus Golf, a manufacturer of specialized clubs to help golfers improve their swings.

Other major manufacturers and distributors and their products include:
- Goodyear Rubber Co., hose
- Ceco Building Systems, metal buildings
- Alaniz Ltd., high quality printing
- Mackay Envelope, envelope printing
- Nypro, plastic injection molding
- Lomont Industries, plastic injection molding
- City Carton, cardboard and paper recycling
- Mid-America Lumber, building products distribution
- Pioneer Hi-Bred International, seed corn

Mt. Pleasant's oldest industry is Staats & Co., Inc., established in 1898. Staats is nationallly known for supplying county and state fair prize ribbons and rosettes. It has expanded in recent years to provide products and services to a variety of markets in the awards and recognition industry.

The Van Allen Family

Prominent in the history of Mt. Pleasant is the Van Allen family, George Clinton Van Allen moved to Mt. Pleasant in 1862 from upstate New York, built a home and established a three-generation law practice. His son, A.M. Van Allen, served as mayor and helped bring electric lighting to the city. A.M.'s four sons left their mark on their community, state and nation. George practiced law and served as district judge. William headed Howard Hughes aircraft company in London. Maurice chaired the University of Iowa Department of Neurology. James, an Iowa Wesleyan College alumnus, is famed for his discovery of the radiation belts that bear his name, and other space exploration activities. He headed the University of Iowa physics and astronomy department until retirement in 1985. The family home at 502 West Washington is owned by the Van Allen House Heritage Center.

MIDWEST OLD THRESHERS REUNION

The Old Threshers Reunion, always held the five days ending with Labor Day, offers fun for the entire family with farming demonstrations, tractors, steam engines, trains, trolleys, great food and entertainment. Since its first show in 1950, Old Threshers has become the largest event of its type in North America, attracting more and varied types of events and visitors than any other.

Old Threshers today is a feast of sight, sound, smell, taste and hands-on experience. You can learn

The Henry County Courthouse was completed in 1914.

Mt. Pleasant IOWA

to drive a tractor, take in a saloon show, ride a steam-powered carousel, train or electric trolley, enjoy a country music show by big-time artists from Willie Nelson to Lone Star to Brad Paisley, or enjoy a home-cooked meal served up at a tent run by churches and civic groups. Hundreds of volunteers give thousands of hours of time to make the reunion a lasting success, but it takes a year-round staff, a board of directors and a foundation as well. Facilities cover 180 acres, including a 60-acre campground served by restored electric trolleys that shuttle campers to the reunion. Midwest Central Railroad operates a steam locomotive that carries passengers around the reunion grounds.

"The Old Threshers Reunion is a place where you can see more things, eat more food and have more fun that you ought to – and afford to bring the whole family," says CEO Lennis Moore.

Tragedy & Triumph

City Face Dark Days

Near the end of a regular City Council meeting on Wednesday night, Dec. 10, 1986, 69-year-old resident Ralph Davis walked into council chambers with a semi-automatic handgun, firing into Mayor Edd King and council members Ron Dupree and Joann Sankey before he was disarmed. Mayor King, who had helped lead Mt. Pleasant's industrial surge in the 1960s and 1970s, died hours later. Sankey and Dupree were seriously injured. The shock, grief and sudden loss of leadership are keenly felt by residents years later.

Davis was convicted and imprisoned for the murders. A sense of security and well-being has long since returned to Mt. Pleasant. The Edd King Fountain in Central Park is the community's lasting tribute to the progressive mayor.

The rise of Tom Vilsack

A year after the shootings, the Mt. Pleasant News reported "the town has managed to put itself together, and one ironic, unintended consequence...has been an increase in interest in city issues." Civic leader Ernie Hayes said the council "worked together to do what Edd had been working on" and noted more people running for office and a broader base of citizens working on various projects. One of those persons was a young lawyer, Tom Vilsack, who ran successfully for mayor.

Born Dec. 12, 1950, in Pittsburgh, Pa., Vilsack attended Hamilton College in New York State, where he met his future wife, Christine Bell, of Mt. Pleasant. Vilsack earned

Mt. Pleasant's old high school has been converted to a community center and library. Right, the Edd King Memorial Fountain, honoring the late mayor.

Mt. Pleasant

his law degree at Albany Law School, Union University, in 1975, and joined his father-in-law Tom Bell's law practice in Mt. Pleasant, where he became active in civic affairs, leading efforts to build the Mapleleaf Athletic Complex. Vilsack served as mayor from 1987 to 1992 and two terms in the Iowa Senate. He was elected Governor in 1998, winning reelection in 2002.

As Governor, Vilsack has worked for stronger funding for schools, an emphasis on biotechnology and creation of the Iowa Values Fund to help recruit higher paying jobs to the state. First Lady Christie Vilsack, a former teacher and journalist, has campaigned for libraries and literacy, as well as candidates and issues, wearing her colorful, trademark hats. Vilsack is the second governor to be provided by Henry County. Joshua Newbold served from 1877 to 1878.

HIGHWAYS A VITAL LINK

Highway construction and amenities to enhance the quality of life have been themes for the community in the past decade, along with continued emphasis on industrial development and education. Agriculture continues to be important – Mt. Pleasant is located in the middle of some of the world's richest farmland – but the community has worked hard to diversify its economic base. As a result, population has steadily increased, reaching 8,751 in the 2000 census.

Highways have been vital to Mt. Pleasant from 1853, when the Plank Road was finished, connecting the community with Burlington. In the 1970s, Ernie Hayes coined the term, Avenue of the Saints, and launched a campaign for a four-lane highway linking St. Paul, Minn., with St. Louis, Mo. Mt. Pleasant leaders have been fighting for better highways since. Banker Don Carmody, has been at the forefront for the past two decades, leading delegations to Des Moines and Washington, D.C., lobbying, calling and writing officials to keep projects on track. Carmody, who was appointed in May 2002 to a seat on the Iowa Department of Transportation Commission, explains importance of highways this way: "Whenever you have good arteries–two major four-lane highways–to get raw materials in and finished goods and services out, you will prosper. That, along with the safety aspect, has set Mt. Pleasant up to burst at the seams in the coming years."

The four-lane Avenue of the Saints and the Burlington to Des Moines Freeway, upgrading U.S. 34 and 163 to four-lanes, are both nearing completion in Iowa. For Mt. Pleasant, access to two four-lane U.S. highways is a boon to current and future industry, an opportunity for local attractions such as Old Threshers, and a convenience to residents, making travel safer and easier to and from surrounding areas. Development is flourishing around Mt. Pleasant's new interchanges. Shottenkirk Automotive Group, Hy-Vee, Wal-Mart and Farm Credit Services have invested in sparkling new facilities near the bypasses. Further growth is expected. The transportation system is complemented by a city-owned airport with a 4,000-ft. runway and serviced by two navigation aids, NDB and VOR approach systems.

Henry county Health Center is recognized nationally as one of the "Top 100 Hospitals."

Mt. Pleasant

United Thru Play Playground

Health, recreation facilities abound

The community cares about its health. Henry County Health Center is a 74-bed facility staffed by more than 25 resident physicians, 50 visiting specialists and some 300 employees. Since admitting its first patient in 1921, the public hospital has continually upgraded physical facilities, technical and innovative equipment and the skills of associates. HCHC has been recognized at the state and national levels as one of the "Top 100 Hospitals" and the "Top National and State Ambulance Service." Healthy Henry County Communities, an organization working to promote healthy lifestyles, conducts substance abuse prevention programs, works to improve childcare and children's readiness for school, offers education to pregnant women and young parents through Mentoring Moms and the

Activity Abounds

Nest, sponsors a Diversity Action Team to integrate immigrants into the community, and administers a program to improve the nutritional environment for youth.

The health-minded also benefit from an extensive park system including an aquatic center, lighted tennis courts, driving range, soccer fields, baseball diamonds, horseshoe and sand volleyball courts, archery range, fishing lake, playgrounds and picnic shelters. Year-round fitness is available at the community Recreation Center. The facility houses a swimming pool, racquetball courts, basketball and volleyball courts, running track and workout equipment. Year-round educational and fitness programs are offered.

The Henry County Recreational Trails Association has laid out 10-mile loop with the second segment under construction. Citizens raised $148,000 and volunteered their time and tools to construct the elaborate United Thru Play playground in a week in the summer of 2002. The unique structure features racing slides, bridges, and upside down room, rocketship and more.

Located four and one-half miles south of Mt. Pleasant on the scenic Skunk River, Oakland Mills County Park provides fishing access, hiking trails, camping and picnic facilities and a nature center. Built around 186-acre Lake Geode in southeast Henry County, Geode State Park offers boating, swimming, hiking, fishing, camping and picnicking opportunities. A bowling alley, movie theater, fitness centers and country club with 9-hole golf course round out Mt. Pleasant's leisure time offerings.

Passion For Education

Education has always been a priority for Mt. Pleasant. A strong public school system and a private Christian school provide kindergarten through high school education. Two colleges are available to traditional age college students and provide life-long learning opportunities for adults. Residents backed a $10.9 million bond issue in 1996 for construction of a new high school on the city's south edge and to improve neighborhood
elementary

Mt. Pleasant

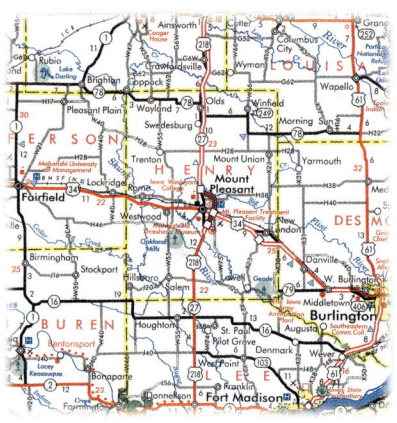

Learn More

Mt. Pleasant is located at the intersections of U.S. Highways 24 and 218-27.

For more information please feel free to call the Henry County Convention and Visitors Bureau at 800-421-4282 or visit websites at:
www.henrycountytourism.org
www.mountpleasantiowa.org

Story Contributors

*Emery Styron
Publisher, Mt. Pleasant News*

*Don Young
Historian*

*Martha Hayes
Preservationist*

Veterans Memorial

schools. Mt. Pleasant Christian School offers faith-based teaching and cooperates with the public school on transportation and extra-curricular activities.

Voters also backed a $3 million bond issue in 2002 to fund renovation of the old high school downtown into a library and community center. The project is partially-funded by a $1 million Vision Iowa grant. The facility is expected to open in winter 2005. Refurbishing of the art deco auditorium is a key component of the project. The existing 1903 Carnegie Library will be traded to Southeastern Community College, which will expand its Mt. Pleasant classes, and work closely with Iowa Wesleyan.

Iowa Wesleyan provides 26 majors, five degrees and a variety of pre-professional programs, along with 12 intercollegiate mens and women's sports. Home to the Southeast Iowa Symphony, IWC brings guest speakers, artists and entertainers to the community. Mt. Pleasant Community Theater productions and repertory theater productions are staged at the historic Iowa Wesleyan College Chapel. Summer theater is also provided at the Repertoire Theatre Museum on the Old Threshers grounds.

The college recently completed the Howe Activity Center, providing spacious athletic and meeting facilities to the campus, and in May 2004 received a $15 million challenge grant from Stan and Helen Howe.

"Mt. Pleasant is a community of civic boosters who are always building on the town's past endeavors for its future economic success," wrote Gary A. Mattson, researcher for the Iowa State University College of Design, in a 2003 study of rural county seats in Iowa. He identified Mt. Pleasant as a community with willingness to make investments in social capital and public service features to keep the community's children interested in the town instead of moving to more urban areas.

Mt. Pleasant: "Always building"

John Freeland, Mt. Pleasant's mayor, sums it up this way: "Mt. Pleasant, the Heritage City at the Crossroads, has a rich history of accomplishments.

As our city looks to the future, we will continue to promote our history of cooperation and leadership to make Mt. Pleasant a great place to live, work, raise a family and enjoy a remarkable quality of life."

Come for a weekend, but be careful. You may want to stay for a lifetime.

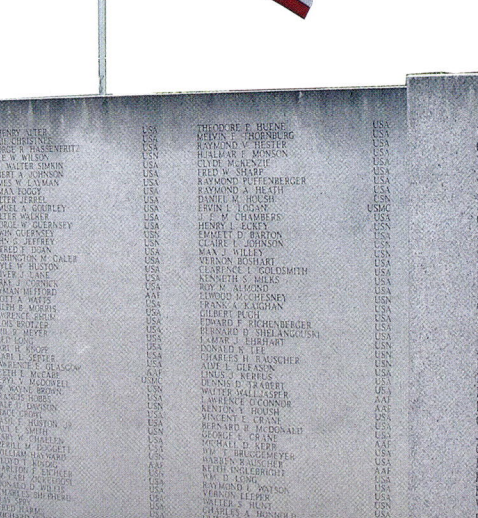

Pride In Our Hometowns.

P·O·R·T·R·A·I·T·S
OF
Nevada

NEVADA

Heartland, Heritage and Horizons

After the first pioneers settled in Nevada in 1853, the town was quickly shaped into an upstanding community with strong schools, businesses and churches. Today, Nevada is one of the best small towns in America. Its residents maintain their pride in being from the nation's Heartland, honor their rich heritage and grow, literally and figuratively, toward their horizons.

Nevada's motto, "Heartland, Heritage and Horizons," represents pride in the town's ability to draw from tradition as it grows into the future, making the community one of the best small towns in the nation.

Pride In Our Hometowns.

P·O·R·T·R·A·I·T·S
OF *Nevada*

Heartland, Heritage and Horizons

Story County's first courthouse, built in 1855, towers above a busy downtown business district.

A Snapshot

This community, named after a mountain range hundreds of miles away, is located on land that was not considered the highest quality in the mid-1800s. In stark contrast to its Sierra Nevada namesake, this land was low and wet. But early settlers such as T.E. Alderman, considered by many to be the "father of Nevada," saw great potential in the area and its rich soil. Strength in times of hardship, high moral standards and an ability to celebrate special occasions as a community helped Nevada quickly develop as a town with a strong sense of itself and its future. More than 150 years since its humble but optimistic beginnings, the pioneering spirit of Alderman and other early settlers continues to thrive in Nevada. In 1995, the community was declared the 26th Best Small Town in America by the Prentice Hall Publication, "100 Best Small Towns in America." The land that was considered undesirable in the 1800s now boasts some of the highest property values in Iowa. Located in the heart of both the state and the nation, Nevada is comprised of highly productive people, a diverse economic base and a strong commitment to future generations.

In 1853, seven years after Iowa became a state, the area for which Nevada would be county seat was formed and named after Supreme Court Justice Joseph Story. At first, Story County grew slower than the surrounding areas due to

Left: The railroads through Nevada were an important part of the town's early success. Right: "Heartland, Heritage, Horizons," officially or unofficially, has been Nevada's motto for more than 150 years.

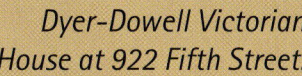

Dyer-Dowell Victorian House at 922 Fifth Street.

History

Nevada was declared Story County's county seat on June 27, 1853. Prior to that the land in this area belonged to Benton, Polk and Boone counties. Alderman was present when a group of commissioners located the county seat in Nevada. He was hunting for a good place to build a mercantile business and decided at once to settle in the town and establish a general store for the pioneer trade. He bought two lots located west of where the courthouse would be built in 1855. This was the location of Nevada's first log cabin, which served as the general store, post office and residence. The building site is still honored with a monument with the inscription, "Nevada founded here October 11, 1853 by T.E. and Hannah Alderman."

More people bought land in Nevada, more homes were built and more businesses sprouted. The first building to be used as the Story County Courthouse was built in 1855, but in December of the next year, that building was destroyed by fire. Thankfully, most of the county records were saved. Shortly after the fire, another courthouse was built in the same location as the first. In 1876, a large new courthouse was erected on the same site, with much of the brick for the construction manufactured by the McHose Brothers tile factory, which was

the damp soil that accounted for a large number of lowlands, marshes, ponds and sloughs. Prior to the arrival of white settlers, even Native Americans avoided residing in this area.

"Meet you at the bell!" is a common phrase for students at Central Elementary.

The business district on Sixth Street includes several historical buildings, including the Camelot Theatre.

Nevada, IOWA

located on Seventh Street, south of the Rock Island railroad.

In 1966, a new courthouse was constructed at the location. That building now houses Story County Administration offices, such as the recorder, assessor, treasurer, auditor and board of supervisors. A new $14 million justice center housing a jail and courthouse opened in 2002 and is located on the southeast side of town.

Early settlers of Nevada brought their religious beliefs and traditions with them. Among the religions represented in those early years were Cumberland Presbyterian, Baptist, Norwegian Lutheran, Dunkard, Methodist, Christian Disciple, Episcopal, United Brethren, Evangelical, Presbyterian, Catholic, Congregational, Adventist and Protestant Methodist.

In 1866, W.G. Allen, a pioneer historian, wrote: "Nevada has as good schools, perhaps, as we have any where in Central Iowa. Its citizens have regard for quiet and order within its limits. Lager beer and whisky are 'few and far between.'"

Social and cultural features in Nevada flourished with an opera house; several social and fraternal groups grew year after year. From the beginning, education was a very important issue in Nevada, starting with a wooden schoolhouse and expanding to a present-day modern and extensive school system.

Several organizations in Nevada work to ensure the heritage of this community will continue to be honored and acknowledged. At the forefront of this mission is the Nevada Community Historical Society, which is making great strides to preserve the town's history, including the publication of a 341-page book titled, "Voices from the Past: The Story of Nevada, Iowa."

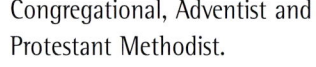
Nevada City Hall and Police Department at 1209 Sixth Street.

Story County Medical Center at 630 Sixth Street.

Like most pioneers, early Nevadans suffered their share of hardships – prairie fires, tornadoes, floods and drought. Despite the challenges, early residents stayed to work the land, tend their businesses and raise their children. The population rose steadily from 300 in 1855 to more than 1,600 in 1890. The 2000 Census cites Nevada's population as 6,658, a growth of almost 10 percent from 1990.

Hardships

In the early-1940s, tragedy claimed an architectural jewel and the main source of health care for most of eastern Story County. With most of the funding coming from the Seventh Day Adventist Association, a Sanitarium was constructed on what is now known as Academy Hill at the south end of Eighth Street between downtown Nevada and U.S. Highway 30. The beautiful three-story porch-lined building was dedicated Aug. 16, 1909. It contained an operating room, treatment rooms, nursery, patient rooms and X-ray facilities.

The Sanitarium burned to the ground on Jan. 30, 1943, leaving only the huge chimney and part of the outside brick walls. The loss to the community was immense, especially as building supplies and permits were in short supply due to the war effort. Even the Nevada Fire Department was short-handed as firefighters rushed to answer the call in sub-zero temperatures. A blizzard had nearly blocked roads in the Nevada area a few days before, and temperatures were as low as 25 degrees below zero. The fire spread so rapidly there was no hope of saving the building. There was one fatality in the fire, a 23-day-old infant. The cause of the fire was never discovered.

Briggs Terrace/Evergreen Lane at 1204 H Avenue.

Even in tragedy, the community-mindedness of Nevada residents was apparent. During the fire in 1943, many residents braved the bitter cold and the raging flames to help their fellow townsfolk – physicians and nurses from downtown helped at the scene, even students at Oak Park Academy helped by bearing stretchers.

That sense of togetherness continues in modern day Nevada. It comes in many forms: financing for parks and buildings, fund-raisers for neighbors facing disease, clean up after a storm. It comes at good times, as well: cheering

Children play in the beach area of Fawcett Aquatic Center.

Nevada IOWA

the Nevada Cubs at an athletic event, waving at friends in the parades during a wealth of community celebrations, attending or participating in the community's variety show. If there's something to do, Nevada residents can get it done. That ability to focus together on goals makes them worthy of the title of being one of the best small towns in America.

Nevada residents place a high value on healthy living. They proved this by strongly supporting the creation of Story County Outdoor Recreation for Everyone (SCORE). The 58-acre SCORE recreation athletic complex boasts the Fawcett Aquatic Center, pavilion and soccer fields. The Fawcett Family Aquatic Center opened for its fourth season in 2004. The Aquatic Center includes lap lanes, a deep-water area and provides a zero-depth entry area. It also features a sand volleyball court and water slides.

A Pavilion has been constructed that will be rented for meetings, parties and events. The Pavilion has a full-service kitchen and inside seating room for 130 people and a covered outside area with picnic table seating. In the first year of operation alone, nearly 50,000 patrons used the pool area. When completed, the area will also offer softball diamonds and baseball fields.

The community offers a large variety of other parks, a bowling alley, dance school and three local golf courses. Hickory Grove Lake between Nevada and Colo offers fishing, non-motorized boating and camping.

Story County Medical Center offers state-of-the-art facilities for treating disease and injuries. It also focuses on preventative medicine by holding exercise classes and featuring speakers on health topics. The facility features a 24-hour

Fawcett Aquatic Center is part of the 58-acre SCORE park.

A memorial at 935 Lincoln Highway honors past and present Nevada firefighters.

A mural on main street promotes Nevada's annual celebration.

emergency room with ambulances and paramedics, an outpatient clinic and a two-story long-term care wing. A number of other health-care providers, including physicians, dentists, chiropractors and pharmacists, care for residents of Nevada and the surrounding area.

The family of one of the town's early mayors bequeathed a large sum to Nevada for its school, cemetery and library. William Gates, an Irish-born blacksmith, moved to Nevada around the 1860s where he operated a very successful blacksmithing business. Gates served as mayor six times and was also elected to the city council several times. His daughter, Mabel Gates Wadsworth, then of Longmont, Colo., died in 1939 and willed that, upon the death of her husband, three-quarters of her estate would go to the town with the intention of creating a community center as a memorial.

In 1963, at a cost of $280,000, Nevada constructed Gates Memorial Hall at 825 15th St. The 16,000-square foot facility offers an auditorium with a stage, two meeting rooms and a fully-equipped kitchen. Gates Hall received a $1 million facelift in 2001. Through the years, the building has hosted many events for the school and the community. Those activities include Nevada High School's prom, dramatic performances and musicals, the ABWA's twice-annual craft fair and the Festival of Trees.

The Nevada Public Library offers a large selection of books and other media for its patrons. Located at 631 K Ave., the 11,000-square foot building was completed in 1992 and serves Nevada and rural Story County residents. The library's circulation is about 150,000 items annually with approximately 12,000 registered users. The library also maintains a full program of events and activities for youth and adults alike.

Since its earliest years, education has always been a top priority in Nevada. One-room schoolhouses

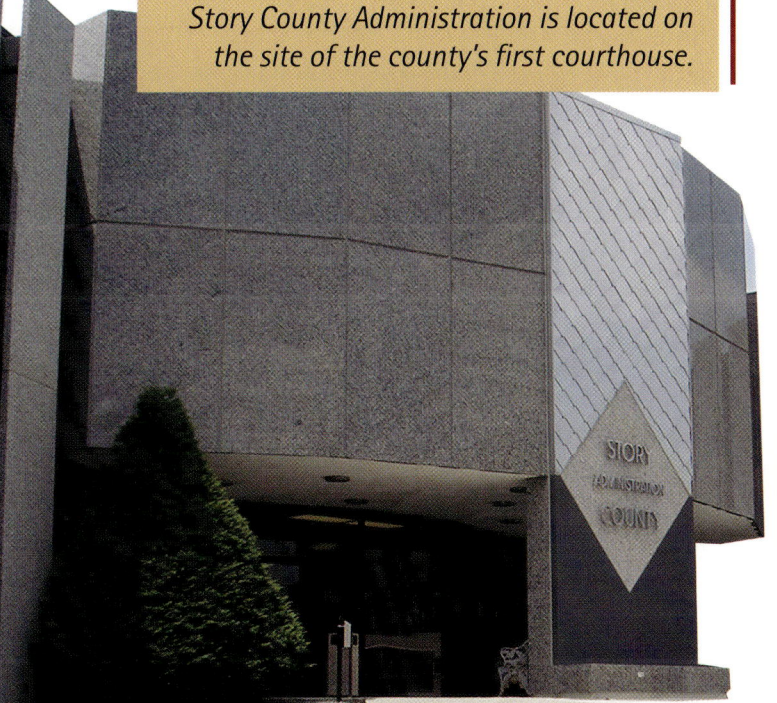

Story County Administration is located on the site of the county's first courthouse.

NEVADA HIGH SCHOOL

Nevada IOWA

were constructed from native timber as areas of Story County were developed. Nevada Township had the highest number of frame-structure schools in the county. The 1874 Halley School, which was used through the 1944-45 school year, still remains an honored building in Nevada. In November of 1858, the county's first brick school building was constructed at the present corner of Fifth Street and I Avenue. It was a two-story building, and was built at that location as it was near the only bridge that spanned the slough.

By 1870, the Nevada school district was in need of a larger school and a high school. A brick building, Central School, was constructed at the corner of Ninth Street and J Avenue. At a cost of $16,000, it was one of the leading schools in the state. In 1884, a new section with a bell tower was added to the south side of the facility. By 1900, Nevada had three schools with the construction of North School at Fifth Street and R Avenue and West School at Third Street and K Avenue. North served Danes who had settled in this part of town, and young students living west of Sixth Street attended West. North and West schools were torn down in 1971 and 1966, respectively. The first school, however, is now Central Elementary and remains a bustling hub of activity for younger students. The bell from the school's original bell tower is a well-known fixture on the elementary grounds.

Shipley School in Grant Township, Fernald School in Richland Township and Milford School in Milford Township were constructed in the early 1900s. The district used the Shipley and Fernald buildings until the 1960s and continued to use Milford as a middle school until the decision was made in 1989 to construct a new middle school in Nevada. Nevada High School and Nevada Middle School, along with athletic facilities, are located on 15th Street. Quality education remains a top issue with Nevada residents.

SCHOOLS

The Chicago Northwestern depot in 1900.

Like giant guardians overlooking the schools on 15th Street, two wind turbines quietly generate energy. Harold and Marjorie Fawcett and Harold's sister, Josephine Tope, donated generously to purchase three turbines, two for the school and one for the hospital. The Nevada school district was first in the state to have two wind generators. The first turbine, a 250-kilowatt machine, was erected in 1993 and the second in 1994. The school's windmills generate about one-quarter of the electricity used by the Middle

A wind turbine at the athletic fields rises high above Cub Country.

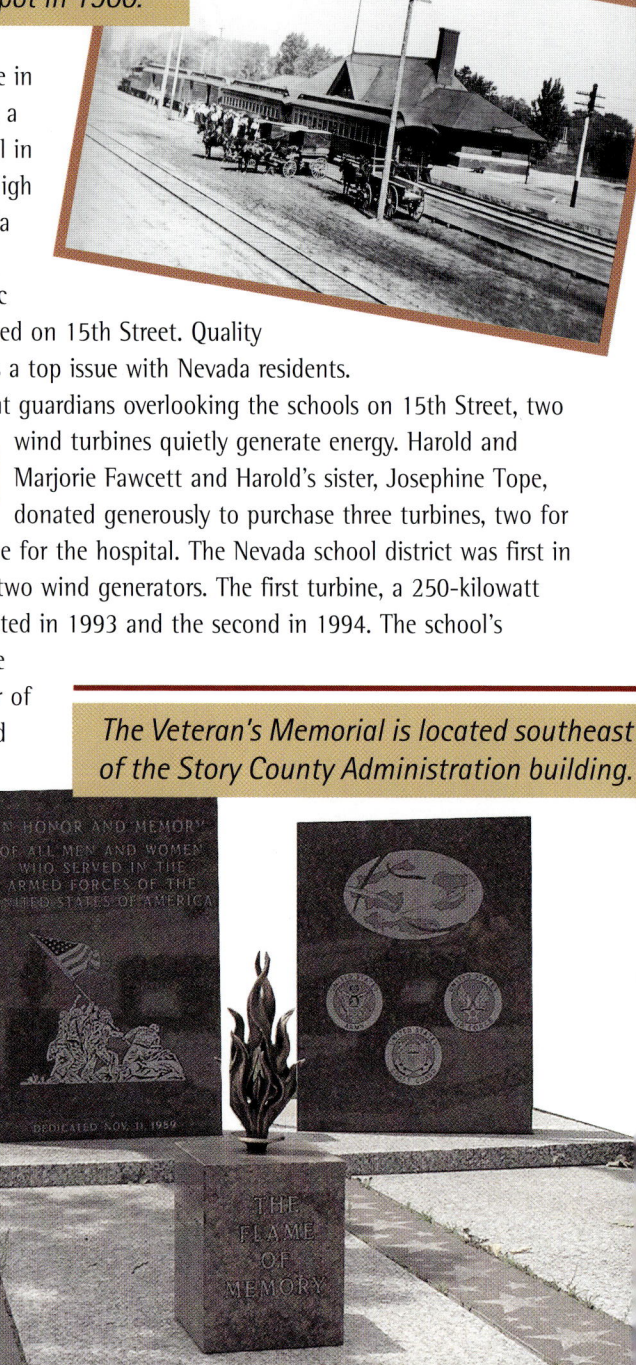

The Veteran's Memorial is located southeast of the Story County Administration building.

The home of the Cubs, Nevada's high school colors are purple and gold.

School and the High school, saving Nevada schools about $72 a day. The third windmill was installed in 1995 next to the water treatment center. Story County Medical Center sells the electricity to the city of Nevada, which uses it to power the sewage treatment plant. The plant runs almost exclusively on the turbine's electricity. The turbines are 132 feet tall and weigh about 40,000 pounds. Each rotor weighs 9,250 pounds and each blade is approximately one ton. Three blades attach to each rotor and have a blade span of less than 83 feet.

Nevada is home to many businesses, both large and small. The area continues to be strong agriculturally including Hertz Farm Management, which oversees 1,700 operations in several states. Burke Marketing is one of the nation's leading manufacturers of pizza meat toppings. Almaco produces farm equipment that is used around the world.

The town has three grocery stores, Fareway, Smitty's and Cook's, as well as many convenience stores. Nevada also offers a variety of restaurants including national chains and hometown favorites. Construction trade businesses continue to thrive in the area along with self-employed contractors. Other businesses, from car dealerships to daycare providers, also make a good living in this community.

Nevada's downtown historic district was approved for listing in the National Register of Historic Places in 2003. The approval places a three-block section of

Story County Courthouse at 1315 South B Avenue.

NEVADA'S SCORE PARK

Nevada

Learn More

Nevada is located in central Iowa, 6 miles east of the intersection of I-35 and Hwy. 30.

For more information, please call the Chamber of Commerce at (515) 382-6538 or the Nevada Economic Development Council at (515) 382-1430 or visit Web sites at:
www.ci.nevada.ia.us
www.nevadaiowa.org
www.nevadaiowajournal.com

Story Contributor

Ronna Lawless is a freelance writer living in Ames.

the central business district on the register and qualifies a majority of the 39 buildings within it for rehabilitation tax incentives.

The Camelot Theatre reopened in 2002 after closing in 2001, an occurrence that was devastating to many residents and left a gap in the downtown atmosphere.

Nevada residents have historically enjoyed community celebrations. In 1855, nearly all the residents of the county gathered in a grove of the southwest cemetery for a Fourth of July celebration. A grand Independence Day celebration every year remains a huge part of Nevada's personality. Another big celebration, Lincoln Highway Days, is held each August. This celebration honors the transcontinental highway that starts in New York, cuts right through Nevada and ends in San Francisco. With the Story County 4-H Fairgrounds within its city limits, the annual 4-H fair is also a large attraction for people in the county.

The Nevada Journal was founded in 1895 and continues to publish a weekly newspaper, which comes out on Thursday, and the "Story Today" is released on Wednesday. The Nevada Journal provides in-depth coverage of local issues and sports and is the official newspaper for the city of Nevada. The Journal offers some of its articles at its Web site, www.nevadaiowajournal.com.

Many of the things that make Nevada special today are what most people would think of as quintessentially American for a small community. The residents of Nevada are proud of their pioneer forefathers, proud of the people who helped make the community strong today. Nevadans are especially proud to have a family-oriented community with exceptional schools, businesses, churches and parks to pass on to the next generation. **Nevada is a small community with big sense of pride and works hard to be one of the best small towns in America.**

Nevada's connection to the Lincoln Highway is apparent in many places in the community.

Pride In Our Hometowns.

P·O·R·T·R·A·I·T·S
OF
Orange City

DISCOVER THE DUTCH!

*They're a distinctive folk, the Dutch.
Industrious, clean, thrifty. Orderly. Opinionated. Stubborn.
And the Dutch who settled Orange City came with a deep faith
in God... a persistent faith.
All of that translates to a community that's quaint, tidy, and
progressive, with a few idiosyncrasies.*

And it's really quite lovely.

*Orange City also has a good measure of hospitality. The
invitation is open to all—to discover the Dutch.*

ORANGE CITY

Pride In Our Hometowns.

P·O·R·T·R·A·I·T·S
OF *Orange City*

DISCOVER THE DUTCH!

Visit Orange City in May and you'll [see] hundreds of tulips and lots of cute kids

A Snapshot

When the first Dutch folk settled Orange City in 1870, they were amazed at the beauty of the prairie and the richness of the soil. They had come from the Netherlands, when that land was rife with poverty, food shortage and religious conflicts. Once in America, many headed for southeast Iowa, but when land prices skyrocketed to $30 to $60 per acre in Pella, they set up a committee to investigate land farther north and west.

A spot near Cherokee was chosen, but by the time the Dutchmen returned to claim their land in '69, speculators had snatched it, hoping to make a tidy profit. Those Hollanders would not be cheated, however. They headed on, with maps, compasses and surveying equipment, and staked out a couple of townships... and a hill-top site for what is now Orange City.

It was spring, 1870, when several wagon trains left Pella for the 19-day, 250-mile journey... to what would become their new Holland.

Why Orange?

The town is named after William the Silent, the Prince of the House of Orange-Nassau. He and his son Maurice had led the Dutch in their long war for independence in the 16th century,

Welcome to 'the back garden,' a little Dutch courtyard. Welcome to Orange City!

166

Orange City IOWA

against the powerful Spanish.

Henry Hospers gets the credit for the town's name. According to local historian Nelson Nieuwenhuis, Hospers was a man of "quiet demeanor and winning speech." He was kind and sympathetic, a person who put his caring for others into action. He was, according to Nieuwenhuis, "a born leader, and without doubt, the greatest man in the early years of Sioux County."

Hospers came to the U.S. as a 17-year-old, sent ahead of the rest of his family. And he became a prominent citizen of Pella.

But Hospers wanted to join the adventurers in northwest Iowa.

In Orange City, he sold real estate and published a paper, **De Volksvriend**, or **Friend of the People**. He opened a bank… and when, one Sunday morning, church-goers heard an unfamiliar whirring, pattering sound, and those grasshoppers demolished the crops… Hospers obtained state aid and made personal loans to farmers. Crops were destroyed for several years in the 1870s, and a few families returned to their motherland.

Henry Hospers

But Hospers visited the Netherlands in those early years, speaking to hundreds about the benefits of immigrating to Iowa.

He served on the county board of supervisors for 15 years, and later in the state House and Senate.

He was devout, and certain of God's watchful eye… as most Orange City Dutchmen were.

"Imagine yourselves a little over 12 years ago, standing on this place," he spoke at a school dedication in 1882. "Wheresoever your eye wandered, only the clear

> It's a good guess that 99 percent of Orange Citians love sports, especially when the Knights, Dutch or Red Raiders are on the field. And local athletes excel. Northwestern College men's and women's basketball teams both won the NAIA Div. II national championship on the same night in March '01. NW was only the second college or university at any level to have the men's and women's teams win national titles in the same year.

The windmill visitor's center is the Chamber of Commerce office in Orange City… 76 feet tall with dome and blades that weigh 14 tons.

Orange City

skies and the prairie, bounded alone by the horizon... This was the place for centuries destined for our homes by the Creator of the universe."

A judge who knew Hospers well called him "one of God's noblemen."

THE HUMONGOUS SAFE

Dutchmen are stubborn, and proved it in 1872... when the huge county safe was forcibly moved to Orange City.

Orange City was not Sioux County's first settlement. The county, of course, was named for the Sioux tribe... and acquired through a treaty in 1830.

Early in 1860, adventurers founded Calliope, along the Big Sioux River south of present-day Hawarden, at the western edge of the county. By June, Calliope, population 10, became the county seat.

Corruption was the order of the day, however. In 1871, William Runyan spoke for a group of dissenters: "All northwest Iowa has been the general headquarters of a reckless, unprincipled banditti of sharks and swindlers that would disgrace the inmates of a penitentiary."

Some Dutchmen, and others, decided to take charge. On Jan. 22, 1872, at 2 a.m., they set off on 20 sleighs.

"I was in Calliope when the crowd came... and moved the county seat," said a witness, quoted by historian Nieuwenhuis. "They took an ax and chopped the back end of the courthouse out where the safe stood, and rolled it out to a bobsled and hauled it to Orange City."

Ten days later, the sheriff and several deputies came, with a court order, and returned the safe to Calliope.

Later that year, though, county citizens voted 121-45 to move the county seat to Orange City... and since there was no courthouse, the safe was temporarily stored in a rented shed.

The safe rested peacefully for 100 years until one night in 1975, when a group of men from Calliope-Hawarden secretly stole into Orange City and located the historic safe, unused at that point and stored in a shed at the county farm. After much huffing and puffing, they got it onto a truck and transferred it to Hawarden... the place where it "rightfully" belonged.

The safe is now on display in Calliope Village in northwest

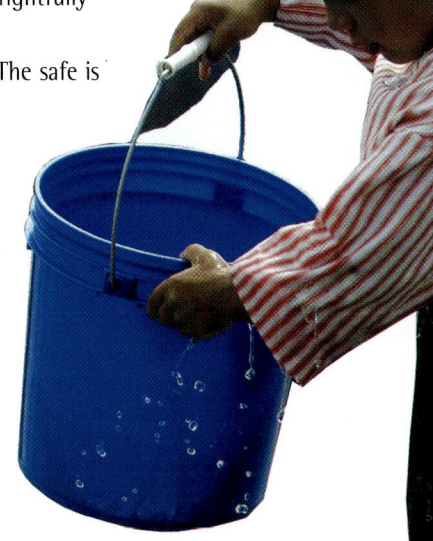

The Dutch word for clean and be are the same: schoonheid. But w was cleaning so much fun?

Horse-drawn street car at Tulip Festival.

Orange City IOWA

Hawarden.

But the county seat is still Orange City,

In 1977, the Sioux County Courthouse was listed in the National Register of Historic Places.

where the 100-year-old Sioux County Courthouse stands in grandeur. It's one of the finest examples of Richardsonian Romanesque architecture in Iowa, made of red Minnesota sandstone, with white sandstone trim and tile roof, and topped with the majestic Lady Justice. Sioux County employees number 140.

SCHOOLS AND CHURCHES

The first Orange City buildings were the home of A.J. Lenderink, a carpenter... whose house was east of the present Windmill Park, and a schoolhouse, erected in that village center.

Soon afterwards came First Reformed Church and First Christian Reformed Church. Both the Reformed Church in America and the Christian Reformed Church are sister churches to those in the Netherlands.

Of course, occasional feuds have stirred up the locals. After several years in America, many insisted on continuing to worship in the Dutch language. Those who wanted services in English began their own congregations.

What's permissible on the Sabbath has also been a subject of debate.

Later, disagreements on baptism and the role of women in church led to more new congregations.

Now Orange City boasts 11 churches plus MOC-Floyd Valley Public School, Unity Christian High, Orange City Christian School–now 100 years old–and Northwestern College... all vitality important in the community.

Northwestern College began as a classical academy in 1882, classes meeting in a church and public school. But Henry Hospers had donated some land on the south end of town, and a majestic hall, in the Romanesque Revival style, was erected. Zwemer Hall is now listed on the National Register of Historic Places.

Northwestern, affiliated with the Reformed Church in America, grew into a junior college, then a four-year college in '61. The liberal arts college has grown by 35 percent in the last 15 years, with its 1,285 students coming from 29 states and 13 countries... and from 25 denominations. Over

Northwestern's Zwemer Hall, built in 1894 for $16,000, was restored in 1997. In the early years, it was a favorite site for college student pranks. One Halloween, a group of students disassembled a large piece of farm equipment, then reassembled it on top of the main Zwemer roof.

Orange City, Iowa

half of its facilities have been newly constructed or significantly renovated in the last 15 years.

Committed to integrating the Christian faith into all aspects of college life, Northwestern offers 35 majors leading to the Bachelor of Arts degree, and off-campus programs in the U.S. and 15 countries.

Northwestern has consistently been named as a top-tier Midwestern comprehensive college by U.S. News and World Report, and as one of the nation's best college buys, according to an independent research firm.

VOGEL AND HIS PAINT

Orange City has its share of legendary characters, like Henry Hospers. One is Andrew Vogel.

Vogel was born 66 years after Hospers, in the Netherlands, and immigrated with his parents and nine brothers in 1913. Of course he mixed his own paint, as everyone did in those days... but when others saw the quality of Vogel's paint and asked to purchase it, the ball started rolling.

What began in his home and barn - Orange Brand Paint - is now Diamond Vogel Paints, with eight manufacturing plants, more than 80 retail centers and 900 employees.

Vogel, whose 103 years spanned three centuries, was a character from day one. Grandchildren tell of him, at almost 70, diving off the high board into the lake... always with his glasses on, occasionally summoning the family for a lost spectacles search. They tell of him pulling out stumps with his new Cadillac; of painting the roof of his metallic gold Olds red, so people could see him coming; of traveling to the vacation cabin with grandkids sitting on five-gallon cans of paint, paint destined for customers in northern Minnesota.

When the old Vogel plant burned in '64, and staff were trucking remains to the dump and salvage yard, Vogel was busy painting a sign: "We've moved... to the city dump."

He never minced words. He never pretended to be anyone other than himself. He was compassionate. He is remembered by nearly everyone who met him.

He left the business with family members in leadership positions. One of his sons, Frank, took over the company, and now Frank's son, Drew, is president. And the company recently underwent an $8 million renovation project.

Andrew Vogel, always busy, built "The Old Mill" during his

Northwestern College's Christ Chapel features a Dutch 57-rank organ. Another Dutch organ is located at American Reformed Church.

Below: Art Vogel demonstrates the carving of wooden shoes. Right: Andrew Vogel.

Orange City IOWA

retirement years, a working windmill with a 120-year-old mill stone from the Netherlands. It includes small living quarters, furnished with antiques from Holland.

Vogel, true to himself at age 99, was checking a windmill problem before Tulip Festival a few years ago, according to his daughter Margaret: "He was crawling on the roof, hanging half-way to heaven on the blades..." It's not hard to picture.

Vogel's original paint factory is now The Old Factory, a local shop where, for special occasions, Vogel's son Art demonstrates the carving of wooden shoes.

HOMEGROWN

Vogel Paints is not the only homegrown business in town.

- Paul Korver founded MED-TEC, a company that designs, manufactures and distributes radiation oncology equipment, for precise cancer diagnosis and treatment. Three thousand hospitals in 85 countries purchase oncology equipment from MED-TEC.

Korver, who began MED-TEC in Dallas, Texas, moved the company back to his hometown in 1988... and his son Clayton also moved to Orange City to serve 10 years as CEO. The company has since grown from five to 110 employees. Today David Van Gorp is chief executive officer.

New recreation areas in town include Landsmeer Golf Club, Kinderspeelland children's playland, the aquatic center, a seven-screen movie theatre, and Northwestern's theatre and art centers and athletic complex. The public library was expanded in 2003.

Orange City IOWA

MED-TEC's vision is to think globally and act locally, so the company offers employees paid time off for charitable and community work.

• Tom Kohout founded K-Products in northwest Iowa in 1947, and moved the company to Orange City in '67, where it became a leading manufacturer of logoed merchandise. As the result of several mergers, the company is now American Identity, and in 2002 was named the leading promotional merchandise company in the U.S. It remains at the top, based on volume of sales.

The company serves more than 350 corporations of the Fortune 1000, plus hundreds of small hometown businesses.

American Identity facilities are located across the country, with the Orange City office and manufacturing plant employing 400.

• The Orange City Health System, employs 479, including eight family practice physicians, five surgeons and a radiologist. Groundbreaking for its new $30 million facility was June '04.

• Other large employers are Russell's Ready Mix, operating 13 ready mix plants in northwest Iowa; Advance Brands, which processes and distributes frozen meats, and recently underwent a $16 million upgrade; and Revival Animal Health, producing animal care products and vet supplies.

Northwestern presented "And God Said" in its new DeWitt Theatre Arts Center in spring, '04. The college touring theatre team has performed Off-Broadway and at St. Paul's Cathedral in New York City.

• Unique local shops sell antiques, Dutch imports, wooden shoes, delft, Dutch lace, and international gifts. Woudstra's Meat Market has been on main street since 1928, and specializes in home-cured dried beef, Dutch ring bologna and Old World sausages. Pluim Publishing has been owned locally for years too, publishing the **Ad-Visor** and **Sioux County Capital-Democrat**.

The city, local business owners, the Dutch Heritage Boosters and other groups have worked to give Orange City a flavor of The Old Country year-round. Many local shops feature architecture reminiscent of 19th century Holland.

Orange City IOWA

One of the early Tulip Festival floats, the Flying Dutchman, is based on the 1600s legend of the ship doomed to sail around the Cape of Good Hope forever. Far right: Girls handle the brooms during the Festival street scrubbing.

- Twenty new commerical and industrial structures were built in Orange City in the four years from 2000 to 2003, and 22 renovations completed. Nine construction projects happened in churches and schools, and four other facilities were built just outside of city limits... including the new Sioux County Public Safety Center. Over $52 million were spent on those projects.

Eighty new residences and 241 residential renovations were done in those same four years... totaling $13 million. Three new housing developments are in the works at present.

The industrial park is being developed also, providing 80 new acres for light and heavy industry. Recent improvements have been made to all utilities in town. It's an industrious place.

AND THERE ARE TULIPS

Tulips were 'discovered' in Turkey in the 1500s, by an Austrian ambassador, and a Dutch botanist brought bulbs to the Netherlands. They were prized... so much so that during tulip mania in 1636-37, one precious bulb sold for as much as $10,000. Now Hollanders grow fields of tulips.

So why wouldn't the Dutch in Orange City want to grow tulips in their new home? These days there are thousands of tulips blooming in town each May, and Don and Mary Lou Vander Wel have created a garden with umpteen varieties of tulips... in their backyard, and open to the public.

In 1936, some Dutch folks planned the first Tulip Festival, in honor of their heritage. And it's grown to a major tourist attraction in the state.

Hundreds of community members, maybe thousands, spend many volunteer hours on bringing a bit of 19th-century Netherlands to Orange City. It begins the third Thursday in May each year and goes for three days, and includes everything from

Orange City

Orange City is located in northwest Iowa on Hwy. 10... 40 minutes NE of Sioux City, IA and 70 minutes SE of Sioux Falls, SD.

authentic Dutch costumes to folk dancers. Bicycles are big in the Netherlands, and Orange City has bicycle singers. The Dutch, always practical and economical, made their own wooden shoes... a necessity for keeping feet dry in a country largely below sea level. So Orange City demonstrates the crafting of those shoes.

Other highlights of the Festival include street scrubbing; colorful parades featuring the award-winning Pride of the Dutchmen band, which marches in wooden shoes; Sioux County Heritage Center; Dutch puppet show; flower show; Dutch folk arts; the Century Home; horse-drawn street car tours; quilt show; Vogel Windmill tours; Dutch song and dance show; road race; fly-in breakfast; ArtBurst; Dutch street organ; amusement rides; an open-air market; and food, both Dutch and non-Dutch – poffertjes (little Dutch pancakes), almond patties, pigs in the blanket, bratwurst, dried beef, pea soup, funnel cakes, Dutch puppies. The Festival ends with a community worship service in the park on Sunday morning.

A highlight for the locals is that Tulip Festival not only brings new people to town, but it's also an all-town reunion. Hundreds of former Orange Citians return for the Festival each year, just to see old friends.

Tourists come to Orange City at other times of the year also. Sinterklaas Day and the Christmas Tour of Homes is the first Saturday in December. And, year-round, visitors come to experience a flavor of the Old Country. Dutch architecture, a Dutch pump in the center of town, a courtyard behind The Little White Store, a tree-lined downtown... all are reminiscent of 19th-century Holland. A collection of windmills, recently donated to the town, is being erected at Korver Pond.

Guided tours and Dutch food are also highlights for visitors.

DIVERSIFYING

Orange City's Dutch roots still dominate, but the town of 5,500 is diversifying. At the 2004 Tulip Festival, one could see not only Dutch dress, but a few kilts, saris and kimonos. One could hear not only English and Dutch languages... but also Spanish.

Even the chair of the 2004 Festival has no Dutch blood. But Bill Kepp, who has lived in Orange City or nearby all of his life, feels like he's an adopted Dutchman, he said.

He, along with mayor Daryl Beltman, invite you to visit Orange City, to discover its beauty and hospitality... to discover the Dutch.

LEARN MORE

Mayor Daryl Beltman invites you to ca Orange City Chamber of Commerce for information, at 712-707-45 e-mail octulip@frontiernet.r tulip@orangecitycomr Or check our web www.orangecityiowa www.octulipfestival

STORY CONTRIBUTOR

Janine M. Calsbeek, author portrait of Orange City, wr the Sioux County Ca Democrat. A special than to local photographe historians, especially G. Nieuwenhuis, au Siouxland, A History of County, Iowa and Hospers Cent

Tulip Festival features bright costumes, brilliant flowers and lots of smiles.

Pride In Our Hometowns.

P·O·R·T·R·A·I·T·S
OF
Oskaloosa

PRIDE, PROGRESS AND TRADITION

Oskaloosa, county seat of Mahaska County, has a population of around 11,000, but draws visitors from afar with its historic sites, recreation facilities, innovative industries and history and continuing tradition of music.

The entire downtown square and surrounding buildings are on the National Register of Historic Places. With help from Main Street Iowa and other grants, renovations are improving building facades and utilizing second- and third-floor space downtown for apartments or other businesses.

Pride In Our Hometowns.

P·O·R·T·R·A·I·T·S
OF *Oskaloosa*

PRIDE, PROGRESS AND TRADITION

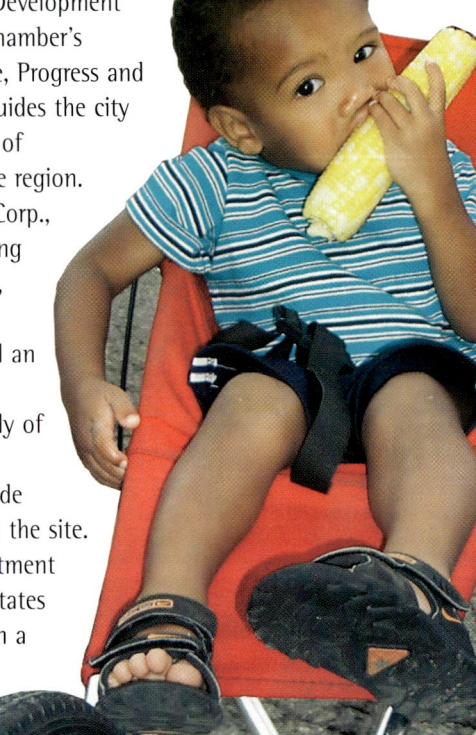

A young man forgets his table manners as he tries to sink his teeth into an ear of sweet corn at Sweet Corn Serenade, held each August. Volunteers roast and serve some 5,000 ears of corn; the event also includes a corn-husking contest, musical entertainment, vendors, corporate games and activities for the kids.

A Snapshot

An unprecedented three-way agreement between Mahaska County, the city of Oskaloosa and the Oskaloosa School District provides sales tax revenue building a new K-5 elementary building and an expanded, renovated high school in Oskaloosa, a $26 million project. Oskaloosa combines rich history with a state-of-the-art community auditorium and public library, and fiber-optic cable for high-speed Internet access, phone and cable TV service. The town views itself as part of Mahaska County, from the Mahaska Community Recreation Foundation to the Oskaloosa Area Chamber & Development Group to the Mahaska County Ag & Rural Development office. The chamber's motto, "Pride, Progress and Tradition," guides the city and its spirit of cooperation to grow the entire region. Oskaloosa is home to Musco Corp., which provides portable lighting worldwide for sporting events, films and many other events. Musco has won an Emmy and an Oscar for its film and sports lighting. Just after the tragedy of Sept. 11, 2001, Musco lighted Ground Zero at the World Trade Center while workers searched the site. The New York City Fire Department gave Musco the first United States flag that flew over the site (on a

This flag, the first flown over the site of Ground Zero after the collapse of the World Trade Center on Sept. 11, 2001, was donated by the New York City Fire Department to Musco Lighting because of Musco's help in lighting the WTC site for search and cleanup efforts. Here it is on display in July 2003 for riders in RAGBRAI (The Register's Annual Great Bike Ride Across Iowa), who made an overnight stop in Oskaloosa.

Oskaloosa

Webster Elementary students did research, wrote the text and made computer drawings for a "Kids' Eye View" of Oskaloosa, showing their favorite sites and explaining their history.

Musco Lighting truck) in appreciation for the company's service.

A subsidiary of Musco, Mahaska Communications Group, has laid underground fiber-optic cable throughout the city and provides high-speed Internet access, phone and cable TV service, putting the world at Oskaloosa's fingertips.

Another longtime Oskaloosa industry, Clow Valve, makes valves and fire hydrants that can be seen all over the United States. Nearby Cargill continues to develop Iowa's corn as sweeteners and other food additives and products. Oskaloosa Food Products does the same for eggs, providing its powdered egg additives for products all over the world. Nearby SoyLink processes soybeans as high-protein food additives, tofu and as processed beans for consumption worldwide.

Local businessman Bob Wersen, president of Panel Components, another of Oskaloosa's major industries, is joining the growing number of grape producers in Iowa. He is building a winery which could begin making wine by fall 2004. He envisions the winery as a tourism attraction for city dwellers looking for a country getaway weekend.

The current Oskaloosa Junior High will become a middle school for grades 6-8 in fall 2004, while the high school adds the ninth grade. The new elementary for grades K-5 will open in January 2005. The town also has a Christian school for grades K-8.

Oskaloosa boasts two colleges. William Penn University was founded by Quakers in the late 1800s; it is now a university with campuses in several locations and a separate college for working adults. Vennard College in nearby University Park has a tradition of educating young men and women for Christian service since the early 1900s. The first "church" in Oskaloosa may have been formed by Methodists, who opened an informal church in the cabin of Isaac Harrell on Six Mile Prairie in fall 1843. Other early settlers were Quakers, Congregationalists and Presbyterians. Today well over 40 churches of many denominations hold worship services and other activities in Oskaloosa.

Native American history

The area's first residents were the Ioway

The new entrance to Oskaloosa High School is on the north side, in an addition built on as part of a $26 million project to expand and renovate the high school and build the new K-5 elementary school. The addition houses the school media center and more classrooms for ninth-grade students, who will start attending four-year high school in fall 2004.

The bronze Chief Mahaska statue as it appears today, after renovation by the Russell-Marti firm with an SOS Conservation Treatment Award, community fund-raising and a George Daily Trust grant. Russell-Marti will continue to maintain the statue and teach local people to carry on the work.

Oskaloosa, Iowa

Indians. The county is named after Chief Mahaska I (White Cloud). In summer 1824, Mahaska and a group of Ioway, Sauk and Fox chiefs were escorted to Washington, D.C., for a council on land treaties. The tribes ceded land in northern Missouri and southeastern Iowa to the United States. After returning from Washington, Mahaska built a log home and took up farming.

In 1833, an Ioway chief was killed by the Omahas. The Ioways looked to Mahaska to lead them in battle against the Omahas, but Mahaska refused, remembering his pledge of peace. The Ioways attacked the Omahas anyway, killing six.

The U.S. government ordered the guilty Ioways arrested, and Mahaska agreed to help capture them. Later, one escaped and, joined by others, killed Mahaska. In 1836, the Ioway Indians took the trail to Kansas and the Great Nemaha Reservation. A bronze statue of Chief Mahaska I commemorates his attempts to keep peace between the Ioways and the United States. The statue, on the west side of the Oskaloosa square, is over seven feet tall.

Chief Mahaska

James Depew Edmundson commissioned the statue in memory of his father, William Edmundson, first sheriff of Mahaska County. Iowa sculptor Sherry Fry made the statue; it was dedicated on May 12, 1909. Ninety years later, the Oskaloosa Historic Preservation Commission began a campaign to restore the badly-corroded bronze statue. A report by Save Outdoor Sculpture! said the statue's corrosion was caused largely by heavy use of coal in Oskaloosa during its early years.

The Chief Mahaska statue was the only Iowa monument to receive an SOS Conservation Treatment Award to help with the $42,000 cost of restoring and maintaining the statue. The commission also raised money from community businesses, organizations and individuals, as well as the George Daily Family Trust.

The statue was rededicated on Oct. 16, 1999. Chief Mahaska's great-great-great-great-grandson, James Rhodd, spoke at the ceremony and thanked the city for its preservation efforts. Drummers from the White Cloud Reservation in

A 19th-century steam engine chugs back into the barn at the 2003 Nelson Pioneer Farm Fall Festival in September.

Oskaloosa elementary students and Superintendent Carolyn McGaughey, far right, break ground for the school district's new K-5th grade elementary building, scheduled to open in January 2005.

Oskaloosa

Kansas also performed at the rededication. The site for the city of Oskaloosa, named after the Creek Indian princess Ouscaloosa ("Last of the Beautiful"), was staked by the First U.S. Dragoons, led by Lt. Col. Stephen Watts Kearney, with second-in-command Nathan Boone, son of Daniel Boone. The Dragoons stopped at the future site of Oskaloosa on June 11, 1835, on a high ridge between the Des Moines and Chiquaqua (Skunk) rivers known as "The Narrows."

The site was chosen for a small fort, and when the territory was opened for settlers in 1843, the fort was a post between the Mississippi and points west. Today's city bandstand sits on this exact site.

Oskaloosa was established in 1844; then it was a pioneer village with 13 cabins and two stores. Oskaloosa was chosen as county seat for Mahaska County in May 1844. By 1853, when the town was incorporated, Oskaloosa boasted 1,000 residents.

Railroads were important to Oskaloosa's history, and especially to the coal industry. The first railroad was built in 1864, and ran from Keokuk to Eddyville. Eventually it became part of the Chicago, Rock Island and Pacific Railroad in 1878. The Rock Island Depot still stands in Oskaloosa; the building has been restored and renovated as a bar and grill.

Bandstand, town square

The centerpiece of Oskaloosa's square is the bandstand, which has hosted concerts by the city band and many of the world's great band conductors and composers for over 125 years. The first wooden bandstand was built in 1876, and replaced in 1882. In 1912 the current concrete, iron and copper bandstand was built. A replica of the original Oskaloosa bandstand was placed in President John F. Kennedy's Inaugural Parade by the Musicians' Union of Washington, D.C. The entire square and bandstand were lovingly restored in 1991; well-known artist P. Buckley Moss painted the bandstand to help raise money for the project, which included new landscaping, sidewalks and lights for the entire square.

The square is the heart of the city; the county courthouse, law

Famed Iowa artist P. Buckley Moss painted a limited-edition print of the Oskaloosa bandstand as part of a campaign to raise money to restore the bandstand and the Oskaloosa square.

Children tumble toward the finish line in an old-fashioned sack race at Nelson Pioneer Farm's Fall Festival, held each September.

The old Rock Island Depot, formerly one of two major railroad depots in Oskaloosa, has been renovated into a bar and grill, complete with caboose.

Oskaloosa

enforcement center, public library and city hall are nearby, as well as downtown shopping and restaurants, including Penn Central Mall. In addition to successful businesses such as J.C. Penney and McGregor Furniture, the mall hosts craft shows, baseball card shows, an annual used book sale and other events. It is a handy facility when inclement weather drives downtown events indoors. The square hosts events year-round, including Art on the Square in June, Sweet Corn Serenade in August, weekly Oskaloosa City Band concerts in summer, the Mahaska Ruritan Farmers' Market from late spring through fall, an annual Halloween parade for kids, high school and college Homecoming parades, and the Lighted Christmas Parade in early December.

The Lighted Christmas Parade was begun in the late 1980s as a fun way to promote holiday shopping downtown.

By 1994 the parade had over 100 entries, and was expanded from one to two nights. Main Street Iowa has voted Oskaloosa's Lighted Christmas Parade Iowa's No. 1 Holiday Event.

Thousands of people come to Oskaloosa during parade weekend. Other activities include church suppers and street food vendors, living window displays, entertainment in the bandstand, a concert at George Daily Auditorium, and the Festival of Christmas Delights at Oskaloosa Christian School.

Mahaska County Courthouse, on the east side of the square, was built in 1886, and rebuilt in 1917. It was remodeled in 1934, and again in 1988-91. A bell tower with a 2,000-pound bell was removed during one of the renovations.

Daily Trust

George Daily was a brilliant, eccentric and reclusive Oskaloosa native whose generosity continues to help Oskaloosa grow. Most people knew him only as a shabbily-dressed man living

Oskaloosa's many churches emphasize the religious meaning of Christmas in their entries in the annual Lighted Christmas Parade. Here a chorus of angels sings to the crowd lining the streets.

Oskaloosa Public Library's renovation and expansion was completed in 1997. The original building is on the right; the new main entrance is the beginning of the addition, which continues on its other side. OPN Architects have earned many architectural and historic preservation awards for their design.

Oskaloosa's square was packed as Marvin Leese, a local minister, spoke from the Oskaloosa bandstand near dusk at a 9/11 memorial observance in September 2002.

180

Oskaloosa, Iowa

The Knights Templar Band of Oskaloosa. This appears to be the model for the P. Buckley Moss print of the bandstand; 100 special-edition prints were sold to raise money to renovate the bandstand and the square in 1991. (Photo courtesy of Patricia Patterson)

in a tumbledown house, often seen playing checkers in the park - until he died and left the City of Oskaloosa $6 million. The money was put into a trust, with grants for community projects made from the trust's interest income. The Daily Trust has contributed to many projects involving education, recreation, restoration of cultural and historic treasures and human service organizations. The trust's philosophy is to provide "a seed for growth," to help projects with seed money. Local composer Iola Cadwallader spent months researching Daily's life, then months more writing a musical to honor his memory as well as the fifth anniversary of George Daily Auditorium, completed in 1997.

The auditorium at 1800 N. 3rd St., cost some $4 million and opened in August 1997. The George Daily Family Trust, Oskaloosa School District, and local private donors provided funding for the 700-seat auditorium, which includes an orchestra pit and state-of-the-art lighting and sound systems.

Manager Randy Wright, who teaches drama at next-door Oskaloosa High School, uses the auditorium as a training ground for high school students interested in learning the technical aspects of theater. In 2003, a full-time children's theater coordinator was hired to operate a summer theater camp for kids, and after-school children's theater workshops and classes all year.

The auditorium hosts school Christmas programs, spectacular magic shows and national touring musicals such as "Fame" and "Grease." It has hosted the Aquila Theatre Company from London, England, with their production of "King Lear," as well as popular performers from Branson, Mo. The auditorium board tries to program acts to appeal to a wide variety of tastes, and corporate sponsors often chip in to keep ticket prices affordable.

The auditorium also hosts the Oskaloosa Symphony Orchestra, formed shortly after the auditorium opened, under the direction of Tony Y. Chang. The orchestra, which

Tents covered the gently-rolling hills of Edmundson Park, as well as other camp sites, in July 2003 when RAGBRAI made a stopover in Oskaloosa. Here riders relax after pitching their tents. Vendors and hauling trucks are parked down the hill.

The north side of the Oskaloosa square includes these restored building facades in "the Centennial Block." The entire square is listed on the National Register of Historic Places.

Oskaloosa

includes local and regional musicians, performs three to four concerts a year, including multi-media performances with film and lights, holiday concerts with high school musicians and singers, and accompanying international touring and recording soloists.

Another of Oskaloosa's musical traditions goes back to C.L. Barnhouse, founder of Barnhouse Music Publishing Co. in 1886 and a former director of the city band. Under Barnhouse's direction, the band was known nationwide and played for the Iowa State Fair and the St. Louis World's Fair.

Barnhouse Music Publishing began by publishing band marches and circus music.

Today, Barnhouse is known worldwide for its band music for all levels of school bands, marching, concert and jazz bands. Another famous Oskaloosan, Frederick Knight Logan, wrote well-known songs such as "The Missouri Waltz."

But it is his mother, Virginia Knight Logan, who left a bigger mark on her community. She helped found the Oskaloosa Women's Club, which established Oskaloosa's first lending library. It began as a reading room, and evolved into a complete library with funds from industrialist and philanthropist Andrew Carnegie. Designed by Oskaloosa's Frank Wetherell, the building was completed in 1903. In the mid-1990s, the library was fast out-growing its space and technological constraints. The Cents for the Library Committee formed and convinced Oskaloosa voters to approve a local-option sales tax to renovate and expand the current library, as well as build a new law enforcement center to replace the old jail. OPN Architects was hired to design the library extension and renovation. The result is a seamless transition between old and new buildings, preservation of the library's traditional charm with modern climate control, wiring and cabling, computer labs, a music listening center, a children's program room and handicap access with an elevator to all levels. The library has won many

> *Oskaloosa's state-of-the-art George Daily Community Auditorium hosts everything from school holiday programs to summer theater camp to national and international performers. At the auditorium entrance is a sculpture of Daily as many Oskaloosans remember him - sitting on a park bench playing checkers. The auditorium was built with help from the George Daily Family Trust.*

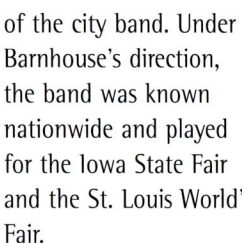

> *McNeil Mansion: The stone mansion was built in the early 1900s by a local coal baron named McNeil. It had fallen into neglect and disrepair until it was purchased by Virginia and Gary Walker. They have renovated the mansion with painstaking attention to period detail, and made it into a bed and breakfast.*

> *Oskaloosa has been visited by celebrities over the years, as when President Herbert Hoover planted the Hoover Elm during William Penn College Commencement, 1925; and in 1912, when President Theodore Roosevelt dedicated the old YMCA at 301 High Ave. East in 1902. Today's YMCA (above) is located at 414 N. 3rd St.*

architectural and historic preservation awards.

Oskaloosa's first hospital was another Oskaloosa Women's Club project. The club raised money to build the original Oskaloosa Hospital in 1907 at 1229 C Ave. East. In 1929, a new building was built to the east; the old hospital building was demolished in 1962. Mahaska Health Partnership has spent the past several years renovating and expanding to provide a new emergency room, birthing center, physician specialists, outpatient surgeries and treatment, and continues to add new services. MHP has a unique geriatric psychiatric program, and also offers a full range of mental health services, hospice care and more.

Recreation, parks

Oskaloosa cherishes its natural beauty with parks and recreation facilities. Vanderwilt Park, on Green Street past the fairgrounds, was built in the 1970s with ball diamonds and tennis courts. The new elementary school is being built in the Vanderwilt area, so future recreational development is being planned around the school. Edmundson Park was built in 1937 as a WPA project on about 60 acres of land. Nearly 1,000 trees and shrubs have been planted in the park, which is next to the city's public golf course (the town has two other golf courses, Harvest Point and Elmhurst Country Club). Edmundson features fishing ponds, recreation shelters and playgrounds. A newer feature is a disc golf course, which has hosted tournaments attracting hundreds of people.

Voters approved a $1.6 million bond issue to renovate Edmundson Park's pool into an aquatic center with slides, water toys and a zero-depth area for parents with small children. The pool and bathhouse were built by the WPA in 1938; the basic structure of the pool is still sound, architects say, and the old bathhouse, a historic treasure, may eventually be made into an indoor shelter. The renovated pool should open for business in summer 2005. The Mahaska Community Recreation Foundation, funded through a hotel/motel tax, pays for a recreation director who applies for grants toward recreation projects.

In early October, the Oskaloosa Branch of the American Association of University Women holds a gigantic used book sale to raise money for scholarships and fellowships. The sale lasts three days, and is held in Penn Central Mall Center Court.

MCRF has raised millions in grant money toward many projects, including a 15-mile recreation trail around Oskaloosa, with 11 miles in

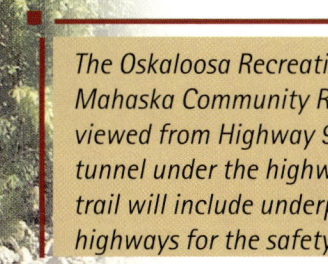

The Oskaloosa Recreation Trail, a project of Mahaska Community Recreation Foundation, is viewed from Highway 92 West; the trail follows a tunnel under the highway. The finished 15-mile trail will include underpasses under major highways for the safety of people using the trail.

Oskaloosa

Learn More

Oskaloosa is located at the junction of Highways 92 and 63 in southeastern Iowa.

For more information, contact the Oskaloosa Area Chamber & Development Group at 641-672-2591, or visit the Web sites
www.oskaloosaherald.com
www.oskaloosachamber.org

Story Contributors

- The Oskaloosa Herald
- Mahaska County Historical Society
- Oskaloosa Area Chamber & Development Group
- Oskaloosa Park Board
- Mahaska County Conservation Board
- Oskaloosa Historic Preservatin Commission
- Webster Elementary fifth- and sixth-grade students
- Chuck and Emily Russell
- Bob Wersen
- George Daily Family Trust
- Researched and Written by Jennifer Swanson, The Oskaloosa Herald

existence so far. Another area attraction is Lake Keomah State Park, seven miles east of Oskaloosa on Highway 92. Keomah also was built with WPA labor. Its lodges, concession area and restrooms at the lake's swimming beach recently underwent $1.4 million in renovations. Other area parks include Russell Wildlife Center, Eveland, Glendale, Cedar Creek and Union Mills Access areas, Cedar Bluffs Natural Area, Rose Hill Marsh, White Oak Conservation Area, Quercus Wilderness Area and others.

Oskaloosa has hosted the county fair since 1852. Today's Southern Iowa Fairgrounds are located on North I Street in the northwest part of town.

The fairground pavilion was built in 1919 by P.W. Sparks, who also built Oskaloosa City Hall in 1912. The round, wooden pavilion was entered into the National Register of Historic Places in 1984; it was said to be one of two remaining pavilions in Iowa built in this style. Today the fairgrounds host activities all year, including gospel and bluegrass festivals, camping and 4-H shows. The dirt race track hosts national stock car and tractor-pull events, harness racing and demolition derbies. The track hosts I.M.C.A.'s All-American Shootout over the July Fourth weekend, with fireworks

Pride, Progress and Tradition

after the races. For a picture of pioneer life, visit Nelson Pioneer Farm, two miles east of Oskaloosa on Glendale Road (T65). The Daniel Nelson house was built in 1853. The Nelson family farmed the 310-acre farm until 1958, then bequeathed it to the Mahaska County Historical Society. The society has preserved the farm as a small village in the mid-1800s might look. It includes the one-room Prine School, a general store, post office, log cabin and blacksmith shop as well as other buildings all dating from the mid-1800s, and also boasts Iowa's only mule cemetery.

The farm and museum are open May through October. Each September, the farm hosts a festival with demonstrations of pioneer skills, including threshing and bailing with an antique thresher, old-fashioned spelling bees and sack races, an antique tractor parade and other entertainment.

Other historic sites include two houses designed by architect Frank Lloyd Wright, and the McNeill Stone Mansion, built by an Oskaloosa coal baron and now renovated as a bed-and-breakfast. Forest Cemetery, where many of Oskaloosa's forefathers and foremothers are buried, is rich in history. The cemetery board recently approved a pet cemetery near the cemetery's lower pond. Forest has had inquiries about the pet cemetery from all over Iowa. **Preserving the best of its history while moving toward the future, Oskaloosa is steeped in "pride, progress and tradition."**

Pride In Our Hometowns.

P·O·R·T·R·A·I·T·S
OF
Ottumwa

"THE CITY OF BRIDGES."

To some historians, the American Indian name for Ottumwa is "land of rippling waters."

One early history book suggests the name Ottumwa was once Au-tum-way-e-nauk, meaning "place of perseverance of self will," a name credited to Chief Appanoose who had a village in what is now the south side of Ottumwa. Another meaning is "at the rapids" or "swift water," referring to the rapids in the Des Moines River which once characterized Ottumwa's site. Iowa's longest river, The Des Moines, runs right through the largest city in Southern Iowa, providing ambiance, recreation, drinking water and water power.

OTTUMWA

Pride In Our Hometowns.

P·O·R·T·R·A·I·T·S
OF *Ottumwa*

"THE CITY OF BRIDGES."

A half-century ago, writers called our state neither an outpost nor wilderness. "She was a restless beach on which waves of settlement washed."

Early history tells of ferries needed to cross the Des Moines River, to take early settlers from American Indian encampments on one side to the growing settlement on the hills of the other side. Today, Ottumwa is known as "The City of Bridges."

Several bridges cross The Des Moines, leading Ottumwans and visitors back and forth to shopping centers, schools, ball parks, businesses and industries and residential homes.

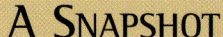

A SNAPSHOT

In 2000 when RAGBRAI came through the city, Ottumwans illuminated one of the bridges, and the city is now the home of the blue bridge.

Ottumwa is rich in heritage dating back to the early 1800s. It is a thriving regional center that boasts numerous cultural and recreational attractions, excellent educational facilities, a multi-purpose event and convention center scheduled to open in 2006, and several industrial areas for economic development. The city offers visitors abundant choices in outdoor recreation and historical

Ottumwa Looking West: Ottumwa High School lower right, Des Moines river winds under the bridges. Courier photograph by Brad Whitney

Ottumwa

Schafer Field: Ottumwa High School Football and Track located at Schafer Field, new field house in foreground. Courier photograph by Brad Whitney

activities close to the city's hub making it an ideal place to live, work, and play.

Ottumwans call the city the heart of Southern Iowa.

Coming into town from the south, visitors crest the last hill, to see the city nestled in the Des Moines River valley, abundant with lush green trees.

The majestic Ottumwa High School stands guard over the downtown area, highlighted by the river which was straightened at great cost to Ottumwans who in the 1950s pulled on their bootstraps and

IT WAS A PROUD MOMENT IN THE CITY'S PROUD HISTORY.

waded into a campaign to raise the money themselves to restrain the rapid water and end the disastrous floods of the previous 50 years.

When flooding returned in 1993, Ottumwans were again ready to bag sand and dig in to repair dike damage, successfully restraining the rising waters and overcoming a major disaster to the city.

Located at the intersection of U.S. Highways 34 and 63, Ottumwa is the Wapello County seat and a major retail, industrial, entertainment and transportation center.

The Beach Slide: Abagail Messer, 7, of Ottumwa slides down a slide in the kiddie pool area at The Beach in Ottumwa. Courier photograph by Brad Whitney

Visitors can find bargains at Quincy Place mall, the growing Wal-Mart SuperCenter and Menards complex west of town, the downtown business district and along Church Street. Ottumwa is home to the John Deere Ottumwa Works, Cargill Meat Solutions, Al-Jon Inc. and American Bottling Co. Ottumwa is the home of Indian Hills Community College. People can splash at The Beach Ottumwa aqautic center or catch a movie at the Capri V theater (a new cineplex is scheduled to be completed in late 2004).

Visitors can drive into town

OTTUMWA HIGH SCHOOL

Ottumwa IOWA

Stearman Biplane: Biplane at the Ottumwa Airport, formerly the Ottumwa Naval Air Station. Courier photograph by Brad Whitney

from each direction, made easier now with the new four-lane highway from Des Moines to Burlington. Ottumwa is in the middle of that stretch of road, and work is under way to finish the highway around Ottumwa and a few other spots along the corridor. Work on the Eddyville bypass is to be completed in 2004, making a straight, four-lane shot for Ottumwans to drive the 84 miles to Des Moines.

A new $1 million airport terminal greets flying guests at Ottumwa Industrial Airport. The airport is the federal government's gift, an air training complex constructed during World War II. The early 1940s hey-days brought the likes of future President Richard M. Nixon to live in Ottumwa for a short time.

Seventy years before that, another president, Benjamin Harrison, helped inaugurate Ottumwa's famous Coal Palace Industrial Exhibit Hall in 1890, a structure that drew the rich and famous to Ottumwa during its two-year duration, including William McKinley in 1891. He would later become president.

And in 1950, President Harry S. Truman celebrated his 66th birthday during a whistle-stop train tour that went through Ottumwa. While Ottumwa awaits the return of a commercial flight service to serve Southern Iowa, Ottumwa Flying Service based at the Ottumwa airport provides plenty of flights for local and area businessmen and other users.

And Ottumwa is one of the few cities in Iowa served by national Amtrak, with trains passing through daily, their whistle blasts echoing the city's early railroad days when 57 freight

Left to right: *President Nixon, lived in Ottumwa for a short time. The Coal Palace Industrial Exhibit.* **Below:** *Ottumwa's Industrial Airport*
Courier photographs by Brad Whitney

Ottumwa

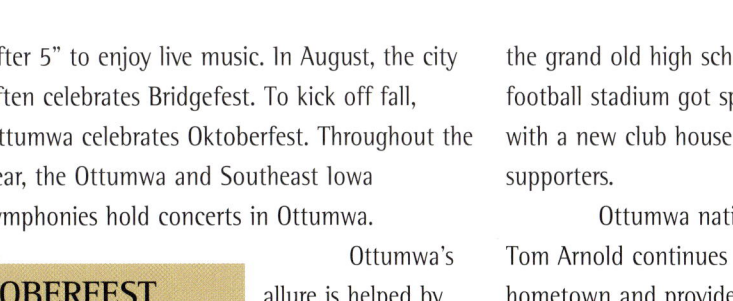

OKTOBERFEST

trains would rumble through town daily. Today's freights haul coal from the western states to

SOMETHING FOR EVERYONE

eastern refineries.

During the summer, Ottumwa hosts the Pro Balloon Races and the 4-H Expo at Ottumwa Park. People also gather in Central Park for "Live After 5" to enjoy live music. In August, the city often celebrates Bridgefest. To kick off fall, Ottumwa celebrates Oktoberfest. Throughout the year, the Ottumwa and Southeast Iowa symphonies hold concerts in Ottumwa.

Ottumwa's allure is helped by nearby Eddyville, a bio-technology hub with an industrial park that is the home of companies such as Cargill, Wacker Biochem and Anjinomoto as well as the Indian Hills bioprocess technician training center.

The Airpower Museum and the Antique Airfield southwest of Ottumwa near Blakesburg is buzzing with activity during the annual Labor Day weekend Fly-In.

Southeast of Ottumwa, Eldon is the home of the American Gothic House, made famous by artist Grant Wood.

Agency, just east of Ottumwa, is the site of Chief Wapello's grave. Many Ottumwans grew up here, moved away, then returned to raise their families, drawn by the city's excellent school system. In 2003, the grand old high school football stadium got spruced up with a new club house provided by the "A" Club supporters.

Ottumwa native and Hollywood actor Tom Arnold continues to be good to his hometown and provided funds for up-to-date work-out equipment for high school students and others. The school district helped provide funds for the new waterpark which remains the jewel in southeast Iowa.

Ottumwans also love their 700 acres of city parks, county parks including Pioneer Ridge Nature Center just south of town and close proximity to the state's largest lake, Rathbun, and also Red Rock Reservoir, both within only an hour's drive. State parks surround the area, and Shimek Forest is

Menards: *The much anticipated Menards Superstore on Venture Drive next to the Wal-mart west of the city.* Courier photograph by Brad Whitney

NATIVE—TOM ARNOLD

Ottumwa, Iowa

Steeped in agriculture, Ottumwa is home to John Deere Ottumwa Works with its $37 million annual payroll. Deere took over Joseph Dain's manufacturing plant a half-century ago. Dain led a revolution in farming, inventing sweeping hay rakes and hay stackers. He received his first patent in 1882 and began manufacturing hay machinery in Ottumwa in 1900. John Deere purchased Dain Manufacturing in 1910. It was wholly owned by John Deere, and the named changed to John Deere Ottumwa Works in the late 1940s.

In The Ottumwa Courier's 2000 Progress edition, Dain was rated by state judges as the

Great LeaderShip

No. 1 most influential person in Southern Iowa in the past 2000 years. No. 2 was labor champion John L. Lewis who grew up in nearby Lucas. Coming in at No. 5 was Ottumwan's own Herschel Loveless, the mayor who led the city's efforts to straighten the Des Moines River through town, and became Iowa's governor and later a favorite son contender for the U.S. presidency.

Ottumwa had felt the effects of devastating floods for decades. An early history book reports "the great inundation of 1851," and later, "The flood of 1903, the largest in the Des Moines river during the present century." They didn't compare, though to the flood of 1947, called the worst flood in history, leaving deaths, evacuations and $20 million in damages. The water rose again two years later, and Ottumwa launched its own flood protection and river improvement

Above Top: *Joe Dain*
Above Bottom: *Herschel Loveless*
Left: *Ottumwa Coliseum*
Right: *Statue of Chief Wapello on the Wapello County Courthouse*

Courier photograph by Brad Whitney

program. A Courier editorial in 1961 told of its successful efforts and the government's plans to build Red Rock Reservoir 50 miles upstream. The midwestern city of 33,751 "rolled up its sleeves and prepared for the future, against some pretty severe odds." The result was a river improvement program, a new $5 million waterworks, a new $2

"WORK IN PROGRESS"

million sewage system and disposal plant, a $10 million highway and bridge relocation program under construction and other improvements.

In 1996, the Wapello County Historical Society launched "Work In Progress: A Patent Point of View" which was tied in to the state sesquicentennial commission and historical society. The project illustrated to today's residents the tremendous impact former citizens had on the world. During the 150 years of Iowa statehood, the creative minds and entrepreneurs of Wapello County patented nearly 1,500 inventions which have sent the names "Ottumwa" and "Wapello County" around the world. Led by innovations of large corporations such as Dain Manufacturing, John Deere Ottumwa Works and John Morrell & Company, the inventions improved lives of everyday residents, from the sad iron to the sewing machine ruffler, to a lawnmower and supermarket stock stamper.

Ottumwa grew the most over 150 years

ago when the Wapello County land was open to settlement in 1843. It also spelled the end of centuries of American Indian influence, some of

Indian Hills Community College looking West. Courier photographs by Brad Whitney

Ottumwa Iowa

Bussiness Growth

which remains in our American Indian rich area.

Today, a statue of Chief Wapello stands atop the county's grand old courthouse, looking down on his beloved river valley. He is buried a short distance away, near Agency, where he and Gen. Joseph M. Street became friends and later worked on the final 1842 treaty which dispossessed the Sac and Fox tribes of their land. Chiefs Wapello, Keokuk, Appanoose and Blackhawk once roamed the Ottumwa area.

Archaeologists still dig in ruins in the area and local historians portray life of those early days. The Wapello County Historical Museum in Ottumwa is a wealth of area history lovingly and factually displayed in the big building which also houses the Amtrak railroad station in the former CB&Q passenger station and office.

Ottumwa's new mall — Quincy Place — heralded in a new decade of growth at the end of the last century. For years, Ottumwans had tried to make the downtown the central shopping area. It took the new mall, a short distance away, to spark growth in the area and raise Ottumwans' hopes for a bigger and brighter future.

That growth is materializing with bigger shopping areas and new restaurants, longtime businesses that have relocated to the growing areas and other longtime business owners who continue to showcase their products and draw customers.

Church spires dot the landscape, and Indian Hills Community College is built on the grounds of Ottumwa Heights College which was served by the Sisters of the Humility of Mary who founded Tally Hospital in 1880, St.

Expansion Quincy Place Mall: Several new businesses have located west of town, large car dealers, Applebees and a new multiplex theater coming soon.
Courier photograph by Brad Whitney

JOHN MORRELL & COMPANY

Joseph's Catholic Hospital in 1914 and remain involved with today's Ottumwa Regional Health Center which is beginning a fund drive for a new cancer treatment center.

The Ottumwa shopping area draws customers from all over southeast Iowa and northern Missouri. Ottumwa is in an ideal location for extended growth which the four-lane Des Moines to Burlington corridor will help promote.

Bridge View Center, the new civic center for Ottumwa, is being designed, and hotels and restaurants are already popping up to capitalize on the crowds that will come to the area.

Ottumwa is a city that didn't die when the largest employer – John Morrell & Company – closed its doors in 1973. It was hard times for years, but Ottumwa did not give up. Other meat packing plants came and went. Today, Cargill Meat Solutions keeps expanding on the former Morrell plant site and has also helped the city diversify.

Today, the city's nearly 25,000 population includes more than 10 percent of Hispanic nationality. The newcomers have added to the town's culture with new restaurants offering delectable Mexican fare, new grocery stores and bakeries.

Ottumwa schools have worked hard to ease the adjustment for these new students, as has the Iowa Workforce Development Center. Ottumwans have learned to embrace diversity and overcome challenge.

Ottumwans straightened their river, ending devastating floods. Ottumwans have welcomed residents from other countries and work hard to provide programs to ease the transition both for the newcomers and the longtime residents.

An active Ottumwa Area Arts Council, the city's two symphony orchestras and a vibrant community players group and children's chorus continue to enrich Ottumwans' lives, providing music and drama for the soul and entertainment for young and old. Dance studios

Mchaffey Opera House: Courier photograph by Brad Whitney

Ottumwa Iowa

thrive as do such worthwhile organizations as a busy, vibrant YMCA, Your Family Center, Boy Scouts and Girl Scouts and a summer 4-H Expo event that draws crowds to the main Ottumwa Park. Civic groups from Rotary to Lions to Kiwanis raise funds to help others.

You can walk the Chief Wapello Trail or take a hot air balloon ride. You can eat a loose meat hamburger or delicious tenderloin sandwich, both are second to none. Ottumwans wait for summer and kids scramble up ladders to ride down slides at the beautiful water park. Fireworks light up the sky not only on the Fourth of July but at other festivals. Horse back riders enjoy a charity horse show, saddle clubs and the Wapello County Fair harness races.

Ball teams play all year long, under the summer lights at a myriad of baseball and softball fields. New soccer parks are now part of the city, and skateboarding kids a few years ago worked hard to get a skateboard area downtown. Golf courses and race tracks abound in the area for fans of all kinds.

A renovated Central Park, a lovely downtown oasis surrounded by the grand Ottumwa Public Library, the county courthouse and Ottumwa City Hall, hosts plenty of music, picnics and fun all summer long with Live After Five on Friday nights and Friday Lunches in the Park.

In the winter, watch a high school basketball or football game, volleyball tournaments and wrestling action.

OTTUMWA PUBLIC LIBRARY

OTTUMWA CITY HALL

Courier photographs by Brad Whitney

Ottumwa

The Indian Hills Community College campus looks like any four-year college campus with new buildings going up often, a cooking school everyone can enjoy and a state-of-the-art robotics program and aviation schooling at the nearby airport. The Indian Hills Warriors are national champions, the baseball team is outstanding and the girls softball games are exciting.

Plays and programs are now given in the newly remodeled high school auditorium, joining the extensive high school remodeling and addition completed earlier. The college auditorium remodeling was completed in 2004.

Ottumwa is often known around the country as the home of TV's "M-A-S-H" fictional character Radar O'Reilly. He may be fictional, but the town is very real. The VIPs who have lived here include Miss Universe Carol Morris; Lee Enterprises founder A.W. Lee; New York City opera coach Margaret Ann Hoswell; UFO expert Donald Keyhoe; Philip B. Hofmann, later the head of Johnson & Johnson; and President Nixon who returned in the 1970s to dedicate Rathbun Lake.

Book authors such as Edna Ferber and Richard Bach have lived here. As have famous book thieves such as Stephen Blumberg.

Our greatest characters have left their legacies. What philanthropist Peter Ballingall did for the city 120 years ago, leading the drive for the Coal Palace, a group of civic minded residents are doing now, putting their faith and hard work into efforts to make Ottumwa the hub of southeast Iowa, from a satellite navigation system added to an outstanding municipal Cedar Creek golf course to a convention center which, with the nearby water park, will help make the downtown area and adjoining river walk a magnet for visitors.

Ottumwa is an All-American City. It's a town that discusses every issue, from gambling to round-abouts to cable TV franchises.

It's heavy Democratic population draws nearly every big political name during presidential races from Ted Kennedy and his clan

CAROL MORRIS
Former Miss Universe

A. W. LEE
Lee Enterprises

Richard Bach
Book Author

Ottumwa

Bridges to Prosperity

to Michael Dukakis to Jimmy and Rosalynn Carter, Al Gore, Howard Dean and John Kerry.

On the homefront, Ottumwans are proud of their police force and fire departments. Residents allow no cuts in these services during lean budget times.

But, they also dig into their pockets when they can help the less fortunate or add ambiance to the community for improved streets, required sewer separations and dreams of a vibrant future in a new civic center complex. Ottumwans agree to disagree many times. But, looking through the years, the city's growth cannot be denied.

The meat packing plant closing in 1973 could have been the city's downfall. But, it wasn't. The city grew again, thanks to the efforts of so many who never gave up and who rose to meet the challenges.

Those challenges continue, but they are exciting ones, as the city works to build on its bridges — the bridges to prosperity and to the good life that an Iowa community can offer.

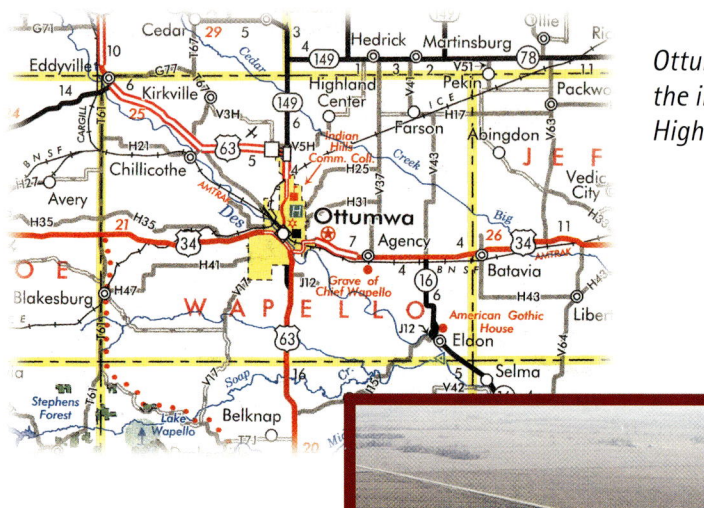

Ottumwa is located at the intersection of U.S. Highways 34 and 63.

Bypass: Interchange North of Ottumwa looking Southeast where Hwy. 34 bypass will connect to Hwy. 63, near Ottumwa Airport

Courier photographs by Brad Whitney

Story Contributors

Judy Krieger
Editor, The Ottumwa Courier

Brad Whitney
Photo Director, The Ottumwa Courier

Pride In Our Hometowns.

P·O·R·T·R·A·I·T·S
of
Pella

"CITY OF REFUGE"

Midway through the 19th century, a band of more than 800 Hollanders under the leadership of Dominie Hendrik Peter Scholte, sought a new home and religious freedom. With bag and baggage and with their gold in a great brassbound chest, they crossed the Atlantic Ocean in four sailing vessels and landed in Baltimore, Maryland. They traveled inland by boat and barge down the Ohio to St. Louis, Mo., and up the Mississippi to Keokuk. From Keokuk they made their way by wagon and on foot to the site chosen by Scholte and named by him "Pella," meaning "City of Refuge."

PELLA

Pride In Our Hometowns.

P·O·R·T·R·A·I·T·S
OF
Pella

"CITY OF REFUGE"

Tradition has led Pella since it's founding in 1847. Early on, Pella's residents had an inkling of things to come in the business world that has led entrepreneurs to establish large and reputable companies. The foundation for all of Pella's Old World charm is its strong economy based on progressive and productive industries and businesses.

As a community that takes pride in its appearance and, with a rich proud history and spectacular festivals, Pella has, through the years, lived up to the meaning of its name truly becoming a refuge for many. But for those who first turned the rich Iowa soil that would become Pella, life was anything but a refuge.

Dominie Scholte was actively involved in the Separatist movement in the Netherlands where many

A SNAPSHOT

declined to follow the state church's dictum as to style of worship that the Separatists believed to be too lax, unduly modern and theologically unsound. For their rebellion, many of the Separatists were imprisoned or fined. Eventually immigration became the only the answer.

The new state of Iowa seemed the ideal location, and a trek from Baltimore, Maryland, began in earnest. Their journey took them over mountains in cable cars, through locks and canals by boat and up rivers via steamboats.

An exploratory group, guided by a Baptist circuit rider, advised Scholte to buy 18,000 acres of land in central Iowa at $1.25 an acre. There the Separatists built houses of sod and roofed them

Dominie (Rev.) Hendrik Pieter Scholte was the leader of the Dutch who immigrated to Pella in 1847, a year after Iowa became a state.

with the branches of saplings with long prairie grasses woven in. The area where these dwellings stood was dubbed "Strooistadt" or Strawtown. The town grew and flourished as immigrant arrivals came at regular intervals for many years to follow.

Residents maintained their religious beliefs throughout much of the town's history. Eventually, Pella became known for its many churches based on a firm Christian foundation.

One of the first churches constructed was the Scholte Christian Church. Dominie Scholte built the church at the same time that his home north of the area known as Garden Square was built. Less than five months after Scholte came to Pella, the church was ready to be occupied.

Many assume that the denomination of the Dutch, the Reformed, was the first religious group to lay down church foundations in Pella. But, the Baptists were in Marion County a few years before the Dutch and had established "Aurora Missionary Baptist Church" six miles south of the present-day city of Pella. The church only had six adult members, but then there were only 502 Baptists in the entire state of Iowa at the time.

In all, there were three distinct cultures in Pella in the early years. In addition to the Dutch and the Baptists, there were the Irish who came with the construction of the railroad in the mid 1880s. After the railroad was built, many of the Irish stayed to make Pella a permanent residence.

The Irish and the Dutch had little in common, as there were language difficulties as well as religious issues. The Irish were Catholic. But, eventually the two cultures blended, and the groups became good friends and neighbors. The Irish were quick in their lessons and generous in friendship. They established a church, and many are buried in St. Mary's Catholic Cemetery north of Pella.

In addition to churches, the settlers built schools.

HISTORY

Scholte built a church while his house was being built (of logs and lumber). He later built a traditional one on W 78th which many years later was razed.

Pella IOWA

One school – Central College – remains today as an important part of the community.

Throughout its history, the college faced repeated challenges. It has withstood financial shortfalls, the death of nearly 20 percent of its male students during the Civil War, a strong challenge from a rival college in nearby Des Moines, two world wars and the Great Depression.

The college first opened its doors as a Baptist Church in 1853 with an affiliated academy for students in ninth through 12th grades. With Elihu Gunn as its president, the school gained its collegiate standing in 1857.

Gunn ushered through the first graduating class of six but spent most of his personal savings to keep the school afloat.

The original Central College building still stands, and is used as the gift shop for the Strawtown Inn.

One of Pella's more famous resident's ancestors also came to America looking for a better way of life.

Pella is the home of the Nicholas Earp family and its most famous member - Wyatt.

The Earp family's English and Scottish descendants immigrated to America in the early 1700s. Like the Scholte band 150 years later, the Earps came to America to escape from Europe's food famine.

Wyatt Berry Stapp Earp, named for his father's neighbor and commanding officer in the Mexican War, was born in Monmouth, Ill., on March 19, 1848. When Wyatt was two years old, his father, Nicholas, moved the family to Pella. While living in Pella, Nicholas was the U.S.

In October 1997, during the visit to our town by HRM Princess Margriet and her husband Pieter van Volenhoven, the courtyard of the Pella Historical Society complex was bright with orange balloons, children and spectators. The children sang Dutch songs and 13-year-old Joy De Haan presented an interpretive dance for the Princess. Photo by Dale Van Donselaar

Flags of The Netherlands' 12 provinces are flown on special occasions at each side of the Tulip Tower. In the foreground is a massive sun dial presented to the city.

Pella IOWA

Wyatt Earp as he may have appeared in Pella as he spent some of his boyhood years here. He was just a teenager when he left this town on his first wagon train. His father put him in charge of providing meals for the family. Photo reprinted from "The Illustrated Life and Times of Wyatt Earp" by Bo Boze Bell© 1993. Used with permission of the author.

Provost Marshal of Marion County.

Wyatt Earp, the famous gun-slinging western marshal, grew up as an ordinary Pella boy, spending most of his time working on his father's farm.

Wyatt's three older brothers enlisted in the Union Army while Wyatt stayed home and tended the farm. Finally, at the tender age of 15, the lure of the Civil War overwhelmed Wyatt. He ran away from home and enlisted in the Army. As luck would have it, the first person Wyatt encountered among the Army ranks was his father, who promptly sent him home – back to the cornfield.

In 1864, Nicholas' hitch in the Army ran out. Although Nicholas was against secession, he disagreed with freeing the slaves. The elder Earp organized a wagon train of 40 families with similar ideas against emancipation and headed to California.

Before the Earps started westward, Nicholas gave Wyatt his first firearm. It was a clumsy weapon - but it proved to be a valuable tool for a wagon train on the move. Wyatt kept the party well supplied with fresh game. Dangers encountered on this trip changed Wyatt from a boy to a man.

Wyatt grew into a handsome, rugged, hard-working man. He was over six feet tall, with powerful flair. Though people knew him to be quiet, good natured and dependable, anyone questioning Wyatt's capability could later testify to his physical prowess.

After the Civil War, the Grand Army

Four young children from Pella display their loyal patriotism in the Fourth of July parade. The Dutch fought in many of our nations' battles whether it be in the American Revolution in the East as the Dutch were very early settlers there ... back in the 1600s.

Pella IOWA

of the Republic made great gains in cities throughout the northern United States. It was a veterans' organization to which most of all the returning Civil War soldiers and sailors belonged. In Pella, the group was energetic, and promoted many encampments for veterans from all over the Midwest. They were also very active in the patriotic events in the community.

After the fighting had ended, two Civil War cannons were mounted on concrete pedestals in front of the monument of "Steen Soldat" or Stone Soldier located in the heart of town. Each of the field pieces had a stack of cannon balls in front of the base, as if ready to be fired at any time. The cannon balls gradually disappeared and probably became cherished souvenirs in someone's living room or den.

Lovingly cared for, the Scholte House built in 1847-48 is lovingly maintained to preserve the aura of the home of Pella's "First Family." The home is the "Grand Dame" of old Pella homes, an example of aristocratic amenities of another era. In a choice location on the north side of the town square, the old matriarch occupies the place with pride.

During World War II, the nation promoted a major scrap drive for the war effort, and the folks of Pella patriotically parted with the old Civil War memorabilia, then more than 70 years old.

However, at the end of World War II, the community would once again obtain survivor weaponry. Area veterans secured two captured Japanese artillery pieces. The larger of the two was set in place where the former Civil War cannon stood. Eventually it was moved to a location in the southwest section of the square. And, the "Big Gun," as it is referred to, still stands there guarding downtown Pella from invaders.

The smaller gun was taken to Oakwood Cemetery to be placed at the Veterans' Memorial site. There wasn't sufficient room, so it was released to a neighboring town for its use as a war souvenir.

A long, hard railroad grade

The Keokuk-Des Moines branch of the Rock Island Railroad generally paralleled the Des Moines River. It ran from Keokuk and Ottumwa up through Pella to Des Moines.

In some areas, the roadbed

A store in the museum features many unusual items including the ones seen in this photo.

followed one of the more prominent creeks in this gently rolling prairie land. When the tracks left the valley to head west of Pella, there was a long grade to climb; and this often proved troublesome for the engines in the early years. The engines were unable to pull the entire train up the steep grade out of the Muchakinock Creek Valley. The area became known as Dutch Gap, so named by the early railroaders in honor of the Hollanders who lived in that neighborhood.

When a long train with heavy tonnage couldn't make the pull up the grade, the train crews would have to "double Dutch Gap." In railroad parlance, this meant that the crews would break the train and take the front section into Pella, put it on a siding and then return with the engine and pick up the remainder of the train. Eventually, the change to more powerful steam engines, then new diesel engines, and work on the roadbed by section crews eliminated most of the problems. In a few years, having to "double Dutch Gap" was a thing of the past.

"Klompen" – Dutch Wooden Shoes

"Klompen" is the Dutch word for wooden shoes. Ancient records make reference to wooden shoes, and it is written that the first guild of wooden shoemakers was formed as early as 1429. Also mentioned were cobblers, skate and last (leather) shoemakers.

People in Pella no longer wear wooden shoes except at Tulip Time when we try to recreate a Dutch atmosphere. A few of our Dutch citizens wear them while washing their cars or for working in their gardens.

Although wooden shoes were once a high-commodity item in The Netherlands, their production was never in the high-profit bracket. "Klompen" makers were often on the rolls of the needy.

In the early days of Pella, about 1850, a shipment of 500 pairs of wooden shoes, shipped to America and stored in a warehouse at the confluence of the Mississippi and Des Moines Rivers, floated down the Mississippi when the warehouse was flooded. The fate of the wooden shoes, each pair tied with twine, is unknown, but it is amusing to imagine the surprise of the fishermen downstream when they saw a flotilla of wooden shoes!

Pella's unique "klokkenspel" located at the Franklin Place Mall is part of a continuing Dutch Front program designed to capture a "Touch of Holland" and provide something out of the ordinary to townspeople and tourists. Several Dutch figures perform to accompaniment of a carillon at regular intervals during the day. The archways in the mall are decorated with beautiful Delft tile scenes.
Photo by Dale Van Donselaar

For many years, the great-grandson of Dominie Scholte has carried the Dutch flag in the Tulip Time parades. Peter Gaass is now deceased and the flag is carried by other descendants of the town's founder.

Pella IOWA

History of Tulip Time in Pella

Growing from a desire to commemorate the sacrifices of the founding fathers and to keep alive the ideals that they cherished, the citizens of Pella came to celebrate Tulip Time. The annual festival is itself a refuge for thousands.

An operetta, presented by the students in April of 1935, was the direct inspiration for Pella's annual festival. The colorful Dutch costumes and the delightful melodies of the production, "Tulip Time in Pella," captured the imagination of some in the audience.

Alert to opportunities for community promotion, community leaders saw the operetta as a "natural" for Pella with its Dutch background.

Since Pella was not yet a tulip town, the planners commissioned George Heeren, a local cabinetmaker, to make wooden tulips - each three feet tall - for the initial Tulip Time Festival. However, it was decided that in the fall of 1935, thousands of tulip bulbs would be planted to provide natural color for future festivals. Despite the lack of real tulips, the historic first Tulip Time set the pattern for the festivals presented thereafter.

In anticipation of Pella's 1936 Tulip Time Festival, thousands of tulip bulbs were planted in the fall of 1935 in lanes along the curbs and in mass plantings in the parks. In February 1936, a bulb grower and broker from the Netherlands came to Pella to advise on the planting and care of tulips.

In 1936, huge crowds attended the festival that had been extended to five days. But the annual celebration wouldn't be without its own challenges.

The outbreak of World War II brought with it rationing of gasoline and other restrictions. Consequently, plans for the 1942 Tulip Time were undertaken with some misgivings.

The replica of Dominie Scholte's church was built in 1976. The original building, much larger, was razed in 1916. The Latin motto means "In God is Our Strength and Refuge".

One of Pella's most recent building projects is the "Molengracht" or mill-canal, built to complement the new Vermeer windmill across the street. A canal flows with a gentle curve throughout the plaza surrounded by copies of 18 century Dutch architecture. Shops, offices, restaurants, a hotel and theater facilities line the brick pedestrian walkways. Photo by Dale Van Donselaar

The beautiful towering Dutch windmill is 125 feet tall and dominates a corner of the Pella Historical Society Museum complex. The Vermeer Mill stands as the tallest working windmill in this country. Authentically designed in the Netherlands, it was reassembled on site. The windmill is a wind-powered grain mill and celebrates the rich agricultural and Dutch heritage. The adjacent Interpretive Center includes a reception area, media room, historical time line along with a fabulous miniature village. A puppet theater is also one of the features in the center.
photo by Dale Van Donselaar

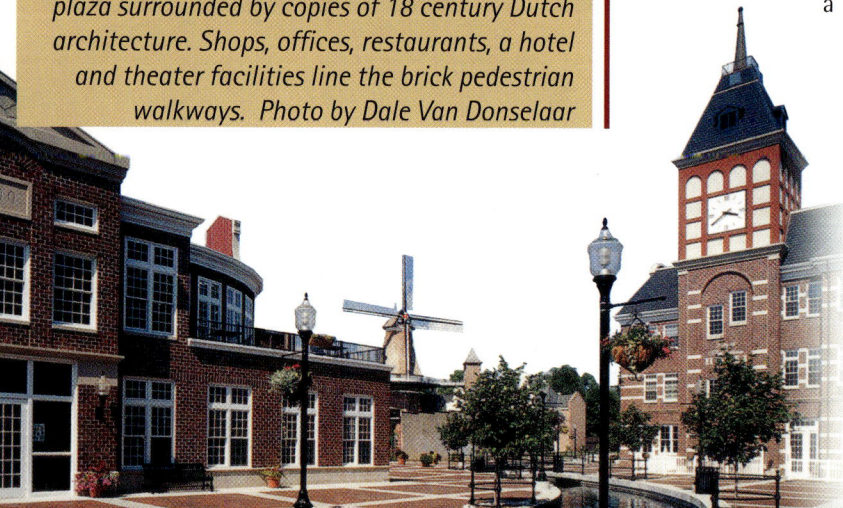

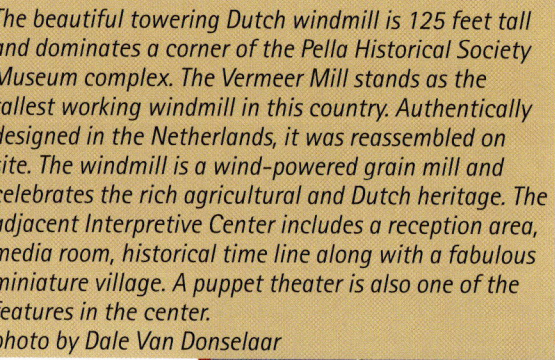

Pella IOWA

However, a three-day festival was held. In 1943 and 1944, despite wartime difficulties, one-day celebrations of Tulip Time were held. No festivals were held during 1945 or 1946.

Sunken Gardens, a few blocks off the square on Main Street, is a true example of the Dutch persons love for flowers, especially tulips. The shape of the pond is that of a wooden shoe.

Now, each spring thousands from all over the United States journey to Pella's Tulip Time.

For a visitor, a typical day begins with morning tours of the points of historic and local interest.

At noon, restaurants offer special foods prepared in the Dutch manner: Snijboontjes (Dutch green beans), erwten soep (pea soup), boonen soep (bean soup), Pella bologna made from recipes unknown except to Pella bologna makers, Dutch "Letters," a baked delicacy with almond paste filling, Dutch Sinterklaas Koekjes (Santa Claus Cookies), Dutch cocoa and more.

The afternoon begins with the appearance of 400-500 Dutch Dancers dressed in Dutch costume and wooden shoes. After the Dutch Dancers, the preceding year's Tulip Queen, dressed in Dutch costume, approaches the Tulip Toren, along with the Burgemeester, dressed in a colorful red and gold robe.

Representatives from 11 Dutch provinces follow the queen and the Burgemeester. Each representative is attired in authentic dress. The beautiful and varied provincial costumes include lace caps and gold head ornaments, waists and blouses ornamented with lovely embroidery and lace, colorful shawls, full skirts and knitted stockings.

At the conclusion of the Parade of the Provinces, the sound of trumpets announces the arrival of the Royal Court. The Royal Court, all in colorful Dutch costumes, proceeds to the Tulip Toren. During the coronation ceremony, the Burgemeester places the crown upon the new queen's head and presents her with a beautiful loving cup that will be hers for a year and upon which her name will be

The Beason-Blommers Mill, a replica of an actual mill that operated in the Pella area in the past. Equipment in the mill is demonstrated and in the adjacent blacksmith shop, a steam engine performs as do blacksmiths. A rare assortment of antique carpenter tools also line one wall, the Lautenbach display.

Pella, IOWA

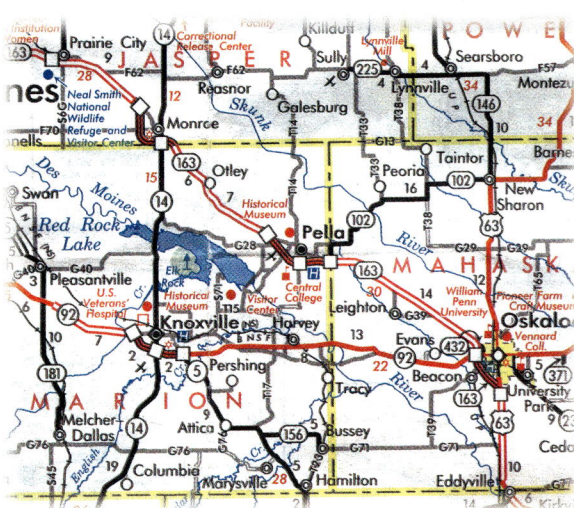

LEARN MORE

Pella is located in Marion County in south-central Iowa.

For more information, contact the Pella Chronicle at:
www.pellachronicle.com or the Pella Historical Society at:
641-628-2409
www.pellatuliptime.com or the Pella Chamber of Commerce at:
641-628-2626.

STORY CONTRIBUTORS

- Murt Kooi, "Pella Past," columnist for the Pella Chronicle
- Loren Vander Zyl of Pella and the late "Buck" Buerkens
- Pella Historical Society (Patsy Sadler)
- Pella Chamber of Commerce
- Pella Historical Archives

---

inscribed along with the names of the queens who have reined before her.

Following the coronation ceremony, the Burgemeester and De Stadtsraad (City Council) proceed to inspect the street for cleanliness. The Burgemeester declares that the street must be scrubbed so that not a particle of dirt will remain when the queen and her retinue pass in the parade. The Burgemeester calls for street scrubbers, and men, women, and children appear carrying large scrub brushes and yokes with pails. They scrub the pavement until every inch of pavement has been washed thoroughly.

Tulip Time is truly a time for celebration and reflecting. Above all, Tulip Time is a beautiful and fun time in Pella. But, Tulip Time is not the only fun time in Pella.

Christmas in Pella

In the Netherlands, the people are in luck in that they have two Christmas days. The first of the two is on December 25 and the second on December 26. Both days are national holidays.

Another celebration for the Dutch at Yuletide is "Sinterklaasavond" or St. Nicholas Eve that occurs on December 5. This holiday is celebrated in a much more jovial manner and is especially enjoyed by children. Down the street comes the old saint on a splendid white horse. His mitre is trimmed with gold, and a rich red velvet cape falls from his shoulders. His hair has turned white and is amassed in a long style complete with a long white beard. On his hands he wears white gloves, and in one hand he holds a gold crosier.

St. Nichols, or "Sinterklaas," as he is known, comes to Pella in late November on the Saturday after Thanksgiving. He arrives on his ship, supposedly from Spain. A large ship float carries the saint to the parade route, and Sinterklaas is accompanied by his splendid white horse (albeit a plastic version!).

A "breakfast with Sinterklaas" is held. There is a list of good children, and their deeds of kindness and helpfulness are read as chocolate letters are received. There just are no bad children!

Today, as with its children, Pella, with its simple and entertaining lifestyle, has truly lived up to the meaning of its name. There just are no bad sides to Pella, for it is still a place of continuous refuge.

"Sinterklaas" aka Jay De Young, dressed in his finery, greets participants at the breakfast in the Great Hall of the Opera House. This is a marvelous experience for young children.

Pride In Our Hometowns.

P·O·R·T·R·A·I·T·S
OF
Shenandoah

THE GARDEN CITY

Shenandoah is a place where beautiful things seem to grow easily. Early in its history, with an abundance of fertile soil, Shenandoah became the seed and nursery capital of America. Through the years the city has enjoyed success and notoriety for its ability to nurture business, the arts and a sense of community. Today Shenandoah is a vibrant town. It continues to fulfill its early promise of a place where beautiful things grow.

  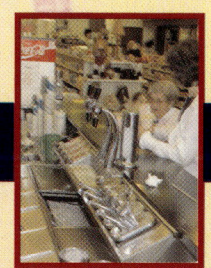 

Pride In Our Hometowns.

P·O·R·T·R·A·I·T·S
OF *Shenandoah*

Shenandoah's Flatiron Plaza is the centerpiece of the new streetscape. Many activities and events are centered around the Flatiron during the summer.

THE GARDEN CITY

A Snapshot

Shenandoah, located in the Nishnabotna River Valley, provided early settlers with a sense of beauty and promise that inspired them to sow the seeds of their families' future on this land. Originally called Fair Oaks, Shenandoah took its permanent name on August 6, 1870. Soldiers returning from the Civil War saw a striking resemblance to the Shenandoah Valley of Virginia.

As with many towns, Shenandoah's growth was spurred on by the railroad. The Chicago, Burlington and Quincy Railroad work was completed in the summer of 1870. The completion of the railroad meant more travelers passing through Shenandoah and more people deciding to call Shenandoah home.

Deeply rooted in the nursery industry, Shenandoah's seeds for growth and opportunity were planted in 1875 with the dawn of the Mt. Arbor Nurseries. Four years prior, in 1871, a young Henry Field was born in Shenandoah. According to company history Henry had sold his first packet of seeds by the age of six. It took another 15 years for a youthful Field to actually grow, harvest and market his own seeds locally. By the time Field passed away in 1949 the Henry Field Company was one of the largest and best-known companies of its kind in the United States.

Another local company synonymous with growing and Shenandoah is Earl May Seed and Nursery. Earl May, a Nebraska man, sold garden seeds in the Midwest and South

Radio Digest declared Earl May the "Most Popular Radio Broadcaster of 1929". He received 452,901 votes in the nationally sponsored contest.

Huge Show Gardens were a tourism draw to Shenandoah. Thousand of visitors would flock to town in the spring and summer to take in the elaborate flower bed designs by local nurseries. This postcard shows the Henry Field's Show Garden.

Shenandoah

to pay his way through college. May moved to Shenandoah in 1915 to work at the Mt. Arbor Nursery. Three years later he founded the company that still bears his name and is known throughout Iowa and three other states.

More than just trees, vegetables and flowers sprung from Shenandoah's fertile soil. Their competitive nature and marketing prowess spurred the nursery owners to success in a far different endeavor. May and Field, created radio stations to broadcast their commercials and entertainment throughout the Midwest and across the country. Field launched KFNF in 1924. Not to be outdone the call letters of KMA were first heard over the crackle of a radio in 1925.

Live broadcasts of music, news and information were beamed from studios and auditoriums built by the stations. Shenandoah became known throughout the Midwest as a stopping point for young entertainers trying to further their way in the entertainment world. Early entertainers lured to the stages in Shenandoah included the Blackwood Brothers in 1940 and other well-known era entertainers.

KFNF Tower Sitter, In 1931 promotional gimmicks like "Tower Sitting" were utilized by both KFNF and KMA to draw crowds and attention during celebrations. Various events would draw as many as 65,000 visitors to Shenandoah in the late 1920s and early 1930s.

EVERLY BROTHERS

The homespun Shenandoah talent of the Everly Brothers also found its way to the KMA stage. Although Don and Phil Everly were born in Brownie, Kentucky the draw of a radio appearance on KFNF brought their musical family to Shenandoah in 1945. After several years they left Shenandoah in the summer of '55. They still consider Shenandoah an important part of their musical legacy. The Everly's went on to national and international acclaim enjoying well known hits with "Bye Bye Love" "Wake Up Little Susie" and "Cathy's Clown".

Even beyond the nursery and radio business Shenandoah's entrepreneurial spirit has helped build a strong independent community. Even within it's own county (Page), Shenandoah is not the largest town, nor the county seat. Yet, it boasts several home-grown businesses that thrive and prove once again Shenandoah's a place where things grow.

Encouraged by the success of their KFNF radio station the Henry Field Co. built their own auditorium for larger live performances.

Shenandoah

*Winfred Brown
Founder, Brown's Shoe Fit Co.*

Seventeen hundred dollars isn't a lot but in 1911 Winfred Brown invested that sum into a twelve-foot wide storefront in Shenandoah. His goal....scratch out a living in the shoe business. His first stroke of genius was to order 1,100 empty shoeboxes with his store label on them. He wanted to give his customers the appearance of a large stock of shoes. Brown's hard work paid off. By February of 1913 Brown was worth $6,000.

Today, Brown's Shoe Fit Stores number eighty-five in twelve different states. The corporate office resides just down the block from the original location and a Brown's Shoe Fit store still occupies a spot in Shenandoah's main shopping area.

Ballparks are just one of the recreational facilities available to residents and visitors. Organized leagues and instruction are a staple of the parks and recreation department.

Much of Shenandoah's industry was focused on helping plants grow bigger, grow brighter or grow stronger. However, in 1958 VET-A-MIX inc. was founded by Dr. Gene Lloyd. Lloyd sought to help animals, not plants, grow stronger and bigger.

LLYOD LABS

A graduate of the then Iowa State College with a degree in Veterinary Medicine, Lloyd built what is now Lloyd, Inc. He received the Iowa's Small Business Exporter of the Year Award in 1990 from the U.S. Small Business Administration.

In the early days Dr. Lloyd's first mixing machine for his animal products was a simple job-site cement-mixing machine. Today Lloyd Inc. is developing drugs for human applications in state-of-the-art scientific labs. In 2002 they received approval of a human New Drug Application. They continue to expand their lab and production operation in Shenandoah and employ more than 70 people.

Charles Parker didn't want to make people feel better like Doctor Lloyd; he wanted to know how they felt. In 1937 Parker established Central Survey, Inc. in Shenandoah. Still thriving today, Central Surveys specializes in opinion-polling in industrial, commercial or matters of public interest. They are well-respected in their field and continue to perform market

*Upper: A home-grown business of Shenandoah, Lloyds Inc. was started in 1958 by Dr. Gene Lloyd. Initially producing vitamins and pharmaceuticals for the veterinary industry, Lloyds Inc. is now producing medicines for humans.
Left: In the early days Dr. Lloyd's first mixing machine for his animal products was this simple job-site cement mixing machine. Today Lloyd Inc. is developing drugs for human applications in state-of-the-art scientific labs.*

Shenandoah

research for Fortune 500 companies throughout the United States.

Shenandoah's small size is no indication of the vast entertainment and recreational opportunities in and around the city. Outdoor enthusiast enjoy the natural beauty and wonders of the Nishnabotna River. Fishing, canoeing, and exploring natures gifts are just a few of many appealing activities.

The Wabash Trace Nature Trail, once a mainline for the Wabash Railroad from Council Bluffs to St. Louis, runs right through Shenandoah. A strong core group of Trace supporters in the Shenandoah area volunteered time and effort to create a superb way to interact with nature. The Trace now offers bicyclist, joggers, walkers and even cross-country skiers a 63-mile corridor of nature to discover. Bird watchers also find The Trace a place to observe and photograph their feathered friends. Benches and shelters dot the trail, which was dedicated in 1999.

Shenandoah's new streetscape makes shopping a pleasure and features the Walk of Fame. Famous Iowans or those influenced by their Iowa days are featured in plaques along the sidewalk.

Community plays, music performances and a triple-screen first run theater add to Shenandoah's draw. The Southwest Iowa Theater Group, Iowa's longest continuous running theater group, calls Shenandoah home. The group has built a strong reputation for quality performances

ENTERTAINMENT-TOURISM

over their 50-year history. Plays and musicals are organized quarterly throughout the year. Additional smaller dinner theater productions are also performed occasionally.

Each summer nearly 160 budding artist descend upon Shenandoah for the Wabash Arts Camp. College art teachers and professionals instruct campers on everything from acting, weaving and painting to hip hop dancing. Thirteen murals, created by students of the art camp, depicting Shenandoah's history and famous works of art adorn buildings throughout town.

Shenandoah's Chamber and Industry Association promote year 'round events to entertain local residents and invite visitors to Shenandoah. Warm weather months feature Thursday at the flat iron. Free live entertainment, refreshments and activities are presented in downtown Shenandoah on the last Thursday of each month. Building upon it's reputation as the Garden City Shenandoah presents the Spring Garden Festival in June, the Garden Shenfest in September and the Holiday Garden of

WABASH TRACE NATURE TRAIL

The original Blackwood Brothers, a well-known Christian singing group, were winners of nine Grammy Awards and were born in Shenandoah.

Shenandoah

Lights in December. They promote Shenandoah as the garden city, a great place to shop for a day, visit for a week or live the rest of your life.

A new, well-received attraction to the community is the Bricker Butterfly House. Dedicated in 2003 the butterfly sanctuary delights both children and adults. Located at the corner of Highway 59 and Sheridan Ave. in Shenandoah, the thousand square foot greenhouse features tropical plants and flowers and butterfly feeding stations. Monarchs, Painted Ladies, Swallowtails, Fritillary and Zebra butterflies are among the butterflies to show their colors after going through the egg, caterpillar and chrysalis stages. The Bricker Butterfly House is free to the public and open to educational groups, clubs and other organizations. The structure was built with funds from the Mabel Bricker Estate.

Shenandoah has built a strong reputation in the region and around the state for it's downtown shopping district. An ongoing Streetscape project, along with active and progressive merchants, has created a downtown atmosphere akin to the heyday of America's downtowns. It's a different pace than the malls

SHOPPING-COMMERCE

in the city. The new downtown streetscape, summer Day Lilies, old-fashioned lamppost with hanging flower baskets and park benches to relax on give visitors and shoppers a relaxed, quaint place to shop.

But Shenandoah's appearance isn't just window dressing. Merchants are friendly and have invested time and resources into their stores. A wide-variety of goods and services await visitors and shoppers to Shenandoah. Just plan on parking the car downtown and strolling from one store to another. China, art, T-shirts, flowers, glassware, linens, antiques, and Iowa souvenirs...it's all here in one form or another. And your clerk is liable to become your friend, while helping you make your shopping decisions.

Women love shopping a variety of clothing stores for children and adults stopping along the way for a cappuccino or other refreshment. Interior design and gift shops are also popular in Shenandoah. And for the man who needs to buy something for the woman in his life, there are clerks who will help him make his decisions. Several nostalgic and unique restaurants provide an enjoyable break from shopping. Shenandoah offers a friendly, family-oriented atmosphere. A call to the Shenandoah Chamber and Industry Association can give you hints on where to

Two major waterslides, diving boards and a zero-depth entry into the pool make Shenandoah's Wilson Aquatic Center a popular destination for residents and visitors.

The Bricker Butterfly House in Shenandoah is home to a variety of butterfly species. This monarch caterpillar munches on milkweed during the second of its four stages during its life cycle. Admission is free. Educational, civic and other groups are encouraged to visit the site and call ahead for specialized tours.

Shenandoah

start.

The Highway 59 corridor, along Shenandoah's western edge offers a very modern shopping experience. That's where you will find Wal-Mart, Hy-Vee, Fareway, several other chain retailers, a collection of fast food and convenience stores. There and beyond, you will discover lumberyards, agri-businesses, hardware stores, furniture stores, banks and more! A day-trip to Shenandoah is a complete shopping experience – more than 200 different businesses are ready to serve your needs.

Shenandoah's ability to furnish industry with labor, an atmosphere conducive to family living and other resources has insured a stable industrial base. Current manufactures, both big and small, continue to grow and expand in Shenandoah's fertile climate.

One of Shenandoah's flagship manufacturers is Pella Corporation. Pella was recruited to Shenandoah in 1991 by the late Dan Offenburger of the Shenandoah Chamber and Industry Association and other members of the community. Today Pella Corporation employs more than 500 at the Shenandoah Operations. The custom window and door plant was expanded by 75,000 square feet in 2001. In addition to producing quality windows and doors Fortune Magazine rated them the number 12 best company to work for in America in 2002. They have made the top 100 list five times.

Eaton Corporation has called Shenandoah a home since 1972. Heavy-duty transmissions are produced in Shenandoah for the automotive and industrial truck industry. Employment has grown steadily with current employee levels topping more than 600. Both Eaton and Pella Corporation have shown a strong commitment to communities.

Eaton Corporation

Shenandoah thinks big but also takes pride in its smaller industry. Of special note are Nishna Productions, Inc., and Triple K Manufacturing. Nishna Productions is non-profit community rehabilitation agency offering vocational and residential services to people with disabilities in Page, Fremont, Mills, Montgomery, Taylor and Pottawattamie counties. The company has enriched hundreds of lives of people with disabilities in its 30-year history. In a vocational sense, the agency provides an opportunity for employers to stay competitive regionally and globally by providing a competitive labor resource to meet a variety of business needs. Triple K Manufacturing, produces private label spices, salad dressing, laundry detergent and other household items. Triple K was born out of the famous maker Kitchen Klatter legacy made popular through the radio show bearing its name.

Residents of Shenandoah and the surrounding rely heavily on the Shenandoah Medical Center for convenient, reliable and state-of-the-art medical services. The SMC Campus includes the

Fortune Magazine has named Pella Corporation to its Top 100 places to work five times. In 2003 Pella was named the 22nd best company to work for by Forbes Magazine. The Shenandoah Operation manufactures custom doors and windows.

213

Shenandoah

MEDICAL

Shenandoah Memorial Hospital, physicians' offices, an out patient clinic, Turnbull Physical Therapy Center and a new Disease Prevention and Wellness Center. With ties to Nebraska Health Systems, Shenandoah's healthcare is aligned with the major medical centers of Omaha, Nebraska. NHS physicians visit Shenandoah Medical Center on a regular basis to provide specialized care or services.

Area veterans from American Legion Post 88 put forth a tremendous effort in 2004 to secure a new Veterans Administration Outpatient Clinic for Shenandoah. The Clinic will be incorporated onto the Shenandoah Medical Center Campus in the coming year. Veterans from a three-state region will travel to Shenandoah's clinic.

Local school activities form a major part of rural Iowa's cultural base. Shenandoah features a strong school system through both academics and extracurricular activities. It is highly visible when the Mustangs and Fillies sports teams are competing. It is just as strong in music, the arts, speech and drama, academics and other pursuits.

Those living in rural America naturally center much of our togetherness at the school. It is no wonder that one of Iowa's greatest strength is the national standing of its

EDUCATION

students. Shenandoah is very proud of its school system. Shenandoah High School was the first of the modern era schools located on the campus at the southeast edge of the city. In 2002, the new award winning building opened for pre-Kindergarten through eighth grade. That was followed by the $2.4 million Turnbull Child Development Center in 2004, offering extended hour care and also education for infants through latch-key kids coming in after

2004 will see the opening of the Turnbull Child Development Center. The center is designed for wide-range of children; from 6 weeks to 12 years

Left: Shenandoah's High School has experienced several new additions since it was built in 1969. Shenandoah's entire school system K-12th grade are located in close proximity to each other on the city's edge.
Bottom: Shenandoah Medical Center takes a proactive approach to healthcare needs of the community. In the recent past an outpatient center, therapy center and disease prevention and wellness center have been added.

This antique Victorian Reed Organ is one of the heirlooms professionally displayed at the Shenandoah Historical Museum. Endless volunteer hours have been spent to assemble and create a glimpse into Shenandoah's past.

school. Located right next door to the schools, the facility can serve 150 children. Marilyn and James Turnbull's generous gift of $1 million to the Child Development Center was just one of their community contributions from their industrial maintenance and bridge painting business.

Iowa Western Community College has a branch in Shenandoah in a newly remodeled building downtown. They award Associate of Arts degrees, certification in a variety of fields, customized training for local businesses, and offer continuing education programs. The main campus is located in Council Bluffs.

FAITH AND CHURCH

Shenandoah is proud of its religious heritage with 21 churches. Given the towns population Shenandoah can boast of having one church for every 245 people. Church street occupies a prominent position in the town's design and is well named. Early pictures of Shenandoah show the area around Church Street much the same as it is today – huge, beautiful well-designed houses of worship dotted the area in the late 1800s and early 1900s. Many of the churches stand today nearly as they were built.

An active community that always seems to be on the move, Shenandoah claims eighteen parks and recreation centers for visitors and residents to utilize. Playgrounds with swings, shade trees, tennis courts, softball diamonds, swimming pools and open areas can be found throughout the town. A round of golf at Shenandoah American Legion Golf Course is convenient. The 18-hole course is located within the city limits. Two sets of tennis courts the Alice and Harold Welch Tennis Center in Gee Park and the Sportsman's Park tennis courts are located at each end of town. If it gets dark, turn on the lights for free. A stroll on the Mustang Field Track is one of the most popular exercises in town. One of Iowa's finest swimming pools is the Ivan and Caroline Wilson Family Aquatic Center that features zero-depth-entry water level and two major water slides. Organized baseball, softball tennis and golf competitions and lessons are offered by the Shenandoah Parks & Recreation Department.

The newest exercise spot is the Shenandoah Medical Center's Disease Prevention and Wellness Center complete with personal trainers, a therapeutic pool, recovery, and athletic acceleration programs. What makes Shenandoah "a place to live the rest of your life?"

It's the "Lifestyle America Needs and Wants" according to the late Dan Offenburger who helped lead the era of development in Shenandoah the last decade as Shenandoah Chamber & Industry Association's Executive Vice President. His SCIA successor, Mayor Gregg Connell is another town leader who initiated a number of improvements in the past 8 years that have made Shenandoah what it is today.

Shenandoah like many towns in Iowa had fallen

The Methodist church of Shenandoah stands today much the same way it stood in the early days of Shenandoah. Early residents were blessed with an abundance of beautiful homes of worship from which to practice their faith.

Shenandoah IOWA

> Shenandoah has been served by a newspaper since 1882 under a variety of names. The Sentinel, Sentinel Post, Shenandoah World, The Evening Sentinel and now the Valley News Today have all appeared in the masthead. At one time Shenandoah could claim to be the smallest town in America with two daily papers. Currently Shenandoah is Iowa's second smallest city (by population) with a daily newspaper.

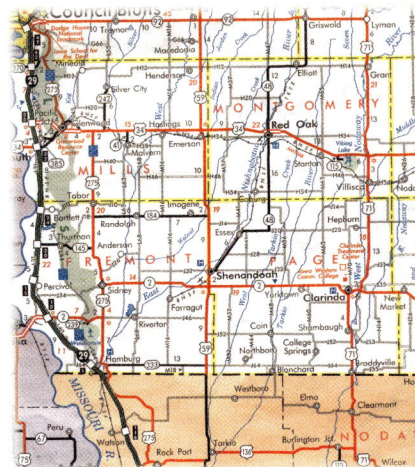

into a period of decline. After the town pulled together in a team effort to recruit Pella Corporation about 14 years ago there was no stopping community activists. The Streetscape, the Aquatic Center, a new school, the new three-screen theater, hospital improvements, new childcare facility.... one project after another has been completed and the development continues. Businesses, the city, and private citizens work hand-in-hand to make things happen. It's tough to find an empty building on Main Street. Shenandoah prides itself in helping industrial and business prospects either to expand here or to re-locate here. A safe, tranquil yet vibrant community it appeals to many for retirement or to raise a family.

The Future...

Shenandoah citizens think big. That's the attitude that led to the development of the West Tarkio Reservoir/Lake project. A 1600 acre lake...midst a park area of up to 4750 acres...with access to the Wabash Trace Nature Trail...multi-purposes for water supply and recreation...fishing, water sports, camping, boating, all types of outdoor recreation. That's how the sponsoring cities of Clarinda and Shenandoah devised the plan for this future lake. They were awarded a $12 million Vision Iowa Grant for the recreation aspects of the lake. It will also provide a clean, abundant water source that will replace Shenandoah's outdated wells. Recreation, jobs, and economic development that will result from the lake project are expected to generate millions of dollars.

Shenandoah's citizens' speak of creating more show gardens, more recreation for youth and the continued growth of the business community. They look forward to the day when phase II and III of the streetscape west on Sheridan Avenue and Hwy 59. Shenandoah was established due to it's ability to help things grow....that continues today.

Left: Shenandoah's Civil War Monument has seen additions over the years to honor veterans from many of America's conflicts. Recently the Veterans Administration has approved locating a VA outpatient clinic in Shenandoah.
Bottom: An old-fashioned community parade is part of Garden Shenfest held the last Saturday in September.

Learn More

Shenandoah is located at the intersection of U.S. Highways 59 c

For more information please feel f to call the Shenandoah Chamber Industry Association or visit websi at:
www.simplyshenandoah.com

Story Contributors

- Shenandoah Historical Museur
- Shenandoah Chamber and Indu
- Association (SCIA)
- Valley News Today
- Shelly Smith of SCIA.

Pride In Our Hometowns.

P·O·R·T·R·A·I·T·S
OF
Sioux City

THE HEART OF SIOUXLAND

When Sioux City was established 150 years ago on Iowa's western border as a gateway to westward expansion, it was cut off from the state's eastern settlements, as well as the rest of the nation. It wasn't cut off, however, from the pioneering spirit that made it one of the fastest-growing communities in the nation. In 1898, in fact, it ranked as the 11th largest city in the United States.

Pride In Our Hometowns.

P·O·R·T·R·A·I·T·S
OF *Sioux City*

THE HEART OF SIOUXLAND

Statue near the north entrance of the Woodbury County Courthouse. (Photo by Jim Lee)

Sioux City was born on the banks of the Missouri River in an area that was to develop at the junction of three states; Iowa, Nebraska and South Dakota. It also formed at the confluence of three rivers: the Missouri, Big Sioux and Floyd. During its early decades, the city grew independently of the rest of the Hawkeye State which sprang up first along the Mississippi River and its tributaries.

The city was forced to forge its own identity as the heart of a boisterous new region—the Heart of Siouxland.

That heart was even on display 200 years ago when Lewis and Clark paid respects to Sgt. Charles Floyd, the only member of their fabled expedition to die, during touching ceremonies on the banks overlooking the river at Sioux City. Sgt. Floyd also happens to be the name of the nautically grounded Visitors Center and Museum. And the first stop for many visitors to Sioux City is the Sgt. Floyd Monument, an obelisk which towers over the city in the Loess Hills above the Missouri.

A SNAPSHOT

And that beating heart crystallized on July 19, 1989, when Sioux City and its Siouxland neighbors earned international acclaim for their amazing and heartfelt rescue efforts following the crash of United Airlines Flight 232 at Sioux Gateway Airport.

Today, the heart beats solidly as business expansion and

The Rose Garden at Sioux City's Grandview Park is a poplular wedding site. (Photo by Jim Lee)

218

Sioux City

housing construction continue apace in the tri-state region. The 2001 completion of the Orpheum Theatre restoration and launch of the River's Edge development project capped more than two decades of remarkable renewal in the heart of Sioux City. Virtually every downtown block has undergone significant change or complete rebuilding. Historic structures have been painstakingly preserved and given new uses, especially along Historic Fourth Street, a bustling commercial district. In 1995, the area was placed on the National Register of Historic Places and was noted for its fine collection of Richardsonian Romanesque styled buildings.

The once stagnant riverfront also has been transformed into a vibrant gathering place.

And the changes have included a splendid increase in cultural and entertainment opportunities, with an impressive new art center, the Lewis and Clark Interpretive Center, riverboat casino and new events center.

Three-term City Councilman (and former mayor) Marty Dougherty says the work done by community leaders over the past decade has made Sioux City a "destination city—and not just for cultural and entertainment events." The same thing is true commercially and with regard to people choosing to move to the city. An "explosion of growth" in the past 5 to 10 years has transformed Sioux City, he said.

VIBRANT GATHERING PLACES

Outside of downtown, Sioux City has experienced growth, particularly to the south with its booming Singing Hills development. Just as European immigrants had played a prominent role in the city's growth and diversity a century earlier, Hispanic immigrants are increasing the population and bringing a new, influential dimension to the community.

Sioux City's physical and demographic changes, in fact, seem a reflection of the civic pride and optimism that was a

Left: Once a rail hub, railroad tracks still cross much of Sioux City. (Photo by Jim Lee)
Right: The Sgt. Floyd Monument in Sioux City became the nation's first national historic landmark in 1960. (Photo by Tim Hynds)

Sioux City

GRANDVIEW PARK BANDSHELL

hallmark of its earliest pioneers.

William Thompson is usually credited as being the first permanent settler in the area in 1848, two years after Iowa became a state. A year later, French Canadian settler Theophile Bruguier established a trading post at the future town site. During the 1850s, explorers, hunters, miners and trappers passed through this gateway settlement on their way West. By the time the settlement was incorporated by the state of Iowa in 1857, Sioux City had a bank, post office, hotels and land registry. The town grew slowly as the last outpost of civilization on the western border of one of the newest states of the Union.

In 1869, the first railroad reached the town and during the next three decades, several railroad companies built tracks which fanned out in every direction, and Sioux City became the boomtown it was meant to be.

By the late 1880s, Sioux City was one of the most modern municipalities in the United States. It boasted an electric company, a telephone exchange, street railways and a Corn Palace. The Panic or Depression of the 1890s, however, struck Sioux City particularly hard, ending the rapid population growth.

Sioux City's agricultural base provided it with a sturdy economy through the 1920s, but it suffered accordingly during the Depression of the 1930s as prices for agricultural products plummeted.

As a major municipality on the Great Plains, Sioux City benefited from many New Deal projects. New Deal initiatives still in use include Stone State Park, the

SIOUX CITY ART CENTER

THE WOODBURY COUNTY COURTHOUSE

Sioux City IOWA

The Lewis and Clark Intrepretive Center is one of the newest Siouxland attractions. (Photo by Tim Hynds)

Federal Court House and the Grandview Park Bandshell, which is the scene of the phenomenally successful "Saturday in the Park," a free music festival that draws nationally recognized musicians to the park every Fourth of July weekend.

You probably know them better as Dear Abby and Ann Landers, but in 1936 the Friedman twins, Esther and Pauline, graduated from Central High School, oft-regarded as the Castle on the Hill, a stately stone edifice given new life as a first-rate apartment complex.

The Depression ended with industrial production for World War II. With air bases being built away from both coasts, Sioux City proved to be an ideal site. Crews trained in B-17, B-24 and B-29 heavy bombers, and thousands of Army Air Corps members were stationed at the Sioux City base.

Today the old air base is home to the 185th Air Refueling Wing of the Iowa Air National Guard. After many millions of dollars in construction at the base, the 185th, formerly a fighter wing, began performing its new mission of air refueling in 2003 as crews switched from F-16 single-seat fighter jets to the four-engine KC-135 tankers.

Following World War II, Sioux City attracted national attention during the polio epidemic of the late 1940s and early 1950s. The city became a testing site for various experiments to rid the nation of the dread disease. In 1952, legendary

Mary Queen of Peace statue at Trinity Heights. (Photo by Jim Lee)

THE SGT. FLOYD MONUMENT

Sioux City IOWA

entertainer Bob Hope visited Sioux City for a benefit show to help polio victims.

On a lighter note came Sioux City Sue, who's hair is red and eyes are blue. She was 19-year-old Gayle Jean Hofstad. After the song "Sioux City Sue" became a hit, the Chamber of Commerce held a contest to find a real Sioux City Sue, and in 1946, thousands of girls went to the Grandview Park Bandshell in hope of winning the title ... which went to Gayle Jean.

While the economy remained relatively strong in the immediate postwar period, major changes occurred in the meatpacking industry. During the 1960s, Iowa Beef Processors (later known as IBP, then Tyson Foods) moved its operation across the river to Dakota City, Neb. IBP used trucks rather than railcars to move its products and it marketed "boxed beef" to outlets throughout the nation. The growth of IBP, however, eventually helped to bring about the demise of the Sioux City Stockyards.

James F. Booge (1833-1911) is regarded as the founder of Sioux City's meatpacking industry. After purchasing a steamboat's water-soaked cargo of wheat, which he salvaged by feeding to a herd of hogs, he later butchered the hogs and shipped them upriver to U.S. Army posts. The profits from these meatpacking experiments led to construction downtown of a three-story brick slaughterhouse, Sioux City's first significant packing plant.

That building later served as the first home of Chesterman and Barrow Bottling Works. The Chesterman Company, Sioux City's oldest bottler, continues in business today in a spacious building complex south of Singing Hills.

Demand for increased production capacity, meanwhile, forced Booge to relocate and expand to a 10-acre site in Sioux City's South

The Anderson Dance Pavillion in Sioux City's Chris Larsen Park hosts many community events. (Photo by Tim Hynds)

STONE STATE PARK

SIOUX CITY CONVENTION CENTER

Sioux City IOWA

Bottoms. By 1884, the James E. Booge & Sons Packing Company was advertising a daily slaughter of 2,500 hogs, 100 cattle and 100 sheep, with an output of $2.5 million in meat products annually.

Eventually the Sioux City Stockyards, which once served such national giants as Swift, Armour and Cudahy's, declined and went out of business.

John Morrell & Co. still maintains a strong presence in the Yards with its pork plant. And Smithfield Foods recently announced that Curly Foods, a Morrell subsidiary, plans to add 120 jobs over the next three years as part of a $25.7 million expansion to its Sioux City facility in the Yards.

Other firms have expressed interest in locating business in the Yards.

Transportation for Sioux City changed greatly in the postwar years. The Army Corps of Engineers built a system of lakes and dams on the Missouri River straightening the many bends and creating a channel for seasonal barge traffic. The federal government also constructed the north-south Interstate 29 through town.

Sioux City has had its share of floods, fires, blizzards, heat waves and tornadoes over the years, but none of these calamities topped in

TRAGEDY

degree the great Floyd River Flood of 1953, which came on the heels of the Missouri River Flood of 1952. When the Floyd River topped its banks, it drove thousands of people from their homes and businesses, leaving millions of dollars of property damage in its wake. Such flooding influenced the Corps of Engineers in its efforts to straighten the Missouri River. Similar channel improvements were made to the Floyd River and, more recently, to Perry Creek,

The Spirit of Siouxland monument in Sioux City's Chris Larsen Park is dedicated to Siouxland's efforts in the wake of the crash of United flight 232. (Photo by Tim Hynds)

Castle on the Hill once served as Central High School. Today, it's an apartment complex. (Photo by Jim Lee)

Sioux City, IOWA

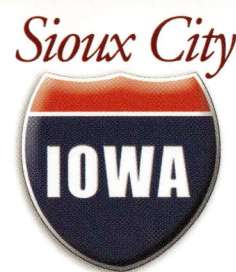

thus taming the last natural waterway through Sioux City.

Never was the Heart of Siouxland beating stronger than on July 19, 1989 when a crippled DC-10 aircraft carrying 296 people was forced to attempt an emergency landing at Sioux Gateway Airport. Though the airport and community were well prepared for an emergency, Sioux Gateway was never meant to handle such a large airplane. But it was Flight 232's best, perhaps only, chance for survival. The jumbo jet en route from Denver to Philadelpia via Chicago was barely controllable following an engine assembly explosion. As the plane appeared, miraculously, to be touching down, the DC-10's right wing tip gouged the earth and the plane burst into a fiery ball as it cartwheeled off the runway into a cornfield, breaking into three parts.

MIRACLE

Ultimately, 112 people died. Yet in what seemed to be a miracle, 184 people survived, thanks in large part to the skillful, compassionate care from a team consisting of city professionals, volunteers from surrounding communities and Sioux City's two medical centers, St. Luke's Regional Medical Center and Mercy (then Marian) Medical Center-Sioux City.

National honors and awards were heaped on Sioux City and its neighboring communities for their professionalism, preparedness and humanity in the crash response. The national media recounted the Sioux City "miracle in a cornfield." And a television movie dramatized the rescue efforts. Much of the film was shot on location, bringing to town such

SIOUXLAND REGIONAL CANCER CENTER

Sioux City

The Rose Garden at Sioux City's Grandview Park was renovated in 2003 (Photo by Jim Lee)

Hollywood legends as Charlton Heston and James Coburn. Within one year, Sioux City was proclaimed, for the second time in its history, an All-America City.

The attention and accolades came as Sioux City was capping a decade of change—its previous claim to fame being as the birthplace of the Friedman sisters and of Fred Grandy, the former "Gopher" of TV's "Love Boat" who was elected Iowa's 6th District congressman in 1986. The community had weathered the economic blows and civic pessimism of the 1970s and early 1980s to redefine itself as the hub of that rising tri-state region known as Siouxland.

A new company, Gateway 2000, excelled in the personal computer manufacturing industry and still maintains a strong presence in North Sioux City, S.D. and Dakota Dunes, a 2,000-acre, $300 million planned community along the Missouri River, also just across border from Sioux City in South Dakota, fulfilled its promise through population growth and job creation, providing a needed boost for Siouxland.

Today, the service only gets better at those medical centers which earned headline praise for their compassionate work following the crash of Flight 232.

St. Luke's recently completed a major expansion. A $31 million construction project created Physician Center Two, home to the busy Same Day Surgery Center, St. Luke's Imaging and Breast Screening Center and a half-dozen physicians' clinics.

Mercy, meanwhile, continued to unveil numerous medical firsts and clinical innovations for Siouxland.

The new six-story

Sioux City's Tyson Events Center was completed in 2003. (Photo by Tim Hynds)

Sioux City IOWA

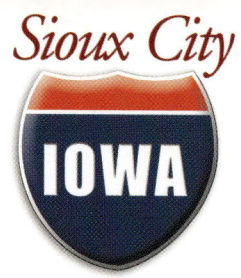

Mercy Heart Center makes it possible for area residents to continue receiving world-class cardiovascular care close to home.

For the good of the community, the two hospitals joined forces in 1995 for an especially worthy joint venture, the Siouxland Regional Cancer Center, which offers a full range of comprehensive services at a downtown location.

Visitors to Sioux City today will also find a wide variety of entertainment and cultural opportunities, historic monuments and museums, a world-class art center, the new Mlr Tym Marina on the Missouri RIver, sporting events and a riverboat casino, Argosy Casino-Sioux City, that just keeps getting bigger.

The Argosy Casino-Sioux City brought a new form of entertainment and an economic boost to Sioux City. (Photo by Tim Hynds)

Sioux City Bandits, semi-professional hockey and football teams, respectively, are enjoying their new home, the Gateway Arena in the recently completed Tyson Events Center, a $53 million structure that also has played host to such entertainment events as Alan Jackson, Smuckers Stars on Ice, Fleetwood Mac, Cher and Aerosmith.

It stands adjacent to the venerable Municipal Auditorium which is getting a $12.5 million face-lift to enable it to become home to a variety of recreation programs.

Meanwhile, the Sioux City Explorers are playing semi-professional baseball at Lewis and Clark Park, a classy ballpark built in 1993 for the X's, whose popularity helped open up the commercial development along nearby Singing Hills Boulevard. The nearby IBP Ice Center and the Sioux City Convention Center downtown also cater to the needs of the Sioux City Musketeers and the

The Sgt. Floyd riverboat museum in Sioux City's Chris Larsen Park also serves as an Iowa Welcome Center. (Photo by Tim Hynds)

A Statue at Sioux Gateway Airport (Photo by Jim Lee)

226

Sioux City

Siouxland visitors, helping to make Sioux City a convention mecca over the past decade.

The metro area, which includes South Sioux City, Neb., also boasts a number of other parks and sports complexes that provide soccer, baseball and softball fields and several first-rate golf courses. Education is not neglected in Sioux City, with a first-rate public school system that boasts three high schools and is complemented by a variety of faith-based schools and early childhood centers. Beyond high school, students can matriculate at Morningside College or Briar Cliff University or perhaps Western Iowa Tech Community College.

Churches of every faith can be found in the metro area, and a synagogue and mosque are available for Sioux City's Jewish and Muslim communities. One of the city's top tourist attractions is the faith-based Trinity Heights which offers a museum and learning center amidst 30-foot statues of the Sacred Heart of Jesus and Mary Queen of Peace.

For entertainment, Sioux City has a new theater complex anchoring Historic Fourth Street downtown in addition to the multiplex found at the always-bustling Southern Hills Mall, the city's largest but not only mall. The Marketplace

A monument to three Presbyterian ministers is located on Prospect Hill (Photo by Tim Hynds)

Shopping Center on the city's north side has completed a major rebuilding project. And a major shopping center is being built in southeast Morningside that will bring Kohl's and Best Buy to town. The luxuriously restored Orpheum Theatre, with a $9.5 million price tag, has played host to world-class entertainers, from Ray Charles to Bill Cosby and Sheryl Crow, touring Broadway productions and regular appearances by the Sioux City Symphony.

The Sioux City Community Theatre is approaching its 60th

HISTORIC FOURTH STREET

Sioux City

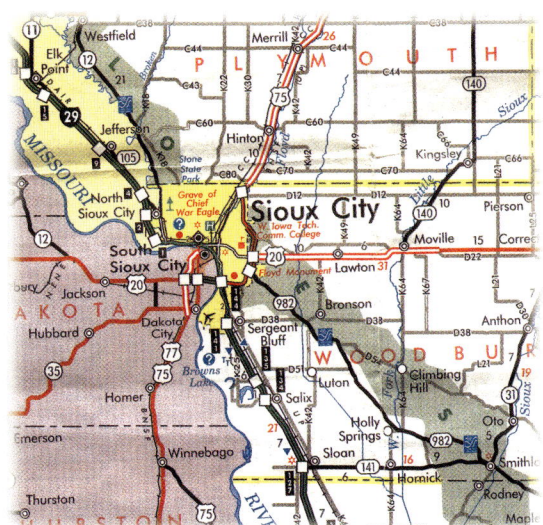

LEARN MORE

Sioux City is located in northwest Iowa at the junction of three states: South Dakota, Nebraska and Iowa.

For more information, go to websites:
www.siouxcityjournal.com
www.sioux-city.org
www.siouxland.net

STORY CONTRIBUTOR

John Quinlan

---

year of existence, and Lamb Productions recently celebrated its 25th season of theatrical productions in what was once a schoolhouse.

Mixing culture with entertainment is the Sioux City Lewis and Clark Interpretive Center, located on the riverfront, in which visitors become active participants in a day in the life of the explorers.

Helping to get people from one place to another in Sioux City is the new $11.6 million transportation center downtown, the Martin Luther King Jr. Transit Center.

Economic development efforts continue to reap dividends in the area, with such stalwarts as Sue Bee Honey, Jolly Time Popcorn, Palmer Candy Company, Sioux Tools, Gelita North America, Diosynth, Prince Manufacturing and other companies maintaining their strong presence.

"I believe one of the greatest things about Sioux City is definitely its people," popular Mayor Dave Ferris said, "the willingness of so many groups to work together to make it a place on the move." Another prominent civic leader, Briar Cliff University President Beverly Wharton, said the people and the community's amenities make Sioux City unbeatable.

"Because we are blessed to have civic and community leaders who are committed to continued growth, I believe Sioux City will continue to flourish."

MORNINGSIDE COLLEGE

Pride In Our Hometowns.

P·O·R·T·R·A·I·T·S
OF
Spencer

GATEWAY TO THE IOWA GREAT LAKES

Spencer offers the best of small town living combined with the conveniences of its position as the region's shopping and entertainment hub.

Spencer wasn't the first place settlers stopped in Clay County on their westward trek through Iowa. In 1855, the first settlers discovered the fertile, northwest Iowa terrain as a good place to lay their claims and make their homes. However, most of those early homesteaders located themselves in the southwest corner of the county, near Peterson. The rolling hills of that corner of the county made travel difficult, so in 1871, Spencer replaced Peterson as the county seat for Clay County.

Today, Spencer continues to lure those in search of the good life. Broad shaded boulevards are a hallmark of the community, as is the friendly nature of its inhabitants.

World class? You bet. From its "world's greatest county fair," the Clay County Fair, to its cutting edge business and industry, Spencer balances its rural history with an eye to the future.

SPENCER

Pride In Our Hometowns.

P·O·R·T·R·A·I·T·S
OF *Spencer*

GATEWAY TO THE IOWA GREAT LAKES

Young and old get into the Flagfest spirit.

A Snapshot

Spencer's beginnings are rooted in the eternal urge of mankind to discover, to spread out and to stake a claim to newly-settled frontiers. In 1859, George E. Spencer, who had lived in Iowa before serving as U.S. Senator from Alabama from 1868-1879 gave his name to the city of Spencer. In less than a year, the settlement grew from 300 people to a bustling town of 1,000.

The first schoolhouse was built in 1866 and the town of Spencer was platted in 1871 and incorporated in 1880 with a population of 884. A small business district that clustered around the depot in the beginning, grew south to the Little Sioux River by early in the 20th century and now has spread along Grand Avenue to both the north and south and includes modern shopping districts and broad, tree-lined streets. The first railroad, the Chicago, Milwaukee and St. Paul, was built in 1878, soon followed by the Minneapolis and St. Louis Railroad. Spencer escaped one of the region's most infamous events, the Spirit Lake massacre, due to a blizzard sweeping over Spencer at the time, forcing the rampaging Indians to pass up the settlement and instead focus its force on the Iowa Great Lakes.

The hardships of the pioneers were to be repeated

Left: Visitors are welcomed to the south end of Spencer by a pair of massive welcoming signs and flower beds.
Right: A recent downtown streetscape renovation captures the Art Deco vibe of the downtown businesses, while also improving the infrastructure of the area.

230

Spencer IOWA

Spencer residents take seriously the community's label as "Flag City of Iowa."

many times over the years. With an early economy rooted in the land, the droughts and ravages by insects were trials the early settlers bore bravely. The famous Clay County Fair has its roots in early Spencer. The Clay County Agricultural Society was organized in 1879 and in 1917, the Clay County Fair Association was formed.

The very first Clay County Fair was held even before that, in 1871. The first fair featured livestock exhibitions and culinary arts programs. For entertainment, there were running races with horses and riders from Sioux Rapids, Peterson and Emmetsburg.

In the years following that first fair, the grasshoppers came and ruined the crops, almost forcing the early settlers to leave the new community. This took its toll on the fair as well, and the next mention of a fair was in 1879, when the Clay County Agriculture Board hosted its event. That fair was located on 30 acres of land northeast of Spencer. The early fairs featured some of the same events and activities of today –livestock shows, exhibits of canned goods and textiles, floral arrangements and farm implement displays.

The first of the "modern" Clay County Fairs was held in 1918 on ground newly purchased by the Clay County Board of Supervisors. That original landstake is still a part of today's fairgrounds.

Today, the Clay County Fair is heralded as one of the largest county fairs in the world, with the added attraction of being one of its most rural-oriented fairs. The implement displays outshine the vast majority of the state fairs in the country, while the grandstand shows rival any large city. Over the years, entertainers like Bob Hope, Johnny Cash and Red Skelton have appeared. Recent years' headliners include Garth Brooks, Martina McBride and Vince Gil among the many favorites. From the original tract of 40 acres, the fairgrounds have grown to over 261 acres. A campground with electrical hookups

The Clay County Fair is heralded as the "Greatest County Fair" in the country, and is one of the nation's largest. The nine-day extravaganza in September draws crowds of over 300,000.

Thunder Bridge is a Spencer landmark, located on the west edge of town, the iron span bridge is lit up with white lights, adding a festive note to the holiday season.

Spencer IOWA

becomes a small city of its own during the fair, as visitors make annual pilgrimages to the site. In 2003, the Clay County Fairgrounds became home to a center aimed at playing host to the region's major activities – the Clay Regional Events Center.

Truly a "community" center, the $4 million, 50,000 square foot facility was supported through donations from individuals and businesses, the support of the city, Spencer Municipal Utilities and county and the infusion of funds from the Community Attractions and Tourism (CAT) grant, a statewide program aimed at supporting the tourism industry in Iowa. The grand opening in November, 2003 showed the area's residents the wide array of uses of the facility, from business meetings and retreats to wedding receptions to large trade shows and expos. Bill Orrison, chairman of the center's advisory committee, expressed the feelings of many in the community about the center. "The Clay County Regional Event Center is the result of a spirit of cooperation with the Clay County Fair Board, the Spencer City Council, and the Clay County Government. This joint effort of these organizations will help benefit all citizens of northwest Iowa."

The center is tied to the community's history not just in its location at the Clay County Fairgrounds, but by its architectural style as well. While cutting-edge in technology and materials, its modern design also pays homage to the fairgrounds' iconic front gates and repeating arches motif. In its first year of operation, the Clay Regional Events Center has shown its worth, truly being a gathering spot for the region. No

Shoppers seeking bargains head to Spencer in mid-summer for the annual Crazy Days event.

The Flagfest parade in June features participants in all modes of transportation.

CLAY COUNTY FAIR

Spencer IOWA

The Miracle on Fourth Street playground at East Leach Park is a child's paradise. The Spencer Family Aquatic Center, built in 1997, features water slides, a zero-depth pool and sand volleyball courts.

history of Spencer could be discussed without a nod to its darkest day, June 27, 1931. On that hot, windy day, two small boys were in Otto Bjornstad's Drug Store. One of the boys lighted a sparkler – someone screamed, and the boy dropped the sparkler into a large display of fireworks.

The fire spread quickly and the main street was soon ablaze. Like lava from a burning volcano, the paving on Main Street (now Grand Avenue) heaved and boiled. Fire trucks from nine surrounding towns joined the Spencer squad, but water was inadequate. The fire chief from Des Moines arrived by plane, bringing explosives, which were used to blast a fire barrier. At the end of that long day, about 50 downtown businesses were destroyed, valued at about $2 million.

The great pioneering spirit of the residents was now revealed. Business was conducted in temporary metal buildings in the streets while the downtown was rebuilt. With the Depression going on, this type of wholesale reconstruction was a testament to the will of the residents.

Today, Spencer is blessed with the unique Art Deco-styled downtown, the largest of its kind in the Midwest. Architectural buffs from all over the nation travel to Spencer to study and enjoy its unique downtown architecture and learn that the community offers a unique type of friendliness and service that is lacking in so many larger metropolitan areas. The jewel of a downtown is supported by a strong central business district, and an organization aimed at keeping it vital. Spencer is a member of the MainStreet Iowa Program, dedicated to preserving and supporting its Main Street businesses. Spencer MainStreet is very active, with several highly-anticipated special events going on throughout the year, including the "Thanks with Franks" promotion and the Grand Meander in December. The arts take center stage as well with Arts on

Spencer residents enjoy their proximity to the wide array of recreational opportunities at the Iowa Great Lakes, located just north of Spencer in Dickinson County.

The Spencer Community Theatre is known for its high quality productions, featuring actors from around the region.

233

Spencer, IOWA

Grand.

Arts on Grand is a facility on Spencer's main street operated by the Spencer Area Arts Council – a non-profit organization funded through memberships, fundraisers and local grants.

The facility offers an exhibit gallery, gift gallery featuring original artworks by local artists, pottery and painting studios. It hosts unique evening events ranging from artist receptions to performances by musical groups.

Classes, workshops and educational programs are offered for artists of all ages throughout the year and are open to members and non-members. Exhibits rotate every five to six weeks and range from work created by local and regional artists to traveling exhibits from all around the country. Classes for children are held on afternoons or days when school is not in session, while adults enjoy evening and weekend classes.

ART & PARKS

How about theatre?

Housed in a renovated grocer's warehouse, dubbed the "Best Little Warehouse," in Spencer, the SCT Playhouse offers quality community theatre experiences for people of all ages.

After over 45 years, Northwest Iowa's award-winning theatre just keeps getting better.

The children's theatre, which recently celebrated a decade in existence, allows youth to experience the thrill of the theatre experience, with the young people both acting on stage and performing the myriad of jobs necessary backstage as well. An extensive array of summer classes and events make for a busy summer for the organizers and youth in the children's theatre program.

SPENCER COMMUNITY THEATER

Spencer IOWA

Looking to the past.

Visitors can step back in time with a visit to the Parker Historical Museum of Clay County. The museum collects and preserves Clay County history and heritage in a 1916 Arts and Crafts period house and the adjacent Duroe Building next door.

The artifacts in the museum's permanent collection date primarily from 1860-1950 and include a rosewood piano, Victorian organ, observatory time clock, 1918 LaFrance fire truck, vintage clothing, china and agricultural tools.

In 2003, the museum expanded its business office into an adjacent vintage home, freeing up exhibit space in the Parker Museum.

> *Buena Vista University's Lakes and Prairie Center, at the Gateway North Center in Spencer, allows residents to seek their four-year degrees close to home.*

> *The Parker Historical Society makes its home in the Parker Museum, an exquisite example of Craftsman architecture.*

Want Recreation?

The Spencer Parks and Recreation Department maintains a wide array of outdoor venues for those wanting to enjoy some time with Mother Nature.

Fourteen parks, including East and West Leach Parks, which form the gathering place for many of the community's outdoor activities, make up the Spencer park system.

East Leach Park features one of the region's most extensive and well-utilized skate parks as well as an array of picnic shelters and a large children's play area.

The Spencer recreational trail system is continually being expanded, and winds its way through the entire community, linking all its parks and recreation areas.

Water Fun

Constructed in 1997, the Spencer Family Aquatic Center offers fun for young and old. The two-acre complex contains two water slides, a children's play area, sand volleyball, five lanes for lap swimming and plenty of lounge chairs for recreation.

A "zero depth" pool, the complex offers plenty of fun water games for the young, combined with the spills and thrills of the exciting water slides.

Is golf your game?

Then you're in luck in Spencer. With two 18-hole courses within the community and 18 more within 30 miles, the golfer is in paradise in

> *The Spencer community worked together on the public art piece, "The Gathering," located in East Leach Park.*

235

Spencer IOWA

The Spencer Municipal Golf Course is a par 72, 6,809-yard course, featuring watered fairways and four sets of tees. The full-length driving range is a new feature of the course, and can accommodate 12-15 golfers, allowing them to practice all aspects of their game, either from the tee box, a practice green or sand bunker.

The clubhouse features a snack shop/lounge and a pro shop.

The Spencer Golf and Country Club also features an 18-hole, par 72 layout.

It has been rated one of Iowa's top 10 courses consistently over the years. The pro shop can fix up the golfer with any manner of attire and clubs, while the clubhouse and lounge offer excellent dining with a beautiful view of the course.

The Spencer Golf and Country Club also plays host to the Northwest Amateur Golf Tournament, a 72-hole tradition.

The event hosts over 385 golfers from 13 states and has been a part of northwest Iowa life since 1921.

The tournament isn't just a Spencer tradition – it's a family tradition for many. Multiple generations of Midwest families gather in Spencer every year for the tournament, a great chance to catch up with one another and with fellow golfers.

Y Not?

Two pools, multiple gyms, a wide array of programming, dedicated staff aimed at helping every visitor have a great experience. That's the Spencer Family Y. The Y provides a wide array of athletic programming, from a large youth swimming program to adult aerobics and league play opportunities in a range of sports.

With well-trained staff dedicated to ensuring a positive workout experience, the Y is Spencer's healthy and fun center.

A fitness center, featuring a newly-remodeled whirlpool is just one of the ammenities of the Spencer Family YMCA.

The Northwest Amateur golf tournament is a tradition of over eight decades for golfers from throughout the Midwest. The tourney, held at the Spencer Golf and Country Club, is one of the largest amateur tournaments in the state.

Youth enjoy Spencer's state-of-the-art skatepark, located in East Leach Park.

Taking to the air

The Northwest Iowa Regional Airport, established in 1942, boasts a 6,000 main runway with an approach lighting system and MALSR/REIL's. The crosswind runway is 5,100 feet.
The airport is maintained by the city of Spencer and managed by the Fixed Base Operator, Leading Edge Aviation. That company provides all aviation services, including 100 LL and Jet A fuel, a fleet of aircraft for air charter, aircraft rental/flight instruction, aircraft maintenance, hangar rental and towing of aircraft.

The Northwest Iowa Regional Airport is home to the annual Spencer Flagfest Flight Breakfast and Air Show in mid-June every year.

Taking care of business

Southpark Mall draws shoppers with its climate controlled comfort and variety of shops.

Spencer is home to a thriving business and retail economy. While nestled amidst the corn and soybean fields of northwest Iowa, the community is also home to an impressive array of industry, including international corporations like Eaton Corporation and home-grown success stories such as Simonson's Iron Works and Tecton. While these companies got their start locally, their operations now reach customers globally. Business is supported by the Spencer Area Chamber of Commerce and the Iowa Great Lakes Corridor of Opportunity, in cooperation with the Spencer Industrial Development Corporation.

Retail magnet

Spencer has long been the retail trade center of northwest Iowa, and it lives up to that reputation with a varied offering of retail outlets. Its downtown plays host to shops including men's and women's clothing, giftware, jewelry and décor. At the south end of Spencer, Southpark Mall has been a shopping magnet since 1981. In 2004, the mall welcomed the Southpark 7 theatres, offering movie-goers the most high-tech film-viewing experience.

Healthy living

The Spencer Hospital, undergoing a $20 million expansion program in 2004, offers area

The Spencer Family Aquatic Center offers wet and wild fun for young and old.

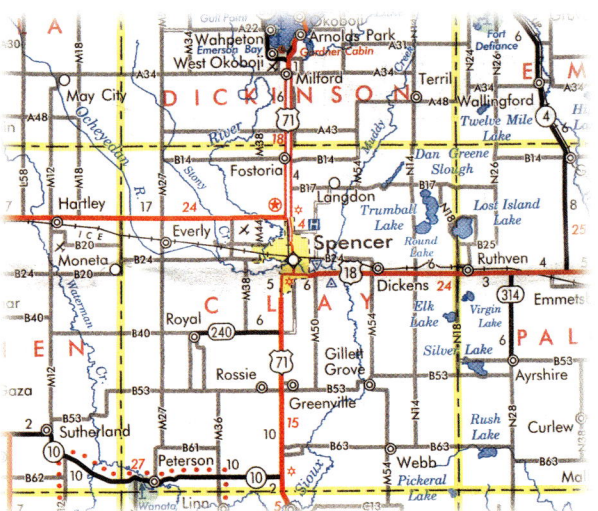

Learn More

Spencer is located at the junction of US Highways 18 and 71 in northwest Iowa, just 20 minutes south of the Iowa Great Lakes.

The Northwest Iowa Regional Airport is a designated Enhanced Service facility, able to handle almost any general aviation use.

For more information, contact the Spencer Area Chamber of Commerce at (712) 262-5860, or online at: www.spenceriowachamber.org/

Story Contributor

Paula Buenger is Publisher of Northwest Iowa Publishing, Inc., which publishes the Spencer Daily Reporter, Storm Lake Pilot Tribune and Dickinson County News.

A Spencer native, she lives on an acreage just outside Spencer with her husband and son Drew.

residents the most up-to-date medical equipment and technology, coupled with the small-town care that comes from its location in rural Iowa. Complete cancer care is available at the Abben Cancer Center and dialysis patients can be treated locally at the Warner Dialysis Center. The latest expansion will create a new inpatient and outpatient surgery center and will allow the hospital to expand its services further.

Add to all the amenities Spencer offers the excellent educational opportunities provided by the Spencer Community School District, home of the Tigers, the Spencer center of Iowa Lakes Community College and Buena Vista University's Lakes and Prairie Center.

A community built on the strong backs of visionary settlers, nurtured through good times and bad by leaders with foresight and ambition as strong as the prairie winds, Spencer has proven that a little bit of heaven can be found on the prairies of northwest Iowa.

Pride In Our Hometowns.

P·O·R·T·R·A·I·T·S
OF
Storm Lake

STORM LAKE

ALWAYS "THE CITY BEAUTIFUL"

*It's the first question a visitor asks.
How on earth did such a pretty, tranquil place get such an angry name?
The locals are happy to tell the tale.
Legend has it that long before the first settlers saw this place, two fueding bands of Native Americans were camped on opposite sides of the lake. The bravest young warrior of one band, and the beautiful daughter of the leader of the other, fell in love. Their respective tribes refused to allow them to see each other, so they made a pact: one dark night when the moon was full and at its highest in the sky, each would steal away from their camp, and they would paddle out to the center of the lake to meet - never again to be parted.*

Pride In Our Hometowns.

P·O·R·T·R·A·I·T·S
OF *Storm Lake*

The Storm Lake parks are full of life, and you might want to keep an eye on your picnic.

ALWAYS "THE CITY BEAUTIFUL"

Storm Lake features the state's largest volunteer driven anti-extinction program for rare trumpeter swans. Here, a mother bird guards her newly-hatched cygnet with care. The main Swan Pond located on Highway 71 north of Storm Lake, where an observation deck and information kiosk allow visitors to learn about the graceful bird is North America's largest.

According to the story, as the two made their way toward each other, a fierce storm blew up, and capsized both of their dugouts, and neither was ever seen again. Both bands of Native Americans were heartbroken at the loss, and blamed the treacherous lake. They called it "The Lake of Storms," and left it behind, never to return.

Just a legend? Yes, but an archealogical crew not long ago came across the site of a prehistoric encampment, on a rise overlooking the lake, which had been abandoned after a short time.

Historians, who tend to take the fun out of such things, insist that the real story of the naming is much less romantic - an early surveying crew encountered a rough trapper when they arrived at the shore of the lake, and invited him to do the honors of naming it for their maps. The traveler, whose name has long since been forgotten

A SNAPSHOT

to time, decided to sleep on the issue and promised an answer in the morning. When a gale blew up overnight and collapsed the traveler's tent, he had his soggy inspiration.

No matter how the place got its name, its reputation is anything but stormy, and both our romantic tribal couple and that old trapper of the history books would certainly be amazed.

Today, Storm Lake is one of Iowa's favorite family attractions, with its sparkling glacial lake, an emerald necklace of public parks surrounding

A massive lighthouse complete with ligthing and landscaping resembling a seascape, serves as a gateway to the Storm Lake community from Highway 71.

Storm Lake IOWA

the water, an impressive campus hosting one of the state's leading private universities, winding walking/biking trails, countless cultural events from theater to art galleries, two major golf courses, museums, celebrations of the city's ethnic diversity, a vital shopping village, and the list goes on.

The Buena Vista Community Theater puts on elaborate annual musicals and traveling shows. Shannon Geisinger reflects on her role as "Maria" in a hit run of the classic "West Side Story" for summer 2004.

It is low-key and relaxing, and although the lake hosts 170,000 visitors each year, it is never a high-crowd, high-traffic tourist trap.

Always an attraction from the days of stagecoach travel and Chautauqua shows, Storm Lake soon became known for its fun appeal. The Casino Beach area once boasted an early bowling alley, Mirror Ballroom, baseball park where the great Satchel Paige is said to have played, hotel and tennis facility, merry-go-round and midway - all reached only by boat. The Cobblestone big band ballroom featured rollerdrome skating, rides, a monkey cage and lakefront bathhouse. Semi pro and barnstorming baseball teams attracted big crowds to two major ballparks, and huge toboggan-style waterslides into the lake made for summer fun.

The city now lures thousands of boaters, campers and recreation lovers to its shores, historical sites, cultural attractions and community events all year around.

The area has a summer-long schedule of automobile racing, a large county fair, Iowa's largest Independence Day celebration for nearly 30 years known as the Star Spangled Spectacular, a Labor Day celebration in the parks, and special shows for bridal, home and farm, a sanctioned marathon run, farmers markets, a Relay for Life to fight cancer, the university homecoming celebration

Hot air balloons in flight over Storm Lake. The city hosted the Great Iowa Balloon Races for many years, and is still home to several balloon pilots. A DARE student flight is an annual event.

Storm Lake

and much more.

The lake has plenty to offer with plentiful boat ramps, two full-service marinas, miles of public access, plenty of public docks and beach areas It is known for the state's best walleye fishing, and also yields plenty of nice catfish and bass.

Eco-tourism is a growing industry, with the opening of one of the country's largest "green energy" windfarms stretching accros the county. Visitors can follow a special windfarm route by car or bike, starting just a few minutes ride from the city's park system.

Since shortly after 2000, Storm Lake been undergoing one of the largest public dredging operations in Iowa history, with the community beginning operations of its own dredge and crew in 2003. The project is considered a blueprint for community water quality activism.

In the planning stages as of this writing is a new $28 million park system that would feature a large lodge hotel in the style of the great western national parks, a huge aquatic center with indoor/outdoor pools and special rides, a new beach complete with a lighthouse and colored water jet fountain, a million-dollar playground for all ages, one of the finest nature interpretive centers in Mid-America nestled into a wetland preserve.

Other projects include a $26 million cutting-edge Science Center on the campus of Buena Vista University completed in fall of 2004, complete with exhibits sure to pique the curiosity of students and visitors alike.

Coming for the future are a proposed new golf course housing development; a new state park to encompass the nature-rich Casino Beach area of the lakefront; a new community-wide elementary school under discussion, a new student center at Buena Vista

The Storm Lake Organization of Boaters and Sailors - yes, the SLOBS - put on an exciting Storm Lake Regatta each year that draws catamaran competitors from several states.

Artists Alley is one of the region's top shows for artisans and craftspeople from all over the midwest, set in the shady scenery of Sunset Park with its winding walks and comfortable benches. Anne Wangui Ferguson, creator of African art and jewelry, is one of the scores of talented people who return each year.

Storm Lake IOWA

University; and hopes for restoring a former train depot and a vacant former ballroom into community showplaces once again.

The ambitious visions of today spring smoothly from the storied past of the community.

Long known to Native Americans dating back to the Mill Creek culture that perhaps lived in the area as early as 1100 A.D., the first pioneer settlers around 1855 found Storm Lake to be an oasis in a sea of waving prairie grass. After seeing it, many westward travelers chose to stay on, and the county's meager population of just 60 in 1860 ballooned to well over 1,600 in the next ten years. Population for the Storm Lake area is now estimated at near 12,000.

Fires have played a part in Storm Lake history, with the burning of Old Main at Buena Vista College as a key moment in the city's past. With a tradition of long-serving fire chiefs, the city has seen only seven men hold the job since 1881.

Timber was scarce, and the initial homes in the area were often constructed of sod - including the original county courthouse.

In 1878, Storm Lake won a long battle to take over as county seat of Buena Vista County, and two teams of horses were taken to claim the safe full of county records from Sioux Rapids. Fearing a fight, the Storm Lakers took along two barrels of apples, and certain other unspecified forms of "refreshment," and no blood was shed.

The area survived record-setting blizzards in 1870 and 1880, several tornadoes, grasshopper plagues, droughts, floods and economic setbacks, but even

...e's a beach in Storm Lake. These youngsters create ... sand castle from the soft sand of Bel Air Beach, a popular stretch of public beach at Lakeside.

The massive "green energy" windfarm is an eco-tourism attraction that surrounds Storm Lake. A driving/biking self-tour route of one of the country's largest renewable energy projects is available.

Storm Lake IOWA

into the new millenium, it proved to be one of the rare rural Iowa communities and school systems to record continued growth.

Interestingly, Storm Lake does not exist on its original location. The town, including a hotel, saloon and post office, is thought to have been established on the south side of the lake. When the Dubuque and Sioux City Railroad came through, the town basically moved across the lake to grow in a crescent around the bosom of its lakefront, and the original site was known for a time as "Old Town." No evidence of the original settlement exists today.

A Civil War veteran named Colonel W. Vestel established the first newspaper in Storm Lake in 1870, the Pilot, and today the Pilot-Tribune is one of the longest newspapers in continuous publication in Iowa. The newspaper has won well over 150 major regional, state, national and international awards for excellence in journalism since 1990, including the "Take Pride in America" Presidentail Media Award presented by President George Bush in a ceremony at the White House.

Buena Vista College dates to 1891 in Storm Lake, springing from a previous Fort Dodge Institute. A number of cities tried to attact the campus when it left Fort Dodge, but Storm Lake won out due to its lovely location and enthusiastic support for higher education. In its early years, the school survived an empty treasury and threats from the faculty to resign if they were not paid. In recent years, the university has had many millions of dollars in a successful endowment, has built innovative new buildings and added several residential halls to handle record-breaking enrollments. With the addition of graduate programs in education, the "college" became a "university." It has been a leader in technology as it became the first fully "wireless" electronic campus in the nation, and provided every student with an

The proposed Little Storm Lake Wetland Interpretive Center as shown in an architect's rendering in 2004. The multi-million-dollar nature center is designed as part of Project AWAYSIS, to feature informative and interactive exhibits, a theater, classrooms, wetland boardwalk and more.

Asian dancers based in Storm Lake perform at Diversity Day, an event to celebrate Storm Lake's multi-cultural appeal.

Storm Lake, IOWA

Do history old-school style in Storm Lake, which features a large museum with an indoor turn-of-the-century Main Street, an original pioneer prairie log home, and the Elk Center one-room schoolhouse, where elementary children come to hold classes each year just as they were done in the 1800s.

integrated laptop computer. The campus has been cited repeatedly as one of the finest educational investments by the leading university rating publications in the nation, and now has learning centers spread across the state.

With the university comes a busy schedule of collegiate sporting events, cutting-edge speakers and nationally-known performers, providing event more options for Storm Lakers and visitors to take in.

Storm Lake is also home to highly-regarded public schools as well as St. Mary's Catholic and Concordia Lutheran schools. It features before-and-after school programs, an alternative high school, a large day care program and a successful campus for Iowa Central Community College.

Storm Lake is also a hub of health care with a thriving medical center, two clinics, surgical paractices, dialysis center, sports rehabilitation center, fitness and health center, and many medical specialty firms. The most recent addition was a massive, multi-million-dollar Center for Women's Health that provides family medical care, education, and prevention programs along with a lending library.

Storm Lake has had its brushes with fame throughout its history. Early on, luminaries like evangelist Billy Sunday, Booker T. Washington, William Howard Taft, James Whitcomb Riley and poet William Jennings Bryant - who was slightly injured in a buggy accident en route to his appearance - graced the

A Latina dancer whips through an energetic routine at the big community celebration of Cinco de Mayo.

Children cheer on jet-ski racers at the Frank Starr Park cove in Storm Lake.

245

Storm Lake, Iowa

Chautauqua stage. Drama stars like Storm Lake's own Sweet Company, staged elaborate productions in the resort city. Vaudevillians including Jack Benny in 1911 played the New World Theater.

Not all of the area's guests were so respected. Legend has it that Jesse James and his gang were spotted in the area, and there are still some relatives of the James family living in the area today. The Bonnie and Clyde gang also made a stop in the city in 1933, stealing license plates that were used in their brutal rampages. The gang robbed a bank at nearby Rembrandt.

The pilot who went down on the ill-fated flight that killed rock music pioneers Buddy Holly, Big Bopper Richardson and Ritchie Valens was a local resident, Roger Peterson, who is memorialized to this day in a local music scholarship.

The Cobblestone Inn attracted a stream of performers from the big band age through the birth of rock 'n' roll. Everyone from Louis Armstrong to Lawrence Welk to Duke Ellington starred there, and in later years, rockers like Jerry Lee Lewis and Tommy Bolin appeared there.

Gene Hackman, the most prolific of Hollywood stars, lived in Storm Lake and attended Storm Lake High School before dropping out of school and lying about his age to join the military.

Many-time best-selling author Marjorie Holmes was a native of Storm Lake, and wrote about the community in glowing terms in some of her books.

Actress Ann Margret and baseball great Bob Feller have served as parade marshalls in Storm Lake. Jesse Jackson has spoken

NOTABLES

There's a great past ahead of you in Storm Lake. Check out a museum complete with an indoor Main Street and a video theater; and visit the Pioneer Heritage Exhibit on the lakefront, with a one-room schoolhouse that hosts actual classes for area schools, an original prairie log home and a pioneer garden.

Storm Lake
IOWA

here, and George H.W. Bush gave addresses here twice, once while serving as vice president and once after leaving the White House.

A freedom lecture series on campus in recent years has attracted the likes of Jimmy Carter, Walter Cronkite, Supreme Court Justice Blackmun and pop scientist Carl Sagan.

Storm Lake has been known as "The World's Hometown," due to its attraction for a rainbow of different cultures and nationalities.

The diversification started in the 1970s, when the community was a leader in resettling Southeast Asian freedom fighter people after the Vietnam War. In the 1990s, large numbers of Spanish-speaking cultures were added to the mix from Mexico, Puerto Rico, Central America. Africans from Somalia and Sudan seeking religious freedom, along with German Mennonites and others made their impact on the mix. Today, about 35 different nations of origin are represented in the city. The diversity is celebrated in the likes of Diversity Day in the school system, International Fairs on campus, a Parade of Nations each July 4th, and shared events such as Cinco de Mayo, Fiesta Latina and Asian New Year.

The city's vast array of churches has grown even as the diversity has taken place, with nearly all of the traditional faiths represented as well as Spanish speaking services and even a small Buddhist temple.

Today, Storm Lake is beaches and shopping, recreation and culture, music and food, diversity and education. It's technology is cutting-edge, its joy for life intoxicating.

The new $26 million Science Center on the campus of Buena Vista University, opened to the public in fall, 2004. It features a "glass beaker" rotunda, a fossil wall tracing the planet's development, cutting-edge labs, a greenhouse that can simulate anything from a rain forest to high desert, and a native prairie plant garden.

Zoo Fun!

The Center for Women at the Buena Vista Regional Medical Center opened in 2003 as a major advancement in family medical care, health education, wellness and prevention.

Storm Lake

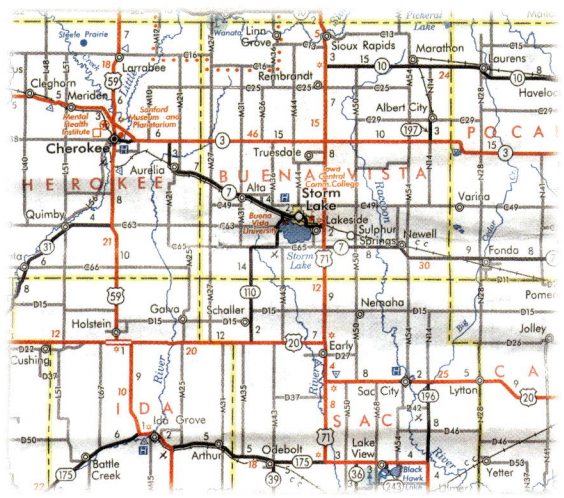

Learn More

Storm Lake is located in northwest Iowa, within three hours of Des Moines, Minneapolis or Omaha. It can be directly accessed by Highway 71 from the north and south, and Highway 7 east and west. Its airport handles small plane traffic.

For information, contact the Storm Lake Chamber of Commerce / Visitors & Convention Bureau at 712-732-3780, or on-line, see www.stormlake.org for a schedule of events, lodging guide and more.

Story Contributor

Dana Larsen is the editor of the Storm Lake Pilot-Tribune and 11-time winner of the Iowa Master Columnist award. He resides in Lakeside with his wife Heidi and children Kathyrn and Christopher.

And at the center of it all, the beautiful 3,000-acre glacier-carved lake still beckons like an oasis.

No one can say if that old tale is true, but only a moonlit night, sometimes young lovers holding hands on their benches beside the shore can almost hear the whispers of a young brave and his princess in the gentle laughter of the colliding waves.

Did You Know

- Storm Lake boasts the country's largest public collection of historic trees in the Living Heritage Tree Museum? One was grown from a seed that traveled to the moon in an astronaut's pocket.
- The new Science Center at Buena Vista University was designed with its glassy rotunda to imitate the classic shape of a laboratory "glass beaker?"
- The city hosts the largest collection of historic Christmas animation figures in the midwest, housed in a Victorian former Carnegie Library, open daily during the holidays and by appointment all year around?
- That in 1871, it was suggested to rename Storm Lake, making the lake "Aegean" and the town "Athens?"
- That the Storm Lake fire department was organized in 1881, and in the 120+ years to follow, only seven men have held the title of fire chief, many serving in excess of 40 years? Historic fires included a prairie burn in 1874 that covered the region from Sac City to Storm Lake; the burning of the showplace Buena Vista Hotel, the destruction of the Nusbaum Sanitarium hospital in 1901, a fire that claimed nearly a block of the area between Lake Avenue and West Fifth Street; and the 1956 blaze that destroyed the landmark Old Main building on the Buena Vista College campus.
- The lakefront statue of "The Little Fisherman," is actually a childhood image of Harold Walter Siebens, the multi-million-dollar benefactor of Buena Vista University, whose ashes were scattered over the lake he so loved?
- The lovely restored Harbor House museum, the oldest surviving home in the city, was once in such disrepair that children considered it a haunted house?
- A clairvoyant in the city's early days was so adept at her skills that authorities used her to locate drowned bodies in the lake?

Pride In Our Hometowns.

P·O·R·T·R·A·I·T·S
OF *Woodbine*

THE BEST IN IOWA SMALL-TOWN LIVING

With a strong commitment to education, a safe environment in which to raise a family and being the home to growing and expanding industries, this small community, named after a flowering vine, is as solid as the historic brick highway that winds through the heart of the community.

Boasting a long and proud heritage, Woodbine, with its population of just under 1,600, is located in the in the heart of the beautiful Loess Hills in the east central portion of Harrison County some 50 miles northeast of the bustling Omaha-Council Bluffs metropolitan area.

WOODBINE

Pride In Our Hometowns.

P·O·R·T·R·A·I·T·S
OF *Woodbine*

THE BEST IN IOWA SMALL-TOWN LIVING

There are a couple time capsules buried on the grounds of the Carnegie Library. This is the site of the centennial time capsule.

Built first as a small trading and grain-processing center and later aided by railroads and the construction of America's first national highway, Woodbine has for decades been a community on the move, slowing but constantly progressing while protecting and preserving the things that really make life important.

One of the first families to settle in Boyer Township in 1849 was Lorenzo and Ann Butler. Mr. Butler is said to have had the first store in the growing settlement. In true frontier fashion, the Post Office was located in the store. Mrs. Butler was the first postmistress and she was allowed to name the office. Remembering the flowering vine that had clambered around the door and windows of her English home, she chose the name "Woodbine." In 1854 a sawmill and corn cracker were built about one mile east of the present town. In 1862 a woolen mill was added, and after the Civil War, a flourmill was built.

A SNAPSHOT

The town of Woodbine was platted in 1866, the same year in which the Chicago Northwestern Railroad began regular runs from Cedar Falls to Council Bluffs. The Illinois Central built its Omaha and Fort Dodge line paralleling the Northwestern in 1899, with passenger service beginning in January of 1900. The Union Pacific also runs through Woodbine. The Illinois Central Building was originally located by the railroad track. As is the case in many Iowa cities whose growth has been closely tied to the railroads that served them, the building has been preserved and relocated to a location known as the "Historical Corridor," which also is home to an Illinois Central caboose. The renovated Illinois Central Freight Depot is one of the last remaining of its kind in America.

But Woodbine is known for more than its railroad ties.

Carl Fisher proposed the Lincoln Highway, the United States' first transcontinental road, in 1912, and the Lincoln Highway Association was organized to promote the establishment of a continuous toll-free highway from the Atlantic to the Pacific Ocean. The highway was to be known, in memory of Abraham Lincoln, as "The Lincoln Highway".

The Woodbine school system boasts an award-winning drama and speech program. Members pictured are, from left to right: John Sullivan, Jim Sullivan, Katie Tremel, Ashley Morrison and Nick Payne.

Woodbine IOWA

Carl Fisher

Carl Fisher proposed the Lincoln Highway, the United States' first transcontinental road, in 1912, and the Lincoln Highway Association was organized to procure the establishment of a continuous toll free highway from the Atlantic to the Pacific Ocean.

History

Most Iowa roads at the time were dirt and, depending on the weather of the moment, either muddy or dusty. Woodbine, not wanting to be left in the mud or clouded in dust, began to act on paving the street. The Lincoln Highway, the segment in Woodbine now called Lincoln Way, runs through the city and is significant as part of the original transcontinental U.S. Highway 30. Woodbine's segment of the highway was bricked in the summer of 1921.

Inflation affects most everything.

In 1921, the cost of a Ford touring car was $450; a 1918 Maxwell touring car with enclosed top went for $250; and a 1917 Ford was $125.

When the Lincoln Highway was built in Woodbine in 1920 and 1921, the cost was a then-whopping $250,000. Some 82 years later, rehabilitating six blocks of that same route required an expenditure of $2.6 million.

The Woodbine leg of the nation's first coast-to-coast highway, also known as U.S. Highway 30, is one of the longest original brick construction sections in existence.

The contract for paving some of the original brick streets was let in late January 1920 - $200,000 for the brick work, plus another $40,000 to $50,000 for curb and gutter construction. The work was completed in June of the following year.

Woodbine's newspaper, The Woodbine Twiner, reported in its June 2, 1921, edition, "About all the cement work is done on the Lincoln Way and a great deal of brick is laid. It should not be many moons until this street is open to traffic."

As the nation's first coast-to-coast transportation route, the Lincoln Highway began in Times Square and ended 3,389 miles to the west at the Pacific Ocean in Lincoln Park in San Francisco.

The highway's advent was a cause for celebration throughout the country.

The Woodbine Twiner, reporting on a 1920 local event, said, "For real enthusiasm, the big country meeting held in the auditorium here Friday evening

White's Floral Garden has been the spot for outdoor wedding ceremonies. A path makes it easy for residents to take a stroll though the garden.

The Believers Training Center is one of seven churches in Woodbine.

Woodbine Iowa

went far ahead of any previous effort in this direction. This meeting was only one of a thousand held the same night from one end of the highway to the other. It was a jollification event, a celebration of the establishment of the national highway, the first in the history of the country.

"Of course, the road is not completed yet. The string of bonfires burning last Friday from the Atlantic to the Pacific, together with feasting and making merry, the eloquent and spontaneous burst of oratory mark the real beginning, rather than the end of this mammoth project. When the golden spike is driven, there will probably be further demonstration."

Lincoln Way's eleven blocks are used as a main thoroughfare for traffic through Woodbine. It is the largest remaining original portion of Lincoln U.S. Highway 30 in Iowa. Picturesque homes of the early 1900's line the brick street. Lincoln Highway

Picture Title

car tours come through each fall. The Lincoln Way renovation was completed in October of 2003 and is on the National Register of Historic Places.

Present Day Woodbine

Beyond the uniqueness of traveling on a beautiful brick road through the heart of the community, Woodbine is a great place to stop and enjoy a moment, a day or a lifetime.

Along the route is the newly expanded Woodbine Carnegie Public Library, the first library in Harrison County, built in 1910. On the library grounds, visitors will find a World War 1 memorial and artillery gun, a refurbished fountain dedicated in 1917 and a replica of the Statue of Liberty, one of only 100 in existence. The interior of the library features a statue, The Goddess of the Cup, a bust of Abraham Lincoln, and documents signed by Presidents Lincoln and Garfield. A $400,000 expansion project for the original library building was completed in 2001.

The library was placed on the National Register of Historic Places in 1997. The federal program, administered in Iowa by the State Historical Society, recognizes resources that are significant in history, architecture and archaeology. The Woodbine library is one of the first Carnegie library buildings that were built in southwest Iowa. Built in 1910 by Eisentraut and Co. of Sioux City, the library is significant architecturally as a well-preserved example of the Type II library plan in Iowa and also is an expression of the Prairie School

Roland and Mary Clark purchased this house in February 1997 from Ida Blackman. The house was bu in the early 1900's, and lived in by the O.W. Rogers family. The house is an American cottage style. The Clarks started a complete renovation project in 1997. Careful replication of the original woodwork, as well restoration of maple flooring, was part of the proces

The Woodbine Alegent Health Clinic stays busy as one doctor and a nurse practitioner is available to assist the needs of the community. The clinic also employs several nurses and a receptionist.

and Mission styles of architecture.

The library's overall design conforms to the Type II Carnegie library plan. The plan consists of a simple rectangular building with an open interior, a bookshelf behind the central delivery desk, a librarian's office in one rear corner behind the children's reading area and a reference or study alcove in the opposite rear corner behind the adults' reading area.

The influence of the Prairie School can be seen in the building's low, horizontal emphasis, wide overhanging eaves and contrasting wall materials, pressed brick with textured stone trim. Both the Prairie School and Mission styles were nationally popular in the early 20th Century. A common feature of libraries of this period was the brick fireplace, which was meant to impart a home-like feeling to the interior.

The Woodbine school system serves the needs of over 500 students with a ratio of one teacher per every 13 children. A general education preschool has been established for three and four year olds as well as a latchkey program, which serves the needs of a growing community.

Schools

The Harrison County Flex Education Program is located in Woodbine. This program focuses on children from the county school districts who are having difficulty completing their education, giving them a second chance to move positively into the future.

Although the main campus is located in nearby Council Bluffs, Iowa Western Community College courses are available to high school students. The academy was established through the joint efforts of the West Harrison, Boyer Valley, Logan-Magnolia and Woodbine School Districts. The benefits of the program are three-fold as students can obtain a possible year to a year and a half worth of transferable college credits prior to their high school graduation. The families will benefit financially, saving thousands of dollars, which would have to be spent for tuition at a college. The school benefits offering a program, which is in high demand, bringing highly qualified teachers to the school. The academy offers general and technical requirement courses.

Tommy Gate Manufacturing Company, one of Woodbine's major manufacturers, recently completed a $1 million plant expansion as product demands continue to grow in the U.S. and in foreign markets. In

Commercial Federal

Below: The Community of Christ Church was originally known as the R.L.D.S. Church. This church is located by the school and is also used by other community organizations.

Woodbine IOWA

business for over 35 years, Tommy Gate has built a national and international network of distributors.

When Delbert "Bus" Brown, founder of Tommy Gate, returned to Woodbine after serving overseas in WW II, he put his engineering and machining skills to work, manufacturing his own line of farm equipment. Eventually, this one-man company became part of a larger local manufacturing firm.

In 1965, Brown again started out on his own with the Woodbine Manufacturing Company. He started the company to manufacture another type of equipment - hydraulic lift-gates for pickup trucks. Named after his son, the TOMMY LIFT® original hydraulic lift-gate was originally designed to help move heavy loads into and out of trucks.

The company is still privately owned by the Brown family and recently the original manufacturing plant, still located entirely in Woodbine, was expanded to twice its previous size to keep up with demand. With customers around the world, each TOMMY GATE® lift-gate is still designed and manufactured entirely at the plant in Woodbine.

The Woodbine Industrial Park boasts a new 10,000-square-foot commercial property, which is home to Phyto-Technologies Inc., Energique Inc., Apotheca Naturale, and Terradyne Naturale Inc.

Phyto-Technologies Inc., a highly respected manufacturer of quality botanical products, announced the debut of its marketing operation, Earth Power Inc. and has tapped a fast-growing, $150 billion global natural foods retail industry.

Energique Inc. also offers more jobs to local residents. Energique has successfully supplied doctors with liquid herbal extracts available in their marketplace for over a decade. They distribute herbals, homeopathic and nutritional supplements worldwide, making over 4,000 natural remedies.

Apotheca Naturale Inc., a manufacturer of homeopathic with worldwide distribution, was founded in 1987 and began as a small family business processing botanicals and manufacturing botanical products. The company has grown significantly. Apotheca Naturale now operates a manufacturing facility with full capabilities to make a range of nearly any type of natural health

Delbert "Bus" Brown, founder of Tommy Gate, returned to Woodbine after serving overseas in WW II, he put his engineering and machining skills to work, manufacturing his own line of farm equipment. Eventually, this one-man company became part of a larger local manufacturing firm.

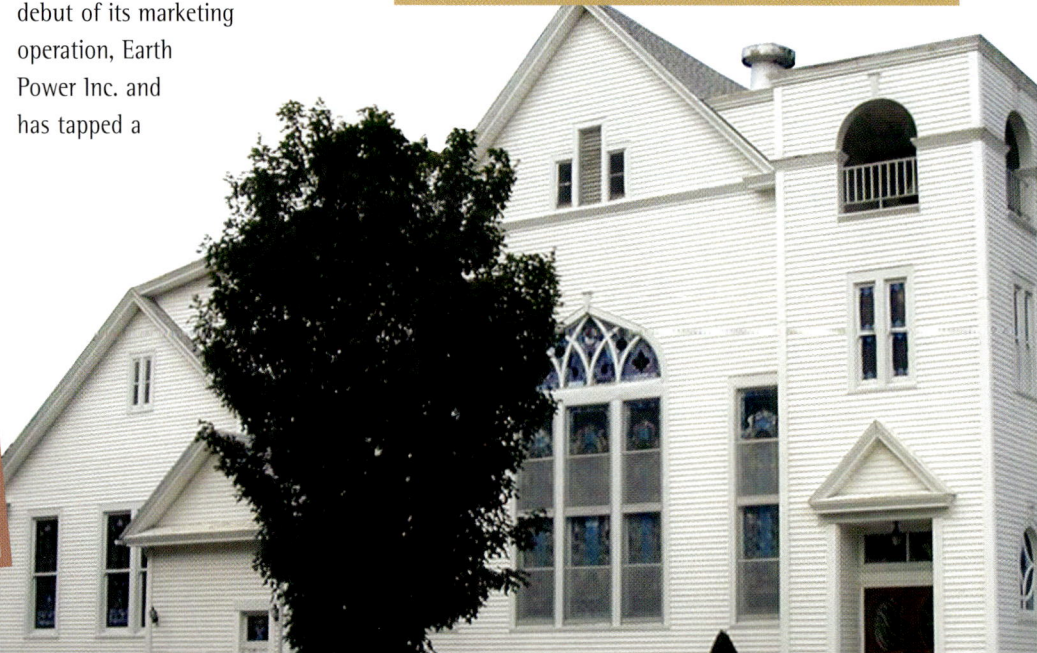

FIRST CHRISTIAN CHURCH

Woodbine IOWA

The Woodbine Girl's Cross Country team has been strong for many years. The current team has represented Woodbine in the state meet for the past two years and all will return for another season. Pictured front row, left to right is: Jessica Kowalsky, Stephanie Straight and Alexia Dunlop. Back row: Jill Lenz, Sarah Kelley, coach Rod Smith, Meghan Hardy and Elyse Harper.

The Woodbine School has an excellent sports program, which is supported strongly by the community. Phil Hummel, who is in the Iowa Coaches Hall of Fame, once coached the Boy's Cross Country team.

care product. They specialize in homeopathic, herbal, nutritional and nutraceutical products. In addition to custom manufacturing and custom formulation, Apotheca Naturale Inc. offers an extensive product line, which can be privately labeled.

Terradyne Naturale, Inc., another manufacturer of herbs sold worldwide, also helps provide local jobs in the community.

Proud of its history, 19th Century storefronts line much of Woodbine's Main Street, although a fire destroyed several buildings on June 10, 1997, forcing progress and modernization with new buildings and businesses. Many of the 19th Century building are entirely made of brick and have very interesting and colorful histories.

The corner of Fifth and Walker streets remains the historic hub of downtown Woodbine, featuring buildings on each corner of the intersection that date back to the late 19th and early 20th centuries. Walker Street, the main thoroughfare through downtown Woodbine, remains, like the Lincoln Highway, a brick street, flanked on either side by brick sidewalks.

At the intersection, the former Oddfellows Hall and Rebecca Lodge now houses LJ's Café and Whitmore's Home Decorating. Across the street, Hometown Hardware is a traditional hardware store that has operated in the same location – with different owners – since 1914 or earlier. The McDonald Building, once the home of a bank that closed during the Bank Holiday of the 1930s, now houses a real estate and insurance agency and a beauty shop.

Woodbine residents pride themselves in being about kids and offering people a safe environment in which to raise them. It has an extremely clean and well-kept city park with much to offer. Among the parks features are a large, heated swimming pool; a bath house; three concession stands; a lighted tennis court; a lighted softball field; a lighted baseball field; a lighted little league field; two soccer fields: a third located at the industrial park; two picnic shelters; a stage;

FOUTS FUNERAL HOME

Fouts Funeral Home recently added a parlor to hold funeral services. The business has been family owned and operated for several years.

Woodbine IOWA

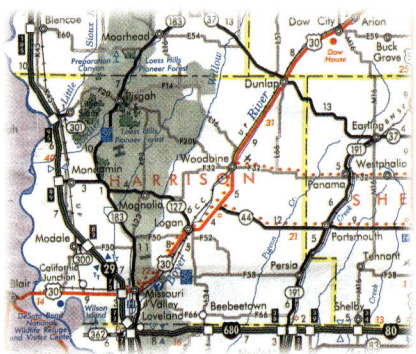

LEARN MORE

Woodbine is located in Harrison County within the West Central Region along the banks of the Boyer River between Logan and Denison on US Highway 30.

For more information please feel free to call the Woodbine City Offices at 647-2550 or visit websites at:
www.woodbineia.org
http://woodbineia.areaguides.net
www.ohwy.com/ia/w/woodbine

STORY CONTRIBUTOR

Kim Barry

Jon Leu,
Managing Editor
The Daily
Nonpareil

---

playground equipment; rodeo grounds; an RV and trailer dump station; a horseshoe area; a 400 meter track; and a football field.

Woodbine offers a number of annual events, drawing visitors from Iowa and surrounding states.

Every July the Woodbine Saddle Club sponsors a rodeo, which is kicked off with Kid's Day activities. It's no ordinary event. Everyone can enjoy the sportsmanship and good "clean" fun. The evening is full of games, foot races, face painting, clowns, and a Dunking Booth. The event also includes the famous "Mutton Busting" and "Dressing a Sheep" competition.

On the last Saturday in September, thousands of visitors converge on the town to participate in the annual Applefest celebration. The popular celebration, started in 1989 as a means of celebrating the formation of an apple growers cooperative in Woodbine, frequently swells the city's population by ten-fold. Residents and visitors alike have come to see Applefest as a return to simpler times, an opportunity to see remarkable one-of-a-kind items, to sample sensation food – and apple pie – and to just have fun.

Some of the popular events include the "Show & Shine' car show; an antique tractor show; doll show; quilt show; street entertainment; food vendors; bike races; Genealogical Society tours; Illinois Central freight depot & caboose tours; black powder shoot and buckskin encampment; apple, apple pie and apple item sales; chicken noodle dinner; and an airport fly-in and plane rides. The main kicker of the event is the huge craft show and flea market stretching out for several blocks.

PROSPERITY AND PROMISE

Woodbine's "Lights On" festival, a city and countywide lighting contest for the Christmas season, rounds out the list of annual activities. Festivities start on Main Street the first week in December as the community Christmas tree is installed. Children from school walk downtown to decorate the tree. Evening events include the Kiwanis Soup Supper; cookie walk; arrival of Santa; and late night shopping.

Woodbine also boasts two county parks within six miles of town. Schaben Park and Willow Lake Recreation Area both offer fishing, no-wake boating, camping, hiking trails, play areas, bathhouses, seasonal hunting opportunities, picnic shelters, fire pits and grills. Willow Lake also offers two large cabins and three camping cabins along with a swimming area and beach.

Proud of its heritage, Woodbine is reflective of the best in Iowa small-town living and is poised to capture the prosperity and promise the future holds.

Need brief desception of the picture to fill this space. Box can be expanded to some degree